"Being an educator, coach, and parent who has lost a child to suicide, I truly believe that a comprehensive program such as Lifelines Prevention has the potential to help educate all those involved. If through this program we save one child's life and the pain and grief associated with this journey, it is educational time well spent."

CRAIG MILES, THIRTY-YEAR EDUCATOR, COACH, AND SPEAKER

"My son's thirteen-year-old friends knew he was contemplating suicide but did not know how to appropriately respond to this crisis. There was no suicide prevention education program at his Vermont school. Our young people are on the front lines every day; they are typically the first potential responders for a peer at risk for suicide. It has always made sense that education is our best tool to ensure that first response is appropriate. Lifelines Prevention is by far the most comprehensive, evidence-based program I have come across."

JOHN HALLIGAN, MOTIVATIONAL SPEAKER, WWW.RYANSSTORY.ORG

Hazelden Lifelines® Prevention

Building Knowledge and Skills to Prevent Suicide

SECOND EDITION

Maureen Underwood, LCSW

John Kalafat, PhD

The Maine Youth Suicide Prevention Program,
Led by the Maine CDC

Hazelden Publishing
Center City, Minnesota 55012
hazelden.org/bookstore

ISBN: 978-1-61649-751-4

Notice and Disclaimer
This curriculum is for educational and informational purposes only and should not be considered, or used as a substitute for, professional medical/psychological advice, diagnosis, and treatment. Hazelden Publishing makes no warranty, guarantee, or promise, express or implied, regarding the effectiveness of this curriculum in the prevention of suicide in specific situations. Hazelden Publishing does not take responsibility for any loss, injury, or damage caused by using the curriculum information, and in no event shall Hazelden Publishing, its employees, or its contractors or agents be liable for any special indirect or consequential damages or any loss or damages whatsoever resulting from injury, loss of income or profits, whether in an action of contract, negligence, or other tortious action, arising in connection with the use or performance of any information contained in the curriculum or associated materials. Hazelden Publishing does not monitor and is not responsible for statements made by instructors or others, or for the quality of instruction provided in conjunction with this curriculum.

In the stories mentioned in this publication, the names, details, and circumstances have been changed to protect the privacy of those involved.

Readers should be aware that websites listed in this work may have changed or disappeared between when this work was written and when it is read.

22 21 20 19   2 3 4 5 6

Cover design: Kathi Dunn, Dunn + Associates
Interior design and typesetting: Trina Christensen and Terri Kinne

Contents

···

For My Colleague John Kalafat

When the *Lifelines Prevention* program was first conceived, it was the early 1980s, and the rates of youth suicide had tripled in the preceding thirty years. School-based programs to address what was considered to be a public health epidemic were virtually nonexistent. John Kalafat and I were colleagues at a community mental health center in a suburban New Jersey town when we were asked by the director of guidance at a local high school to develop a curriculum about suicide prevention for students.

Our community backgrounds—I am a social worker and John was a community psychologist—helped us understand the need to translate the mental health concepts of suicide awareness and prevention into practical, easily understood lessons. We believed the curriculum needed to fit into the regular school schedule and be taught by faculty members to reinforce for students that they could find approachable, helpful adults within the school.

Our mutual appreciation for the importance of systemic program commitment led to the development of program components for all levels of the school community, from administrators to faculty and staff, students, and parents/guardians. The program was piloted, tested, and revised numerous times. In 2000, John became a project consultant for the Maine Youth Suicide Prevention Program, and *Lifelines Prevention* was implemented in a number of Maine schools.

The field of youth suicide prevention has grown slowly and cautiously since those early years. It has finally reached a point where evaluation data have demonstrated that well-constructed school-based programs can be effective tools in youth suicide awareness. And John Kalafat was one of the field's pioneers and preeminent leaders.

John died suddenly in October 2007. With his colleagues in Maine, he had just completed the process of submitting the final *Lifelines Prevention* evaluation data to the National Registry of Evidence-based Programs and Practices (NREPP) for evidence-based practice review, and he and I were working together on the manuscript for the original *Lifelines Prevention* publication.

While his loss is certainly profound for me on both a personal and professional level, it is an even greater loss for the field of youth suicide prevention. John had a passionate and career-long commitment to the implementation and evaluation of school-based prevention programs. He was a pragmatist who understood that successful, effective program development took time, and he championed the need for programs to set appropriate goals and be carefully evaluated. He understood the importance of programmatic continuity and insisted on providing training to ensure program fidelity and on developing strategies for program maintenance.

Yet despite his extraordinary level of academic and intellectual sophistication, John was a consummate egalitarian. He nurtured collaborative relationships with colleagues from all mental health disciplines as well as with the people who benefit from suicide prevention programs—teachers, school staff members, and students—whose contributions he genuinely valued equally. In the *Lifelines Prevention* curriculum, for example, he was most moved by the young boys whose help-seeking interventions for a friend are described in one of the original curriculum's videos, *One Life Saved*. "These kids are the real heroes in suicide prevention," he often said.

Those who worked with John miss his intellect, compassion, wit, and contagious sense of curiosity about the world around him. Those who are fortunate enough to be exposed to the work he left behind will be impressed by his thoroughness, intellectual rigor, and obvious commitment to evaluated interventions that effectively address identified suicide prevention needs.

John's legacy to youth suicide prevention lives on in the *Lifelines Prevention* program. Even in this edition, John's wisdom continues to infuse the content on each page. As you implement this in your school, I have no doubt that you will share John's observations that your students are the real heroes in suicide prevention.

But in my mind's eye, John Kalafat was one of its real heroes too.

—*Maureen M. Underwood*

Acknowledgments

A monumental distance exists between having an idea and turning it into a reality. From start to finish, *Lifelines Prevention* has been inspired by the scores of dedicated mental health professionals and school staff members who shared our belief in the critical importance of youth suicide prevention. Especially in this second edition, the broadening of content to address not only middle school students, but late elementary and high school students, was championed by educators across the country who knew long before national data was released that suicide had become a serious problem at even younger and older ages. These educators also believed us when we told them that their suggestions would be incorporated into this second edition, and although there are too many people to list individually, we hope they all know we are extraordinarily grateful for their help in making the content so vibrant and timely.

Some people deserve special recognition, however, and should be considered coauthors of the expanded content in this revision.

- Julie Geddes from the Oklahoma Department of Mental Health and Substance Abuse Services. Julie walked through this document page by page to add her expertise and wisdom. Her sensitivity, knowledge, and compassion are reflected in every section, and her experience as an educator has kept the content right on target for its intended audiences.

- Jan Bryson, author. We were so inspired by Jan's book *A Walk in Her Shoes* that we asked her to become part of our team and help provide a realistic youth perspective to our understanding of adolescent communication, especially as it relates to social media.

- Nathan Levy, author. The well-known author of the *Stories with Holes* series generously responded to our request to use one of his stories for our middle school curriculum. It is truly a brilliant metaphor for an abstraction of thinking, and we want to give Nathan all the credit for its ingenuity.

- Judith Springer and Michelle Scott, *Lifelines Intervention* authors. The experience of these two professionals with older high school and college students provided the foundation for the grades 11–12 curriculum, which they graciously wrote. Their support and vision helped guide the *Lifelines Prevention* curriculum to another level of professionalism.

- Nicole D'Amore, the next generation of suicidologists. As a young researcher and trainer, she brought a fresh eye and a contemporary perspective to the entire *Lifelines Prevention* project.

Other professionals who made significant contributions include Susan Tellone, Laine Smith, Denise Wegeman, Liza Morales, and Dianne Thompson. Finally, I'd like to recognize one additional person:

- Lincoln Underwood, my grandson. With the wisdom and honesty of a sixth-grader, Lincoln reviewed and edited the curriculum materials to "make sure they make sense." They have, we are pleased to report, received his seal of approval.

The Hazelden Lifelines Model
for Creating a Competent School

....

COMMUNITY FOR YOUTH SUICIDE PREVENTION

The concept of the school as a learning community based on shared beliefs, mission, and values is not new; it dates back to the ancient Greek academies. In the last several decades, however, this concept of community has expanded to include the idea of "competence." In relation to a school, it reflects the fact that the school values each member of its community, can recognize when one of its members is in need, and knows where and how to get appropriate helping resources.

What's inherent in this definition is an understanding that the school community comprises all of its members—administrators, faculty and staff, parents and guardians, and students—and that each has a critical role to play in creating community competence. Too often the responsibility for a new school-based program is delegated to a single person, its implementation is often perceived as a burden, and the program only continues if that person remains at the school.

The Hazelden Lifelines® model is different. It recognizes that unless everyone in the school has a role in suicide prevention, the impact of even the best program may be minimal and unsustainable. Although the responsibility begins at the administrative level with the adoption of board-approved policies and protocols, everyone who attends or works in the school has a role to play. Not only faculty, but all staff—including bus drivers, cafeteria workers, and office personnel—are provided with information that clarifies their critical but limited role in the prevention process: to recognize signs of risk and make referrals to appropriate school resources for further assessment. Parents and guardians receive information on how to be alert to suicide risk in their children or their children's peers, and students are actively engaged in knowing how to get help for themselves or a peer. Because Hazelden

Lifelines is grounded in the mission of the school, it is not designed to provide mental health information about complex diagnoses. Instead, its focus is on observable changes in students' behavior and help-seeking from trusted adults.

From this perspective, the idea of suicide prevention can be easily incorporated into existing school programming, from elementary school through high school. In addition, the program simplifies the presentation of a consistent message to everyone in the school by providing a shared language that outlines the role of each member in suicide prevention.

This thread of community competence is woven through each book in the Hazelden Lifelines trilogy—*Lifelines Prevention, Lifelines Intervention,* and *Lifelines Postvention*—and provides an organizing principle that can easily be applied to other prevention programs as well.

How to Access the Program's Digital Materials

This Hazelden *Lifelines Prevention* manual comes with digital handout files and a DVD of videos. The digital handout files are downloadable, printable resources for administrators, school faculty and staff, parents or guardians, and students, including all the handouts and presentations needed for implementing *Lifelines Prevention*. The resources are all in PDF format and provided on a flash drive that accompanies this manual. The files can be accessed using Adobe Reader®. If you do not have Adobe Reader, you can download it for free at www.adobe.com.

To use the flash drive, insert it into a USB port on your computer or other device.

This is what the credit-card USB flash drive looks like when it is closed.

Place your thumb at the right center edge of the card and press down. The tab will flip open.

Insert the chip into the USB port in your computer.

Handouts are compiled in packets by curriculum section, and blank pages have been added to the packets for easy double-sided printing. Be sure to read the Preparation Needed list at the beginning of the faculty/staff presentation, the parent/guardian presentation, and each student curriculum session for printing instructions before printing full handout packets.

Whenever you see this icon 📄 in the manual, the paragraph beside it mentions one or more handouts or other resources that are provided as digital files. An SP symbol (SP) near the icon indicates a Spanish version of a document is also available in the digital files.

These resources cannot be modified, but they can be printed for use without concern for copyright infringement. For a list of accompanying digital files, see the List of Digital Materials near the end of this manual or the digital Read Me First document.

This curriculum's DVD contains video scenes that are used during the sessions. When you see this icon ▶ in this manual, it means the video can be found on the DVD. The manual's List of Digital Materials also details these video scenes.

Introduction to Hazelden Lifelines

WHAT IS THE HAZELDEN LIFELINES PROGRAM?

Based on the authors' work in youth suicide prevention in schools and communities for more than forty years,[1] the Hazelden Lifelines® trilogy—*Lifelines Prevention, Lifelines Intervention,* and *Lifelines Postvention*—is a comprehensive school-based suicide prevention program whose components address youth suicide from a three-pronged perspective. With the ultimate goal of creating a safe learning environment where all suicide is prevented, Hazelden Lifelines also recognizes that school staff need to be trained to identify and respond to potentially at-risk students and respond in the event a suicide does occur.

Here is a brief description of each of the three Hazelden Lifelines components:

Lifelines Prevention: Building Knowledge and Skills to Prevent Suicide

Designed for implementation in late elementary schools, middle schools, and high schools, *Lifelines Prevention* targets the whole school community by providing suicide awareness resources for administrators, faculty and staff, parents and guardians, and students. The evidence-based curriculum portion of this program fits easily into health class programming and lesson plans. *Lifelines Prevention* educates students on the facts about suicide and students' role in suicide prevention. It provides information about where to find suicide prevention resources in the school and community. Training materials are included for faculty and staff that provide accurate and practical information on identifying and referring students who might be at risk for suicide. *Lifelines Prevention* also includes a presentation for parents and guardians that answers questions about youth suicide and prevention, and involves them in the school's suicide prevention activities.

Lifelines Intervention: Helping Students at Risk for Suicide

The *Lifelines Intervention* program is based on a three-tiered approach:

- The first tier addresses early identification and assessment of at-risk students.

- The second tier provides guidance on making referrals to community resources for additional services.

- The final tier enhances the protective factors that increase student resilience and provide buffers from stress.

Hazelden Lifelines is based on the firm belief that schools are not mental health centers; the schools simply take the first step in helping direct students to the care they need through community mental health resources. Targeting school resource staff, the *Lifelines Intervention* program reviews a protocol for an assessment interview, outlines and demonstrates specific strategies for engaging students and parents and guardians in the assessment process, and calls attention to special categories of students who might be at elevated suicide risk. It also provides direction for the establishment of programs that enhance student resilience.

Lifelines Postvention: Responding to Suicide and Other Traumatic Death

Lifelines Postvention is a comprehensive whole-school best-practices program specifically designed for primary and secondary school communities. This unique program educates everyone in the school community about how to successfully address and respond not only to suicide, but to any type of traumatic death that profoundly affects the school population. With in-depth references and detailed plans, this resource outlines a response strategy that reflects the challenges schools face in dealing with a death within the school community. Also included are references and support materials that allow school leaders to recognize and reduce the risk of suicide contagion (or "copycat") behavior within the school.

WHAT IS THE PROCESS FOR IMPLEMENTING THE THREE-PART HAZELDEN LIFELINES PROGRAM IN A SCHOOL?

Just as the content of the three-part Hazelden Lifelines program is presented in a structured manner, the order for implementing the three components is clearly delineated. Implementation training from Hazelden Publishing trainers is highly recommended. Training in the trilogy of *Lifelines Prevention*, *Lifelines Intervention*, and *Lifelines Postvention* generally occurs over the course of an academic year, although the schedule of training can be adjusted to an individual school's needs. For more information on how to receive training for your school, contact Hazelden Publishing at 800-328-9000 or visit hazelden.org/lifelines_national_training. Both the full program and training is rolled out in the following order:

Lifelines Postvention is the initial six-hour training day that includes selected administrators and staff who have been designated to be part of the school's crisis team. This training reviews current school protocols for responding to traumatic deaths like suicide, outlines a best-practice model, and provides specific tools to assist a school in model implementation. This training is presented first because of its focus on the tangible policies and protocols that need to be in place to ensure administrative commitment to a comprehensive approach to suicide prevention. In a school that has recently experienced a traumatic loss event, starting with *Lifelines Postvention* can also be especially helpful.

Lifelines Intervention is scheduled next, primarily because schools usually see an increase in referrals to school resource staff after the *Lifelines Prevention* curriculum is implemented. *Lifelines Intervention* training is done over one to one-and-a-half days and is directed toward school mental health staff such as counselors, psychologists, and social workers. Additional staff may also be included at the discretion of school administration. This training reviews the implications of developmental issues on intervention techniques and provides an age-appropriate, conversational model for assessing suicide risk, engaging parents and guardians in the process, and making referrals.

Training for *Lifelines Prevention* is then presented over one to one-and-a-half days to selected school staff who will teach the *Lifelines Prevention* curriculum to late elementary, middle school, or high school students. In addition, content for suicide awareness presentations to school faculty and staff and for parents and guardians is reviewed. The process of curriculum implementation is also discussed.

The following School Implementation Process offers an outline of how this implementation process would flow. A reproducible copy of this implementation process is available in the program's accompanying digital files.

Just as the content of the three-part Hazelden Lifelines program is presented in a structured manner, the order for implementing the three components is clearly delineated. Implementation training from Hazelden Publishing trainers is highly recommended.

School Implementation Process

CONSULTATION WITH SCHOOL ADMINISTRATOR

Distribute the Readiness Survey

Confirm the training schedule

POSTVENTION TRAINING

Review policies and protocols and postvention readiness questions

Establish/train a crisis team as part of the training

ADMINISTRATORS	**STAFF**
Review and revise school policies	Review protocols

INTERVENTION TRAINING

Review the readiness assessment regarding intervention

Create assessment and referral protocols with documentation templates

Develop a local resource list

PREVENTION TRAINING

Review the readiness assessment regarding prevention

Train staff who will teach the classroom curriculum

Determine the schedule for the classroom curriculum

Determine the resources needed for faculty/staff training
and a parent/guardian workshop

IMPLEMENT CURRICULUM

FOLLOW UP WITH THE TRAINER/CONSULTANT

CAN YOU TELL ME MORE ABOUT *LIFELINES PREVENTION*?

Lifelines Prevention is a comprehensive, evidence-based suicide prevention program that is an outgrowth of programs initially developed by the authors in the 1980s in response to requests from schools for help in dealing with an increase in suicidal behavior among students. Although *Lifelines Prevention* provides basic information about youth suicide, it is primarily directed at helping everyone in the school community recognize when a student is at potential risk of suicide and understand how and where to access help.

The objectives of *Lifelines Prevention* specifically reinforce the goals of the competent school community by increasing the likelihood that these effects will occur:

- Members of the school community can more readily identify potentially suicidal students, know how to initially respond to them, and know how to rapidly obtain help for them.

- Students who are potentially at risk for suicide are aware of and have immediate access to helping resources and seek such help as an alternative to suicidal actions.

HOW IS *LIFELINES PREVENTION* DIFFERENT FROM OTHER SUICIDE PREVENTION PROGRAMS?

Like most school-based programs, *Lifelines Prevention* is a universal program, which means it's directed at the entire population of a school or a grade level. Besides being strongly evidence-based, it is unique even in the field of universal programs in several ways:

- It was created in schools, for schools. The program is firmly grounded in theoretical knowledge and best-practice mental health concepts; however, the objective of the program is to integrate youth suicide prevention into both the culture and mission of the school, which is to provide a safe learning environment for its students.

- It is a comprehensive universal program with specific, detailed content for all four school community populations—administrators, faculty and staff, students, and parents and guardians. Many other programs target only one or two school community components.

- Program content is devoid of clinical or mental health jargon and presents information in language that is accurate and easily understood. Even the curriculum, in its consistency with school mandates and culture, is not designed with a primary focus on mental health. Unlike some other programs, it does not aim to screen students for suicide risk or address suicidal feelings or behaviors. Instead, classes emphasize help-seeking behaviors and are aimed at students who encounter at-risk peers.

- Outcome measures are rooted in measurable objectives that are relevant to school functioning.

- The student lessons, which are forty to forty-five minutes long, fit easily into class periods, and content is correlated with national academic standards.

- *Lifelines Prevention* is designed to strengthen internal school resources by training teachers to present the student curriculum instead of using outside resources.

- It provides a consistent message about suicide prevention that is reinforced by the development of policies and protocols that address the prevention, intervention, and postvention components.

- *Lifelines Prevention* is designed to be sustainable in a school by integrating the prevention component into the student curriculum. No hidden expenses are involved in either program implementation or continuation.

Lifelines Prevention can also be used effectively in schools already using the *Olweus Bullying Prevention Program* (OBPP). (For a detailed description of how to coordinate the two programs, see the handout titled Connecting Hazelden *Lifelines Prevention* to the *Olweus Bullying Prevention Program* provided in the digital files.)

WHAT ARE THE *LIFELINES PREVENTION* PROGRAM COMPONENTS?

Lifelines Prevention consists of four components that are considered essential to a comprehensive school-based approach to youth suicide prevention. These are the four components:

1. Administrative perspective

2. Training for school faculty and staff

3. Parent/guardian workshop

4. Student curriculum

Handouts and additional resources in the program's digital files supplement these components.

Administrative Perspective

This component outlines the school's prepared and planned response to suicide prevention. Setting policies and procedures demonstrates administrative commitment and support for the school's suicide prevention activities and provides guidelines for crisis response to students at risk for suicide or in the event of a death by suicide.

Training for School Faculty and Staff

Addressing the realities of school systems today, this component is generally designed as a twenty- to thirty-minute add-in to a faculty meeting. It provides basic information about youth suicide that has the most practical implications for school personnel, outlines the critical but limited role of faculty and staff in identifying and responding to suicidal behavior, and identifies in-school referral resources. It also briefly explains the *Lifelines Prevention* student curriculum. The role of faculty and staff in suicide prevention is described in this presentation as having four goals:

1. Learning the warning signs of suicide

2. Identifying at-risk students

3. Referring at-risk students to appropriate resources

4. Understanding the role of being a "trusted adult" for students

Parent/Guardian Workshop

This presentation for parents and guardians reviews basic information about youth suicide and provides an overview of the school's response program, as well as brief guidelines for parental response to suicidal behavior. Information about the *Lifelines Prevention* student curriculum is outlined. Resources for additional information on suicide prevention and community support services are also provided.

Student Curriculum

This component cannot be implemented until the first three components have been completed. It would be inappropriate to train students to identify and refer potentially at-risk peers if the adults in the school or at home are unprepared to respond to these referrals.

Lifelines Prevention includes three separate curricula for grades 5–6, 7–10, and 11–12. The grades 7–10 unit was created first in 1987 in response to a dramatic increase in youth suicides from 1950 to 1980. It was targeted at older middle school students and younger high school students and focused on the following learning objectives:

- to review relevant facts about suicide, including warning signs

- to outline a process of identifying how to recognize the threat of suicidal thoughts and behavior and to take troubled peers seriously

- to model positive attitudes about intervention and help-seeking behaviors

- to identify resources, including one helpful adult, and to know how resources will respond

When *Lifelines Prevention* was first conceived, there was no perceived need to address suicide prevention in classroom settings below grade 7. Unfortunately, since that time there has been a gradual increase in suicide attempts by children at younger ages. Data from the Centers for Disease Control and Prevention (CDC) for 2014 found that the suicide rate for children ages ten to fourteen had caught up with their death rate from traffic accidents.[2] Because the risk for these younger children has been a frequent topic at national Hazelden Lifelines trainings, the authors created a four-session curriculum for fifth- and sixth-graders, adapted developmentally from the seventh through tenth grade content. For example, most students in these earlier grades will not necessarily have direct conversations with peers about suicide. They may, however, see things in peers that worry them, and it's important that they know how to identify and approach trusted adults with their concerns. They are also being introduced to the benefits and hazards of social media, which often replaces face-to-face conversation and can negatively affect empathic responses. The grades 5–6 curriculum addresses both these issues and provides an opportunity for classroom discussion and problem solving around these contemporary challenges.

Finally, in recognition of the challenges inherent in the transitions facing upper-grade high school students, a third curriculum has also been added, for grades 11 and 12. This two-session unit addresses the assumptions students may make about their lives after high school and provides them with strategies to use if reality does not meet their expectations.

IS *LIFELINES PREVENTION* AN EVIDENCE-BASED PROGRAM?

Lifelines Prevention is an evidence-based program that is included in the National Registry of Evidence-based Programs and Practices (NREPP, http://nrepp.samhsa. gov). One of the first school-based suicide prevention programs in the country, *Lifelines Prevention* has been revised and updated to reflect both program evaluation and increases in knowledge about youth attitudes toward seeking help.

Lifelines Prevention content is grounded in several areas of research related to youth suicide prevention. It reflects research that has determined most suicidal youths confide their concerns more often to peers than to adults, and some young people, particularly males, do not respond to troubled peers in empathic or helpful ways. It also addresses the fact that as few as 25 percent of peer confidants tell an adult about a troubled or suicidal peer and that school-based adults are often young people's last choice as confidants for personal concerns.[3]

Lifelines Prevention also incorporates the evidence that getting help from their peers is beneficial for youths. Participation in helping interactions can shape positive social behaviors and also reduce problematic behaviors. Finally, the curriculum incorporates research that has shown that a major factor that buffers young people in stressful situations is a sense of connection and contribution to their school or community.

Lifelines Prevention was the subject of extensive research during 2005 in twelve public schools in Maine. This outcome evaluation demonstrates that the curriculum increases students' knowledge about suicide and resources, as well as their expressed intent to intervene on behalf of at-risk peers. Findings also support teacher acceptance of the program and increased student confidence in the school's ability to respond to at-risk youth.[4]

A 2013 evaluation in Delaware, where the *Lifelines Prevention* curriculum was provided to all middle school students, reported a 50 percent drop on a national survey in the number of middle school students who admitted to thinking about suicide after taking the curriculum compared to before the curriculum was administered. There was also a 49 percent decline in the number of students who reported trying to seriously hurt or kill themselves.[5] Additional evaluation is currently under way to determine if the results were sustained for additional academic years.

For more information on the research behind *Lifelines Prevention,* consult the journal articles and book chapters listed in the School-Based Suicide Prevention Resources near the end of this manual.

HOW IS *LIFELINES PREVENTION* IMPLEMENTED IN A SCHOOL?

The implementation of *Lifelines Prevention* begins with an assessment of school policies and procedures by administrators during the administrative readiness consultation. When schools already have such procedures in place, this initial meeting simply reviews school protocols and encourages the involvement of local community mental health providers in the school's response program. If schools do not have these policies in place, consultation is directed at helping them establish guidelines that are in line with nationally recommended standards.

This consultation also identifies the in-school resources to which students identified as at potential risk for suicide will be referred. Because the *Lifelines Prevention* program is designed to increase awareness about suicide risk, it is essential that these staff members be prepared to effectively manage referrals, which often increase as a result of program information about suicide risk. Resources that enhance staff competence by reviewing current protocols for assessment and management of at-risk youth in the school setting are available in this curriculum.

After this review of administrative policies and procedures, a faculty and staff training is arranged. This presentation, which usually lasts thirty minutes (but can be expanded to a longer version if time permits) and is presented by either a member of the school's resource team or an external mental health consultant, can take place in a variety of formats and is structured to emphasize information that has practical implications for educators. It also serves to officially introduce the *Lifelines Prevention* program to the school community and explain the critical but limited role faculty and staff play in its successful implementation.

The third aspect of implementation is the parent/guardian workshop, which reviews the *Lifelines Prevention* curriculum, provides general suicide prevention information, and outlines strategies to help parents/guardians address suicide prevention with their children. Community mental health resources are also reviewed.

The final component and core of the program is the student curriculum. Three units are included to meet the needs of students from fifth through twelfth grade. One unit is designed for students in fifth and sixth grades, the second unit is designed for seventh through tenth grades, and the final unit is for eleventh and twelfth grades. Schoolteachers or staff who have been designated as instructors should receive training to deliver all three curriculum units. This training ensures instructors' comfort with the material as well as fidelity in curriculum implementation.

CAN *LIFELINES PREVENTION* BE IMPLEMENTED IN A NON-SCHOOL SETTING?

Components of *Lifelines Prevention* can be used in non-school settings. The faculty and staff presentation has been adapted for use with caregivers in youth-based organizations, such as Boy Scouts or Girl Scouts, or in faith-based youth groups. It has also been delivered at meetings of school principals and other school administrative personnel as part of a general community education process or as part of an effort to inform school personnel of the need for and the availability of comprehensive suicide education programs.

The student curriculum can also be used with young people in community groups and organizations. The caveat with such adaptations, however, is that when curriculum activities are altered, they may not meet criteria for either impact or effectiveness.

WHAT ARE THE THINGS TO CONSIDER
WHEN IMPLEMENTING *LIFELINES PREVENTION*?

Although an attempt has been made to make the *Lifelines Prevention* program as complete as possible, there are a number of additional things to consider when implementing this program.

1. **Find out early if you need parent/guardian permission.** Depending on the sponsorship of this program—for example, local, state, or federal—you may be required to obtain what is called "active permission" from parents or guardians for student participation. This means that a signed permission slip must be returned to the school even if the parents/guardians have no problem with their child attending the lessons. "Passive permission" only requires the permission slip to be returned if parents/guardians do not want their child to participate in the lessons. If you are in a state that requires suicide prevention education for students, you may not be required to obtain any type of permission.

2. **Training is important.** Although *Lifelines Prevention* is a detailed, field-tested, and comprehensive package, it is not meant for use by inexperienced community consultants or school personnel. That is, *Lifelines Prevention* is best carried out by professionals who have been trained in the process and philosophy of *Lifelines Prevention* implementation. For more information on how to receive training for your school, contact Hazelden Publishing at 800-328-9000 or visit hazelden.org/lifelines_national_training.

3. **Teaching about suicide must be voluntary.** While *Lifelines Prevention* is based on the premise that regular schoolteachers can teach the material, providing education on suicide must be done on a voluntary basis. Certain teachers may decide to opt out or be excused by administration from teaching this material for a variety of reasons. If a teacher opts out, ask a school counselor or other school staff member to teach the lessons.

4. **The teacher is the most important piece.** These materials have been carefully screened and field-tested. However, no materials are as important as the person delivering them. Teachers covering this material need special preparation. In addition to the *Lifelines Prevention* teacher training, teachers who present this material to students must take the time to become thoroughly familiar with school resources and procedures. The many schools that have used *Lifelines Prevention* have found that teachers who teach these lessons are looked at by students as resources and are more likely to be approached about this topic. To respond to inquiries that arise during the

lessons and outside of class, this extra preparation is necessary. The best *Lifelines Prevention* teachers are those who meet these descriptions:

- have rapport with students in and outside of the classroom
- want to teach the program as opposed to being forced to teach it
- are sufficiently comfortable talking about suicide openly and honestly
- know how to link a suicidal student to help

5. **The classroom lessons are designed to be presented in forty to forty-five minutes** or can be combined to address block scheduling needs. However, they are flexible and more time can be used, particularly to accommodate discussions of students' current issues and feelings. Experienced teachers know that it is important to take the time needed to respond to and fully discuss issues that arise in a given class.

6. **Substitute material carefully.** After some experience, teachers may want to substitute their own material for different parts of the curriculum. However, care must be taken to maintain active participation (for example, don't substitute a lecture for an exercise). Alternate exercises should be tested first to check for unanticipated effects, and media must be carefully chosen. Media and exercises should promote help-seeking behavior. There is no place in *Lifelines Prevention* for media depicting or discussing suicidal acts or featuring the stories of people who have made suicide attempts.

7. **The classroom lessons cannot stand alone.** Schools can implement the administrative readiness consultation, faculty and staff training, and parent/ guardian workshop without teaching the curriculum, but they should never implement the curriculum without first carrying out these other components. Also, it is important to be aware that classroom material on problem solving, self-esteem, communication skills, substance use or addiction, sex education, interpersonal violence, and other health topics can supplement and enhance the impact of *Lifelines Prevention*.

8. **Be sensitive to those who may have attempted or lost a loved one to suicide.** While these lessons have a low-key, educational focus, they do generate discussion about suicide. Such discussion might be upsetting to students who have made a nonlethal attempt, those who have been identified as at risk for suicide, or those who have experienced the suicide attempt or death of a friend or family member. If teachers are aware of students who have had these experiences, those students should be approached prior to the class,

informed of the topic, and provided the option of not attending. A general announcement should also be made prior to starting the curriculum that any student who chooses not to attend can be given an alternate assignment. When this is done, affected students often not only choose to attend but also actively participate. Of course, as with any subject matter that may touch on students' personal lives, the teacher must be sensitive to student reactions and follow up after the class with any students who appear to have been distressed by program content.

9. **Be prepared for students who may want to opt out of the curriculum.** Although it has not been common in the schools that have taught *Lifelines Prevention,* some students may not want to participate for reasons they choose to keep personal. A good solution is to inform the class of the upcoming unit before it starts and give students permission to choose an alternate assignment. Create that assignment ahead of time. Rather than focusing on suicide, construct it around resilience or protective factors that buffer youth from stress. Consider having these students present their assignments to the class by adding an additional curriculum session.

10. **What if?** If a school has recently experienced a death from suicide, the *Lifelines Prevention* program should not be started for at least a semester while postvention procedures are carried out. The *Lifelines Postvention* manual contains a one-session curriculum that has been designed to address the needs of students if the school does experience a suicide death. If a suicide death occurs while the curriculum is being taught, the regular *Lifelines Prevention* lessons should be suspended for at least a semester in favor of postvention procedures. Good postvention practices contribute greatly to suicide prevention.

As this rather long list of caveats indicates, providing an effective response to suicide is a complex endeavor. As we, the program developers, learn more about this process, we expect to make further modifications in our approach, and we continue to welcome feedback from those who use the *Lifelines Prevention* program. Finally, probably more than any other community education program that we have developed, we sincerely hope that the need for programs such as Hazelden Lifelines soon passes.

WHAT RESOURCES ARE AVAILABLE TO HELP WITH THIS TOPIC?

It is a good idea to enlist the support of local community mental health resources in your school's suicide prevention activities. Many agencies offer pamphlets and brochures on suicide prevention that could be distributed to your faculty and parents/guardians. They may also have access to material that highlights local resources, which will also be important to share. Most states have developed a state suicide prevention plan. Some state plans are more comprehensive than others, but it's worth taking a look at your state's plan to see whether it offers any youth suicide resources. The list of state plans can be found on the Suicide Prevention Resource Center (SPRC) website (www.sprc.org). SPRC provides information on the most current resources in the field of suicide prevention and offers a weekly e-newsletter called *The Weekly Spark* that is available at no charge; sign-up and back issues are on the site.

The Society for the Prevention of Teen Suicide (SPTS) provides a free online training program for school staff on its website (www.sptsusa.org) that has been designated as a "best practice" by the Suicide Prevention Resource Center. This site also includes a free video for parents called *Not My Kid: What Every Parent Should Know about Suicide Prevention*, also available in Spanish. The website also includes downloadable PDF files for teachers, parents/guardians, and students.

The Youth Suicide Prevention School-Based Guide (http://theguide.fmhi.usf.edu) is designed to provide accurate, user-friendly information. The guide is a tool that offers a series of checklists for schools to assess their existing or proposed suicide prevention efforts. It also provides information and resources, including a section with helpful links, that school administrators can use to enhance or add to their existing program.

For students who are lesbian, gay, bisexual, transgender, or questioning (LGBTQ), turn to The Trevor Project (www.thetrevorproject.org), which is the leading national organization providing crisis intervention and suicide prevention services to LGBTQ young people ages thirteen through twenty-four.

Finally, the Maine Youth Suicide Prevention Program offers an array of resource materials and information for adults and a separate website designed by youth for youth. Visit www.maine.gov/suicide and www.maine.gov/suicide/youth.

INTRODUCTION TO HAZELDEN LIFELINES HANDOUTS

These handouts can be found in the Introduction to Hazelden Lifelines, Introduction to Youth Suicide, and Administrative Perspective packet of digital files.

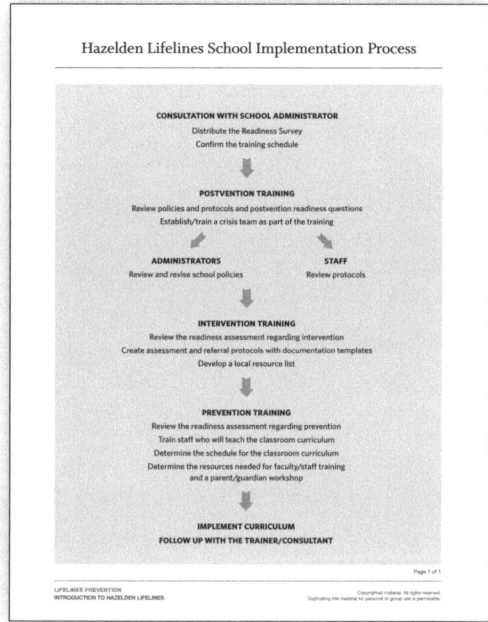

Hazelden Lifelines School Implementation Process

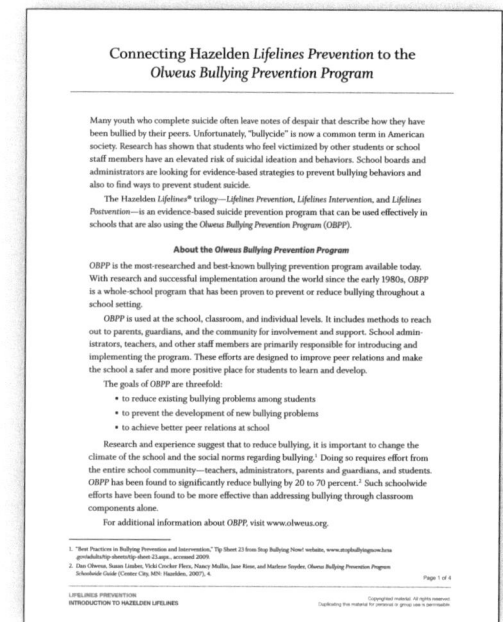

Connecting Hazelden *Lifelines Prevention* to the *Olweus Bullying Prevention Program*

Introduction to Youth Suicide

....

The following is based on a true story.

Nicole and Tanya had been friends with Kate since fourth grade. By the time they were in eighth grade, their friendship circle had widened, but they still sat together at lunch, went on shopping trips, and had sleepovers. That was until about six months ago, when Kate started to act differently.

The girls noticed that she canceled weekend plans suddenly, with excuses that seemed pretty lame. When they questioned her about it, Kate would shrug her shoulders and say she was just tired. She was quiet at lunch, barely eating, and generally looked around distractedly rather than joining in the conversation.

Her grades still seemed good, but she wasn't as enthusiastic about class assignments, and she stopped offering to help her friends with projects the way she had before.

Nicole and Tanya were concerned. They decided they would ask Kate if they had done anything to make her mad at them, but when they approached her, she apologized for not being a good friend and told them she felt like they might be better off without her. She was bored with everything, she said, and wasn't sure she would ever feel better. The girls responded with assurances that Kate was still a great friend. They suggested a plan to go to a new movie they all had been looking forward to seeing, and Kate agreed to go with them.

Early on the day of their scheduled movie outing, Nicole got a text from Kate saying she couldn't go. When Nicole asked why, Kate simply said "good-bye" and signed off.

Nicole and Tanya were frustrated with Kate, so they went to the movie without her. When she didn't show up for school the following Monday, they became concerned. Nicole's mom called Kate's mom, who told her that Kate had tried to take her life and was in the local hospital. She was okay physically but would need psychiatric treatment for what Kate admitted had been a suicide attempt.

For many students like Nicole, Tanya, and Kate, suicide is not something that happens to other people—they are extremely familiar with its unfortunate reality, even in middle school and late elementary school.

So how prevalent is youth suicide? Since the field of youth suicide research began in the 1980s, when the rate of suicide for ten- to twenty-four-year-olds jumped almost 300 percent from what it had been in the 1950s, systematic attempts have been made to collect accurate data about what is a significant public health problem.[1] The primary source of national data collection is the Centers for Disease Control and Prevention (CDC, www.cdc.gov). The CDC reports that suicide in the United States in 2015 was the second leading cause of death for young people ages ten to twenty-four, following accidents.[2] But data about deaths by suicide only tell a small part of the story. Everyone hopes a school will not lose a member of their community to suicide, but that doesn't mean that suicide isn't a problem. Let's look at some other data.

The CDC distributes its Youth Risk Behavior Surveillance Survey (YRBSS) to middle schools and high schools every two years. Data related to suicide risk comes from responses to the following five questions; the percentage listed after the question is the percentage of ninth- through twelfth-grade students in the sample of more than 15,000 who answered that question positively:[3]

- During the past twelve months, did you feel so sad or hopeless almost every day for **two weeks or more in a row** that you stopped doing some usual activities? (29.9 percent)

- During the past twelve months, did you ever **seriously** consider attempting suicide? (17.7 percent)

- During the past twelve months, did you **make a plan** about how you would attempt suicide? (14.6 percent)

- During the past twelve months, how many times did you **actually attempt** suicide? (8.6 percent responded that they attempted one or more times)

- **If you attempted suicide** during the past twelve months, did any attempt result in an injury, poisoning, or overdose that had to be treated by a doctor or a nurse? (2.8 percent)

Extrapolating these percentages to a typical school population provides a clearer picture of how much suicide risk affects schools. Remember, since most suicide attempts by youth remain private, only a very small percentage—2.8 percent in this instance—actually get any treatment.

Unfortunately, the news about middle school students isn't much better. Since 1999, there has been an almost 25 percent increase in suicide attempts among middle school students. And, as stated earlier, it is a growing problem for children in elementary school as well.[4]

WHAT IS THE IMPACT OF YOUTH SUICIDE ON STUDENTS, SCHOOLS, AND COMMUNITIES?

No one whose life has been touched by a teen suicide needs to read these stunning statistics to understand the impact of a self-inflicted death. But the scope of these numbers doesn't matter when you are confronted by the name and the face of a child who has died by his or her own hand. As anyone who has had experience with youth suicide will tell you, the impact is devastating.

The troubling question that is always in the forefront of everyone's mind can be summed up in one word: Why? What often follows is called "an exaggerated sense of responsibility"—the feeling that the person could have personally done something to prevent the death. Even young children struggle to understand why the suicide took place, and they often adopt simplistic reasoning to address their feelings of guilt. For example, a church youth group of twelve-year-olds responded to the suicide of a peer by deciding that the boy had died because the group had made fun of his clothes. They reasoned that if they hadn't teased him, he would still be alive today.

Parents, guardians, schools, and communities experience the same painful search for reasons, which are almost impossible to figure out or comprehend. What could ever be so bad that it would lead a young person to suicide? And what can be done to make sure it never happens again?

This last question is a major concern for school communities, because research tells us that there is a risk that young people will imitate suicidal behavior. Youth copy each other in so many superficial ways, and unfortunately, they copy suicidal behavior as well.

WHY SHOULD SCHOOLS ADDRESS THE ISSUE OF YOUTH SUICIDE?

Very few suicides or suicide attempts take place in schools. But many young people who are at risk for suicide exhibit warning signs in school, and the ability to recognize and act on these warning signs could prevent death or injuries and reduce emotional suffering.

As national data clearly demonstrate, these at-risk youths are sitting in classrooms all over the country. Ignoring their presence does not make them go away. Nor will doing so help their peers who may realize something is wrong but don't know how to help. And pretending the problem doesn't exist will not provide support or direction to their teachers, who also sense there is a problem but are uncertain on whether to intervene.

A suicide prevention education program is a pragmatic, proactive approach that supports the prevention of self-destructive behavior by students. It is grounded in the perspective of the school as a competent community where school officials clearly and consistently convey the vision that all members of the school care deeply about the safety and positive development of each other.

As we suggested earlier, an increasing body of literature suggests that conceptualizing schools as competent and caring communities produces a wide range of positive outcomes, which includes more effectively meeting the needs of both teachers and students.[5] Most schools currently apply this concept of community to the prevention of interpersonal violence. "Safe" school mandates clearly outline responses to threats against others. Suicide prevention programs are the logical extensions of "safe" schools and send an important message to the entire student body: your life is just as important as the lives of others.

And, finally, a suicide prevention program can be positioned as part of a school's efforts to provide social and emotional learning experiences for students.

CAN SCHOOL PROGRAMS REALLY HAVE AN IMPACT?

The school-based suicide prevention programs for students that began in the 1980s tried to encourage student discussion by "normalizing" suicide as a stress response. Unfortunately, these programs gave the impression that feeling suicidal was a normal response to stress. Follow-up studies indicated that some of these programs achieved modest gains in student knowledge and positive attitudes toward help-seeking for suicide, although others had no effect or received negative student response. After the limitations of these early programs were recognized, the emphasis shifted toward prevention programs that focused on skills training (including improvement of student coping skills), the education of school personnel, and screening students for risk through self-report and individual interviews.

Evaluation studies of contemporary programs have shown them to be mostly well received and sustainable. Controlled studies show knowledge gains, improved attitudes toward help-seeking behavior, actual increases in help-seeking, and decreases in self-reported suicide attempts.

There is also evidence that certain programs are not effective.[6] Onetime programs, such as assemblies, do not provide enough exposure to the messages of suicide prevention, nor do they allow monitoring of student reactions. Programs that use media depictions of suicidal behaviors or speeches by young people or adults who have made suicide attempts should not be used, as they could have modeling effects for at-risk youth.

CAN TALKING ABOUT SUICIDE IN A SCHOOL CAUSE MORE SUICIDE?

Absolutely not! There are four main arguments against the myth that talking with young people about suicide will "plant" the idea:

1. Students are already well aware of suicide from their experience with suicidal peers and the media.[7]

2. In the authors' thirty years of hotline experience and twenty years of school-based suicide prevention programming, there has never been a case of planting the idea. The facts about stimulation of suicidal behavior are best summarized by the following quotes from the Centers for Disease Control and Prevention: "There is no evidence of increased suicidal ideation or behavior among program participants"[8] and "Furthermore, numerous research and intervention efforts have been completed without any reports of harm."[9]

3. Several evaluations of school-based programs show increased likelihood that program participants will tell an adult about a suicidal peer as opposed to keeping that information to themselves.[10]

4. Two long-term follow-up studies in counties where suicide prevention programs were provided show reductions in youth suicide rates in the county, although state rates remained unchanged or increased for the same period of time.[11]

Remember, best-practice educational programs are not aimed at suicidal feelings per se, but instead emphasize knowing the warning signs, taking action, and obtaining help.

WHAT ARE THE RISK FACTORS AND WARNING SIGNS
OF YOUTH SUICIDE?

Risk for suicide at any age is extremely complex. It involves a variety of factors that include demographic information, family history, a clinical diagnosis, and the two most critical elements: a previous suicide attempt and access to lethal means (dangerous items that could be used in a suicide act). Just like having risk factors for heart disease doesn't mean that someone will have a heart attack, suicide risk factors do not necessarily predict suicide. Many students will enter a school with risk factors, leave with those same risk factors, and never be suicidal.

The danger happens when a combination of factors come together at the same time and some type of triggering event occurs that escalates risk, almost like a perfect storm. That's when a person may be at increased risk of suicide. So while the causes of youth suicide are multifaceted and determined by many factors, mental health professionals have learned some things about the population of students who may be at an increased risk for suicide.

The current knowledge about the risk factors and warning signs of youth suicide comes from clinical sources and "psychological autopsy" studies of young people who have completed suicide. Researchers interview the family members, friends, school staff, and other significant people who knew the deceased and try to discover the factors that may have contributed to the death.

Let's look first at what we have learned from these clinical studies and then translate this information into a formula that might be useful in a school setting:

- The vast majority of youth who died by suicide had significant psychiatric problems, including depression, conduct disorders, and substance use disorders.[12]

- Between one-quarter to one-third had made a prior attempt.[13]

- A family history of suicide greatly increased the risk.[14]

- Stressful life events such as interpersonal losses, legal or disciplinary crises, or changes for which the young person felt unprepared to cope were also reported.[15]

Young people who are suicidal don't just wake up one day and decide that life is no longer worth living; complex dynamics underlie suicide attempts and completions. These dynamics provide an important foundation for our understanding of suicidal youth, but this information may not be accessible or even relevant in a school setting. What is more relevant to those in a school are the "warning signs" of suicide. These warning signs are attitudes or behaviors that can be observed when a student may be at risk for suicide. The *Lifelines Prevention* program organizes these warning signs with the acronym FACTS, which stands for feelings, actions, changes, threats, and situations. A reproducible copy of these warning signs for suicide are included in the program's digital files.

Feelings

- hopelessness: feeling like things are bad and won't get any better
- fear of losing control, going crazy, or harming oneself or others
- helplessness: a belief that there's nothing that can make life better
- worthlessness: feeling useless and of no value
- self-hate, guilt, or shame
- extreme sadness or loneliness
- anxiety or worry

Feelings

Actions

Changes

Threats

Situations

Actions

- increased use of alcohol or other drugs
- talking or writing about death or destruction
- looking online for ways to kill yourself
- engaging in self-destructive or harming behaviors (like cutting)
- aggression
- recklessness

Changes

- personality: behaving like a different person, becoming withdrawn, feeling tired all the time, not caring about anything, or becoming more talkative or outgoing
- behavior: inability to concentrate, drop in grades
- sleeping pattern: sleeping all the time or not being able to sleep
- eating habits: loss of appetite and/or overeating
- losing interest in friends, hobbies, or personal appearance; isolating oneself
- sudden improvement after a period of being down or withdrawn

Threats

- statements such as "I wonder what it's like to die"

- threats such as "I won't be around much longer" or "You'd be better off without me"

- suicide attempts

Situations

- getting into trouble at school, at home, or with law enforcement

- recent losses

- changes in life that feel overwhelming

- being exposed to suicide or the death of a peer under any circumstances

- being bullied or physically or sexually abused

WHAT SHOULD TEACHERS AND OTHER SCHOOL STAFF DO IF THEY KNOW OR SUSPECT A YOUNG PERSON IS SUICIDAL?

The role of teachers and other school staff in the prevention process is critical but limited. Teachers and staff should follow these steps:

1. Stay alert to changes in student behavior that correspond to the FACTS acronym.

2. Express your concerns to the student, if you feel comfortable doing so.

3. Immediately notify internal school resources (for example, the school counselor, school social worker, school nurse, or dean of students) if the situation seems especially worrisome (for example, the student is making threats or you hear about an attempt). These staff resources have the training and skills to do the following:

   - Talk more in depth with the student.

   - Decide whether assessment by a mental health professional is required.

   - Communicate with parents/guardians to alert them to the school's concerns.

WHY IS TEACHING STUDENTS ABOUT SUICIDE INTERVENTION STEPS IMPORTANT?

Adults are usually the last to know about a suicidal youth. Here are a few of the facts reported in surveys of youth who were asked in whom they would confide suicidal thoughts or concerns:[16]

- Most suicidal youths share their concerns with their peers far more often than with adults.

- Youth who are disturbed (for example, dealing with depression or substance abuse) prefer peer supports to adults more than their peers who are not disturbed.

- Some adolescents, particularly some males, do not respond to troubled peers in empathic or helpful ways.

- As few as 25 percent of peer confidants tell an adult about a troubled or suicidal peer.

- School personnel are consistently among the last people adolescents would choose for discussing personal concerns.

Students consistently cited the following reasons for reluctance to confide in adults in their schools:[17]

- Confidentiality is not respected.

- Adults do not have the time to listen due to school schedules and other demands.

- School schedules and other organizational characteristics prevent students from getting to know adults well enough to feel comfortable confiding in them.

The perceived inaccessibility of helpful adults and reluctance of adolescents to seek out help from adults contributes to destructive outcomes from a variety of adolescent risk behaviors. Contrary to students' perceptions, research has shown that contact with helpful adults may be a protective factor for troubled youth.

There is also evidence that young people themselves benefit from helping others. Participation in helping interactions can shape prosocial behaviors and reduce problematic behavior. In addition, youths practice social competencies that can carry over into other challenging situations. These are some of the reasons students must be taught how to respond to peers who may be exhibiting suicidal behaviors.

INTRODUCTION TO YOUTH SUICIDE HANDOUT

This handout can be found in the Introduction to Hazelden Lifelines, Introduction to Youth Suicide, and Administrative Perspective packet of digital files.

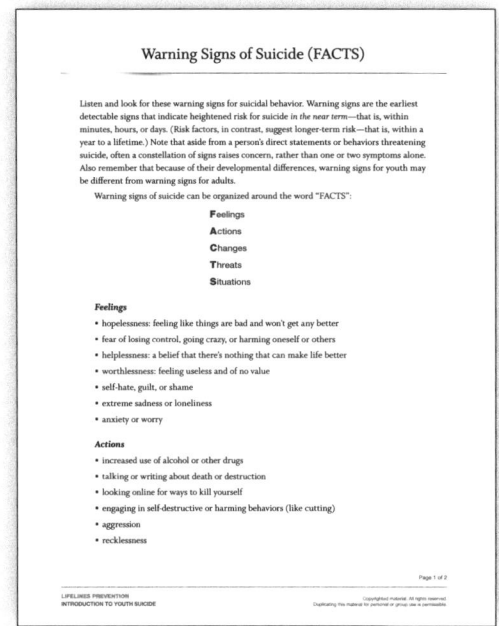

Warning Signs of Suicide (FACTS)

Section 1

....

Administrative Perspective

Administrative Perspective

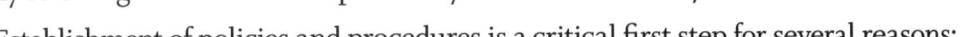

INTRODUCTION

The foundation for any school-based suicide prevention program must begin at the administrative level—including the board of education—by developing awareness and evaluation of the school's suicide prevention and response needs and efforts. (To assist with this step, the board of education and other administrators may be provided with the Questions for Your Board of Education handout, available as a digital file.) With increased awareness comes the development of school policies and procedures that address the myriad issues related to suicide. These policies and procedures are designed to help schools quickly mobilize a coordinated support system for students in crisis and to identify resources within both the school and the local community for responding to suicide emergencies. The emphasis on procedures is part of the school's role as a liaison, clearly referring the treatment responsibility to other community resources.

Establishment of policies and procedures is a critical first step for several reasons:

1. Policies and procedures represent the school's concrete recognition of the special needs presented by suicidal or at-risk youth and, in some ways, a demonstration of the school's commitment to interventions for these students.

2. They can reassure the faculty that a system exists for referral of students who might be at risk. This responsibility will not remain with teachers, who are generally already overburdened with academic responsibilities. A clear definition of a response hierarchy in a suicidal crisis can begin to address faculty concern about assuming yet another responsibility.

3. They recognize that despite the best efforts at prevention, suicide can happen, and a suicide death may have an impact on everyone in the school community. Having a clear, structured response in writing that considers all components of the school community can assist in alleviating the confusion and feelings of helplessness that often accompany a sudden, tragic death.

The intent of protocols and procedures is to provide a coordinated support system for students in crisis in the most efficient manner possible. Written procedures also serve as a concrete reminder that school administration supports suicide prevention. They also reinforce the idea that the obligation to begin possible lifesaving interventions takes precedence over the commitment to student confidentiality. This reinforces the school's role as a competent and compassionate community.

Advanced planning to prevent youth suicide and to intervene in a crisis can significantly improve the ability of school personnel to respond quickly, effectively, and with the least disruption to school routines when suicidal behavior becomes an issue. This can be best accomplished by having these elements in place:

- school personnel or resource staff who have been clearly designated as points of contact and have been trained to respond to the student and collaborate with parents/guardians and local resources

- written referral procedures, which are often formalized as "memoranda of understanding" with local mental health agencies

- clear guidelines that provide ideal responses to various suicidal situations and that are distributed to all school staff

The response chain of command should be clearly stated, with the identification of appropriate backups. Any requirements for written documentation should be created as standard forms and attached to the policies that are given to faculty and staff. A faculty in-service can provide a forum for discussing the policy, the reasons for its implementation, and examples of how it is to be used.

IS YOUR SCHOOL PREPARED TO MANAGE SUICIDAL BEHAVIOR?

Although not an exhaustive list, the questions in the following Readiness Survey will help you assess the comprehensiveness of your school's current policies and procedures and provide direction to help you develop the necessary school policies and protocols to address suicide prevention, intervention, and postvention. (A printable copy of the readiness survey can be found in the program's digital files.) It can be useful to distribute this survey to a variety of school staff and compare responses. First, it will give you a data point upon which to measure your additions or adjustments to your current protocols, and second, it will provide information about the school staff's current level of knowledge about your suicide prevention efforts.

After answering the questions, compare the Policies and Procedures Guidelines that follow this survey with your school's established policies and procedures. Remember, these are guidelines, and they can be modified to fit your school's needs. The overall goal is to provide as smooth, efficient, and maximally supportive response to these situations as possible.

Readiness Survey

Administrative Questions	Response	Priority RANKING OR TIMELINE
A. Prevention refers to proactive activities designed to prepare a school for effective, timely responses to students who may be at risk for suicide.		
1. Does your school have an up-to-date crisis response plan? COMMENTS:	○ YES ○ NO ○ NEED TO CONSIDER	
2. Does the crisis response plan have solid administrative support? COMMENTS:	○ YES ○ NO ○ NEED TO CONSIDER	
3a. Does the crisis response plan have written protocols on how to manage suicidal (student and/or staff) behavior? COMMENTS:	○ YES ○ NO ○ NEED TO CONSIDER	
3b. Does the crisis response plan have written protocols on how to manage a suicidal (student and/or staff) attempt **on** campus? COMMENTS:	○ YES ○ NO ○ NEED TO CONSIDER	
3c. Does the crisis response plan have written protocols on how to manage a suicidal (student and/or staff) attempt **off** campus? COMMENTS:	○ YES ○ NO ○ NEED TO CONSIDER	
4a. Does your school have a crisis team? COMMENTS:	○ YES ○ NO ○ NEED TO CONSIDER	

continued

Administrative Questions	Response	Priority RANKING OR TIMELINE
4b. Are individuals from both the school and the community involved in the crisis team? COMMENTS:	◯ YES ◯ NO ◯ NEED TO CONSIDER	
5. Are crisis team members provided with training? COMMENTS:	◯ YES ◯ NO ◯ NEED TO CONSIDER	
6. Are substitute crisis team members identified in case regular members are not available due to absence, conference attendance, vacation, and so forth? COMMENTS:	◯ YES ◯ NO ◯ NEED TO CONSIDER	
7. Do crisis team members have copies of school floor plans for their use and/or to provide to local law enforcement, if needed? COMMENTS:	◯ YES ◯ NO ◯ NEED TO CONSIDER	
8. Does the crisis team meet and practice tabletop (simulation) exercises on a regular basis? COMMENTS:	◯ YES ◯ NO ◯ NEED TO CONSIDER	

continued

Administrative Questions	Response	Priority RANKING OR TIMELINE
9. Are copies of the school crisis plan readily accessible to all school personnel? COMMENTS:	◯ YES ◯ NO ◯ NEED TO CONSIDER	
10a. Is there an established method for distributing protocols that includes who should receive them? COMMENTS:	◯ YES ◯ NO ◯ NEED TO CONSIDER	
10b. Is there a plan for providing new staff with protocols? COMMENTS:	◯ YES ◯ NO ◯ NEED TO CONSIDER	
11. Has school administration provided clear direction about legal rights and obligations of administrators, faculty, and staff in assisting with a suicidal student? COMMENTS:	◯ YES ◯ NO ◯ NEED TO CONSIDER	
12. Is someone designated to track the number of suicides, suicide attempts, and/or referrals for suicidal behavior? COMMENTS:	◯ YES ◯ NO ◯ NEED TO CONSIDER	
13. Has a policy for maintaining confidentiality of sensitive student information been created and disseminated to all school personnel? COMMENTS:	◯ YES ◯ NO ◯ NEED TO CONSIDER	

continued

Administrative Questions	Response	Priority RANKING OR TIMELINE
14. Does the school have a formal memorandum of agreement (MOA) with a local crisis service provider(s) outlining the services to be provided to the school system such as risk assessments, crisis management, and/or debriefing school staff in the aftermath of a crisis? COMMENTS:	○ YES ○ NO ○ NEED TO CONSIDER	
15. Does the MOA include guidelines for how the school receives feedback on the outcomes of the referrals that are made? COMMENTS:	○ YES ○ NO ○ NEED TO CONSIDER	
16. Have school administrators, faculty, and staff received education and training in suicide prevention? COMMENTS:	○ YES ○ NO ○ NEED TO CONSIDER	
17a. Has an effective student suicide prevention education program been incorporated into the school's comprehensive health education program? COMMENTS:	○ YES ○ NO ○ NEED TO CONSIDER	
17b. Does the prevention education program focus on building help-seeking skills? (*Note:* The student component should be introduced only after protocols have been established, MOAs are in place, staff education has occurred, and key staff have been identified as those who can help with suicidal behavior.) COMMENTS:	○ YES ○ NO ○ NEED TO CONSIDER	

continued

Administrative Questions	Response	Priority RANKING OR TIMELINE
18. Has a discussion with law enforcement occurred so that you know what to expect from the local law enforcement agency in the event of a crisis in school buildings or on school grounds? COMMENTS:	○ YES ○ NO ○ NEED TO CONSIDER	
19. Has the traffic pattern to and from the school been reviewed with emergency response personnel? COMMENTS:	○ YES ○ NO ○ NEED TO CONSIDER	
20a. Has a communication plan been developed in case phone lines to the school are jammed with incoming calls during a crisis? COMMENTS:	○ YES ○ NO ○ NEED TO CONSIDER	
20b. Is there a procedure for handling parents/guardians who show up at school unannounced to sign out students during a crisis? COMMENTS:	○ YES ○ NO ○ NEED TO CONSIDER	
B. Intervention refers to an outline of specific actions to be implemented in response to suicidal behavior.		
21. Do school procedures/protocols identify key people within each building as contacts to help when suicidal behavior occurs? COMMENTS:	○ YES ○ NO ○ NEED TO CONSIDER	
22. Do school procedures designate someone to contact the parents/guardians when suicide risk is suspected? COMMENTS:	○ YES ○ NO ○ NEED TO CONSIDER	

continued

Administrative Questions	Response	Priority RANKING OR TIMELINE
23. Does the school have procedures for when parents/guardians are unreachable? COMMENTS:	○ YES ○ NO ○ NEED TO CONSIDER	
24. Does the school have procedures for when parents/guardians refuse to get help for their child? COMMENTS:	○ YES ○ NO ○ NEED TO CONSIDER	
25. Does the school provide information to parents/guardians about the importance of removing lethal means (dangerous items that could be used in a suicide act) from their home? COMMENTS:	○ YES ○ NO ○ NEED TO CONSIDER	
26a. Does the school have a system to alert staff of an emergency while school is in session? COMMENTS:	○ YES ○ NO ○ NEED TO CONSIDER	
26b. Have volunteers and substitutes been informed about the intervention system? COMMENTS:	○ YES ○ NO ○ NEED TO CONSIDER	
27. Are there protocols concerning how to help students re-enter school after an absence or hospitalization for a mental health disorder, including suicidal behavior? COMMENTS:	○ YES ○ NO ○ NEED TO CONSIDER	

continued

Administrative Questions	Response	Priority RANKING OR TIMELINE
28. Are there systems/teams in place to address the needs of students who are exhibiting high-risk behaviors, such as substance use or addiction, depression, or self-injury? COMMENTS:	○ YES ○ NO ○ NEED TO CONSIDER	
C. Postvention refers to a sequence of planned support and interventions carried out in the aftermath of a suicide (or other tragic death) with the intention of preventing suicide contagion.		
29a. Do the protocols in your school include a section about working with the media? COMMENTS:	○ YES ○ NO ○ NEED TO CONSIDER	
29b. Has a spokesperson been designated? COMMENTS:	○ YES ○ NO ○ NEED TO CONSIDER	
29c. Is there a backup for that person? COMMENTS:	○ YES ○ NO ○ NEED TO CONSIDER	
30a. In the event of a suicide, are there established protocols for identifying close friends and other vulnerable students and plans to support them? COMMENTS:	○ YES ○ NO ○ NEED TO CONSIDER	
30b. Does this protocol include students at other buildings? COMMENTS:	○ YES ○ NO ○ NEED TO CONSIDER	

continued

Administrative Questions	Response	Priority RANKING OR TIMELINE
30c. Does this protocol include staff members who might be affected due to either their relationship with the youth or their own experience with suicide in their families? COMMENTS:	○ YES ○ NO ○ NEED TO CONSIDER	
31. Do the protocols consider the fact that, following a suicide, whole-school and/or permanent memorials are not recommended? COMMENTS:	○ YES ○ NO ○ NEED TO CONSIDER	

Staff-Related Questions	Response	Priority RANKING OR TIMELINE
1. Have all staff members received training about suicide prevention? COMMENTS:	○ YES ○ NO ○ NEED TO CONSIDER	
2. Have all staff members been provided copies of the school protocols? COMMENTS:	○ YES ○ NO ○ NEED TO CONSIDER	
3a. Have trained resource staff members been identified as contacts for when a staff member or student wants to ask about suicidal behavior? COMMENTS:	○ YES ○ NO ○ NEED TO CONSIDER	

continued

Staff-Related Questions	Response	Priority RANKING OR TIMELINE
3b. Has everyone in the building been informed of who the resource staff members are? COMMENTS:	◯ YES ◯ NO ◯ NEED TO CONSIDER	
4. Do staff members know what to do if they come upon or hear about a suicide incident? COMMENTS:	◯ YES ◯ NO ◯ NEED TO CONSIDER	
5. Have confidentiality guidelines been provided and discussed with all staff members? COMMENTS:	◯ YES ◯ NO ◯ NEED TO CONSIDER	
6. Do school protocols guide staff members on what to look for and what to do if they find student work/messages (such as artwork, doodling, homework, term papers, journal entries, or notes) that focus on death or suicide? COMMENTS:	◯ YES ◯ NO ◯ NEED TO CONSIDER	
7. Will teachers receive feedback on students whom they refer for an evaluation of suicidal risk? COMMENTS:	◯ YES ◯ NO ◯ NEED TO CONSIDER	
8. Do staff members understand that it is not their responsibility to assess the seriousness of a situation but that suicidal behavior must be taken seriously and reported using the school protocols? COMMENTS:	◯ YES ◯ NO ◯ NEED TO CONSIDER	

continued

Staff-Related Questions	Response	Priority RANKING OR TIMELINE
9. Do the protocols inform staff members about what to do if there is any reason to suspect a weapon is present/readily available? COMMENTS:	○ YES ○ NO ○ NEED TO CONSIDER	
10. Are procedures in place to brief and debrief staff members in the event of a crisis? COMMENTS:	○ YES ○ NO ○ NEED TO CONSIDER	

Parent/Guardian-Related Questions	Response	Priority RANKING OR TIMELINE
1. Are opportunities provided for parents/guardians to learn about suicide prevention? COMMENTS:	○ YES ○ NO ○ NEED TO CONSIDER	
2. Are there efforts to actively communicate with parents/guardians about risk factors, warning signs, and the importance of restricting access to lethal means? COMMENTS:	○ YES ○ NO ○ NEED TO CONSIDER	
3. Have parents/guardians been told what the school is doing to prevent and address the issue of suicide, what will be done if their son or daughter is thought to be at risk of suicide, and what will be expected of them? COMMENTS:	○ YES ○ NO ○ NEED TO CONSIDER	
4. Are parents/guardians provided with a current list of community resources and agencies to contact if they are concerned that their son or daughter is suicidal? COMMENTS:	○ YES ○ NO ○ NEED TO CONSIDER	

continued

Student-Related Questions	Response	Priority RANKING OR TIMELINE
1a. Are students educated about suicide and how to help a troubled friend? COMMENTS:	◯ YES ◯ NO ◯ NEED TO CONSIDER	
1b. Does this education include practicing an intervention? COMMENTS:	◯ YES ◯ NO ◯ NEED TO CONSIDER	
2. Do students know whom to go to in the school if they are worried about a suicidal friend? COMMENTS:	◯ YES ◯ NO ◯ NEED TO CONSIDER	
3. Are behavioral health services readily available to youth? COMMENTS:	◯ YES ◯ NO ◯ NEED TO CONSIDER	

POLICIES AND PROCEDURES GUIDELINES

The following suicide intervention and postvention guidelines are designed to illustrate for schools what should be included in protocols written to assist at-risk students and intervene appropriately in suicide-related crises. The guidelines are drawn from actual school policies and procedures that were drafted in Oklahoma by the school districts in Norman, Yukon, and Mustang by the Norman, Oklahoma, Public Schools after the district employees completed the Hazelden Lifelines training and are duplicated with the district's permission. The guidelines recognize and build on the skills and resources inherent in school administrative units. School boards and school personnel may choose to implement additional supportive measures to fit the needs of an individual school community. The purpose of these guidelines is to assist school administrators in their planning. The guidelines do not constitute legal advice, nor are they intended to do so.

What you will notice as you read the material is that the customary designations of low, medium, or high suicide risk have been omitted. This is in line with the evolving thinking of suicide prevention experts that these designations of risk formulation are abstract, problematic, and open to interpretation. For example, how many times has your school staff sent a student whom they felt was at high suicide risk for a crisis assessment, only to have that student return to school the next day? Staff members are usually left frustrated and confused in that situation. They may feel that the crisis services are inadequate when, in fact, what seems high risk in a school setting isn't considered high risk at the crisis clinic.

The more pragmatic issue, of course, is what kind of intervention strategies you use for whatever risk determination you have made. As you will see in the sample that follows, the interventions are clearly laid out to clarify who does what when. The following flowchart summarizes this procedure visually for you to gain a general understanding of the way responsibilities and actions might be laid out.

Example of Intervention/Postvention Procedure

(loosely based on Norman, Okla., Public Schools Policy)

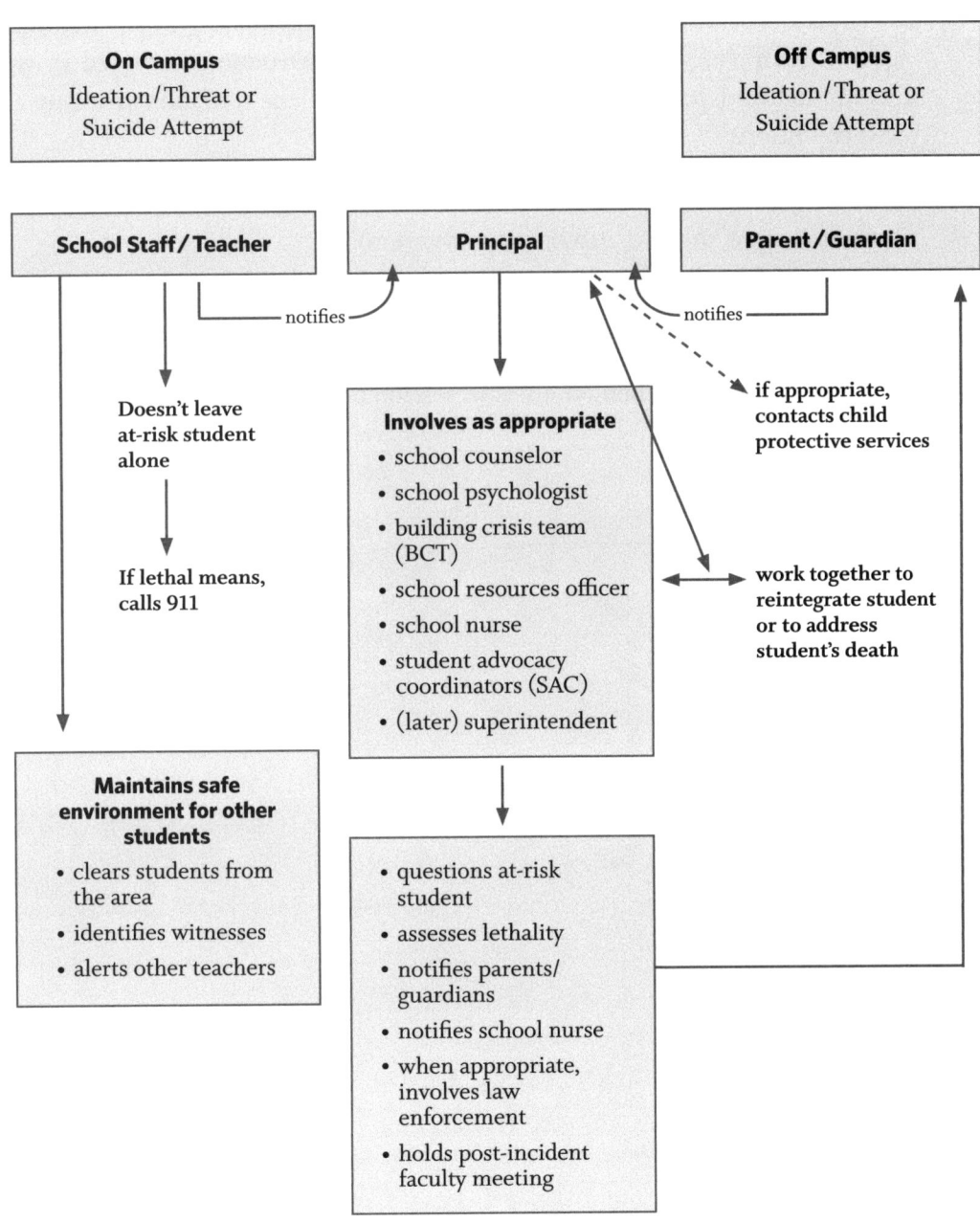

The flowchart provides a snapshot of the more precise and elaborate process that is fully detailed in a school district's written policies. The School District Policy Template for Responding to Suicide: Intervention and Postvention Procedures (in the program's digital files) provides a basis for assembling a district's policies and procedures. The Norman, Oklahoma, Public Schools Policy, which follows, provides an example, showing the detail and clear instructions involved in written intervention and postvention procedures, whether the situation involves any of these conditions:

- on-campus suicidal ideation and/or threats (intervention)
- on-campus suicidal attempt (intervention)
- assisting other students during a crisis (intervention)
- attempt off campus (intervention)
- a student death when school is in session or over break (postvention)

POLICY EXAMPLE
Norman, Oklahoma, Public Schools

Responding to Suicide:
Intervention and Postvention Procedures

PURPOSE STATEMENT

The purpose of this district policy is to protect the health and well-being of students by having procedures in place to prevent, assess the risk of, intervene in suicidal ideation, and respond to suicide completion. This policy covers actions that take place in the school, on school property, at school-sponsored functions and activities, on school buses or vehicles and at bus stops, and at school-sponsored out-of-school events where school staff are present. This policy will also cover appropriate school responses to suicidal or high-risk behaviors that take place outside of the school setting.

INTERVENTIONS

The following are procedures for responding with students who express a desire to harm themselves or dealing with students who attempt suicide while on or off school property.

- All threats of self-harm must be taken seriously.

- Under no circumstances should an untrained person attempt to assess the severity of suicidal risk.

- All assessment of threats, attempts, or other risk factors must be left to the appropriate professionals (that is, school counselors, student advocacy coordinators, school psychologists, mental health therapists, school resource officers, principals, school nurses, and similar professionals). In cases of suicidal risk, the school should maintain a confidential record of actions taken. This will assure that appropriate assessment, monitoring, and support are provided and will document the school's efforts to intervene and protect the student.

INTERVENTION: SUICIDAL IDEATION AND THREATS

When the risk of suicide exists, the situation is managed by the school counselor and student advocacy coordinator (counseling department). The principal and counseling department will direct all steps in this procedure and will document steps in the handling of information.

Steps for School Staff and Teachers

1. During the school day, if a student indicates to any school employee that they are thinking of harming themselves, immediately contact the student's principal, school counselor, student advocacy coordinator, or school psychologist.

2. Do not leave the student alone. Take immediate action to isolate the individual posing a threat and prevent access to potential weapons (if known).

3. The student should be escorted to the counseling department or a principal's office.

4. The individual working with the student shall fill out a Third Party Statement to inform others of the emergency situation. A copy of the Notification of Emergency Conference Form and the Third Party Statement should go to the following:

   a. Parent or guardian or emergency responders

   b. Director of Guidance and Counseling

   c. Confidential file at the school (*not* the cumulative folder)

5. Maintain a safe environment for other students.

Steps for School Principals, Counselors, and Student Advocacy Coordinators (SAC)

ASSESSMENT OF RISK/THREAT:

1. The counselor or student advocacy coordinator will assess the seriousness of the threat and inform the principal.

2. In the case of a life-threatening situation, the student and the staff members involved must understand that the issue of confidentiality shall no longer apply.

3. Trained staff will question the student using the school's risk assessment protocol.

4. If staff ascertains that the student needs a more complete assessment by a mental health professional, or is at imminent risk for suicide, immediate contact with the parent/guardian should be made and require the parent/guardian to come to the site. The Notification of Emergency Conference Form is explained and signed by the parent/guardian. In the event that the parent/guardian cannot or will not come to the school site, law enforcement should be contacted. The student may only be released to a parent, guardian, or law enforcement officer or emergency medical staff.

INTERVENTION: SUICIDE ATTEMPT ON CAMPUS

When dealing with students who attempt suicide while on campus, the situation is managed by the building crisis team (BCT). BCT members may include the school principal, assistant principals, school counselors, student advocacy coordinators (SAC), support staff, faculty, law enforcement, and guidance director. The school principal and BCT will direct all steps in this procedure, and will document steps in the handling of information.

Steps for School Staff and Teachers

1. During the school day, if school staff becomes aware a student is attempting or has attempted suicide on school property, immediately notify the principal, the school resource officer, and the school nurse.

2. Do not leave the student alone. Take immediate action to isolate the individual posing a threat and prevent access to potential weapons (if known).

3. If the student is in possession of lethal means, secure the area and prevent other students from accessing this area. Lethal means must be removed without putting anyone in danger. It is best to call a trained law enforcement officer to remove lethal means. Law enforcement officers have special training to de-escalate a situation that can very quickly become dangerous (such as possession of a gun or knife).

4. If the student is in imminent danger, call 911 immediately and then notify the principal. The principal or nurse will determine if the student is in need of medical attention and make the appropriate additional calls.

5. Maintain a safe environment for other students.

Steps for School Principals, Counselors, and Student Advocacy Coordinators (SAC)

Maintain a safe environment for other students. Initiate lockdown procedures if necessary.

1. The parent/guardian must be notified immediately.

2. The student may only be released to a parent/guardian, law enforcement official, or emergency medical staff.

3. The principal, a school counselor, and/or the student advocacy coordinator will offer support to the family, letting them know specifically the services that the school can offer to their child, and referral information for those services that cannot be provided by the school.

4. The student's absence will be excused and credit will be given for work completed. Nonessential work will be excused.

5. However, if another person was threatened or a weapon was brought to the building, the school's approach may be altered accordingly to match other policies and procedures.

6. The importance of restricting access to means of suicide and general safety planning should be stressed to the parent/guardian.

PROCEDURES FOR ASSISTING OTHER STUDENTS DURING A CRISIS

1. During the crisis, clear the area of other students immediately. Remove students who witnessed the event to a private area where a crisis team member can debrief them. It is best to keep the general student body in current classrooms and provide a supportive presence until the emergency is under control.

2. Alert classroom teachers to the situation through text messages or other previously established methods of communication.

3. Provide teachers with a short scripted message to communicate to students. Unless the entire student body witnessed the event, do not provide information about either the student or situation. Partial information can contribute to chaos. (Use language such as "Our school is having a crisis response drill. We will remain in the classroom until we get further instructions.")

4. The superintendent or designated staff person alerts principals at schools attended by siblings, who in turn will notify school counselors, nurses, and others able to help siblings and other students who might be affected.

5. A faculty meeting may be called by the principal or principal's designee at the end of the day to inform teachers of the event, offer them an opportunity to address their feelings and concerns, and plan appropriate procedures for subsequent school days. Students who may be affected by a suicide attempt should be identified by appropriate staff members by informing the student's school counselor. A follow-up plan should be developed to help support any identified situations where services could be provided via the school counseling department or crisis response team.

6. If a student alerted the staff to the situation, a debriefing for that student should take place and further intervention provided as necessary.

ATTEMPT OFF SCHOOL PREMISES

1. If the suicide attempt is made at home and the parents/guardians share this information with the school, a member of the crisis intervention team will contact the family immediately and offer assistance in whatever way is deemed necessary. The parents or guardians will be informed of the school's policy regarding the need to obtain medical/psychiatric "clearance" prior to re-entry to school.

2. If students are aware of the attempt, follow established procedures for outreach to vulnerable students.

Steps for Re-integration of the Student into School

1. The student and parent/guardian meet with the student's school counselor and/or student advocacy coordinator and a principal to begin a Student Re-entry Plan at least 24 hours before the student returns to school. Among the things that might be discussed would be the student's need to return to school on a half-day or full-day basis.

2. The school counselor holds a conference with the student's teachers to complete the Student Re-entry Plan. If a teacher is unable to attend, the student's counselor or student advocacy coordinator will send the Student Re-entry Plan, in writing, to the student's teachers within 24 hours of the student's return to school. Classroom modifications, concerns, and safety will be discussed. Consider creating a 504 plan (guidelines for implementation of federal disability regulations).

3. If the student is on an IEP (individualized education plan), the teacher of record should be included in the re-entry meetings.

4. The school counselor will adjust the student's schedule, if needed. Classroom teachers do need to know whether the student is on a full or partial study load and should be updated on the student's progress in general. They do not need clinical information or a detailed history.

5. Discussion of the case among personnel directly involved in supporting the student should be conducted in private settings and be specifically related to the student's treatment and support needs. Discussion of the student among other staff should be strictly on a need-to-know basis, that is, information directly related to what staff should know to work with the student.

6. The student should complete a personal Safety Plan with the school counselor before returning to classes. The student should be asked to identify a trusted adult at school with whom he/she feels comfortable. This trusted adult should agree to check in on the student.

When to Notify Child Protective Services

- If the student reveals issues of parental abuse or neglect, notify child protective services immediately and emphasize the possible contributory factors in the suicidal ideation (documented by the school staff).

- If the parent/guardian refuses to acknowledge the student's suicidal intent and indicates no plans to act for the immediate safety of the child (documented by the school staff).

- The parent/guardian is unavailable to be consulted and has not provided consent for treatment authority to another adult (documented by the school staff).

This referral does not preclude the school staff from securing the necessary medical care for the student, such as calling the police for transport to the emergency room.

Notify the appropriate district administrators and determine if further steps should be taken.

The building principal, working with the Building Crisis Team (BCT), will notify the staff through memo or meeting as determined by the severity of the situation.

POSTVENTION: AFTER A STUDENT DEATH WHEN SCHOOL IS IN SESSION OR OVER BREAK

Notify the Superintendent or Assistant Superintendent and determine if further steps should be taken. The principal, working with the Building Crisis Team (BCT), will notify the staff through a site calling tree, e-mail, or faculty meeting.

The BCT will direct all steps in this procedure, and will document every step in the handling of information about the suicide. The following Building Crisis Team Duty Checklist may be used for this purpose with appropriate BCT roles assigned.

Steps for School Principals/Counselors/Student Advocacy Coordinators (SAC)

1. The principal and/or a BCT member should contact the police to verify the death and get the facts surrounding the death. It is important for school staff to know the facts to reduce imitative behaviors.

2. Contact with the parent/guardian should be made by phone or in person by the principal and/or a BCT member. The principal and/or a BCT member should offer support to the family, letting them know specifically those services that the school can offer to any siblings in the school system, and referral information for the services that cannot be provided by the school.

3. Gather any information that the family wants to make known, such as funeral arrangements, visitations, etc.

4. Parental or family permission to release information related to the death is not required, since a death is public information. If the death is officially ruled a suicide, it is up to the parent/guardian to release that information. It is not the schools' role to share that death is due to suicide.

5. A meeting with all staff is advisable as soon as possible. At this meeting:

    a. Inform all staff about the facts known at that point.

    b. Allow time for staff to ask questions and express feelings.

    c. Ensure that all staff have an updated list of referral resources.

    d. Review the process for students leaving school grounds and tracking student attendance.

    e. Announce to staff that the school will interact with the media only through the district public relations office.

    f. Review planned in-class discussion formats and disclosure guidelines for talking to students. Prepare staff for student reactions.

    g. Alert staff of the possible contagion effect and advise to watch for "at risk" students.

    h. Compile a list of all students who are close to the deceased.

    i. Compile a list of all staff members who had contact with the deceased.

j. Compile/update a list of students who may be at-risk for suicide.

k. Remind staff about risk factors and warning signs for youth suicide.

l. Provide information regarding counseling/support opportunities for students and staff.

6. A memo should be distributed to staff for communication to students. Teachers may read the information themselves or chose to have a member of the BCT discuss the information with students.

7. If news of the suicide is received during the school day, faculty should be alerted by the pre-established communication strategy and provided with basic information about the event. Crisis team members should be involved in this notification to faculty members and staff who are known to have had a close relationship or contact with the deceased student.

8. If the death occurs when school is not in session, community crisis team members should be notified to provide support services for school members at community locations.

Announcement of Death to Students

- All memos to be read to students should be time-dated. "This is the correct information as we know it at this time."

- Do not provide morbid details such as the method or location of the suicide.

- The memo should identify the individuals (which may be BCT members) to whom additional questions may be addressed, and where those individuals will be located.

- The final line of the memo should communicate that the staff will be kept informed as new information becomes available. Allow students an opportunity to express their feelings. "What are your feelings and how can I help?" should be the structure of the conversation.

- Explain and predict what students can expect as they grieve (feelings of anger, guilt, shock, anxiety, loneliness, sadness, numbness, or experiencing physical pain).

- Express to students there is no one right way to grieve. It is important to recognize feelings and communicate them.

- Re-orient students to ongoing classroom activities.

- Avoid assemblies for notification and do not use impersonal announcements over the public-address system. Notify students in small, individual classrooms through faculty members or BCT members.

Care for Other Students

Have staff members or the counseling department talk with the most affected friends and determine the type of support needed.

- Designate space for identified students to receive support services, provided by the BCT. Provide necessary passes to release these students from class to receive services.

- Provide a sign-in and -out sheet for students who are seen by a member of the BCT.

- Contact community mental health services, which should be supervised by the BCT. Support services can include local mental health agencies, district crisis team school counselors, community crisis hotline agencies, and faith leaders.

- The deceased student's counselor and/or a principal should follow the deceased student's classes throughout the day providing counseling and discussion to assist students and teachers.

- Establish care stations in the school staffed by BCT members. Make sure that everyone, including faculty, students, and other school staff members, know where these are located. There should be more than one location and locations should be set up in small to mid-size rooms.

- Reschedule any immediate stressful academic exercises or tests if necessary.

- Follow up with parental contacts and referrals if necessary.

Parent/Guardian Notification

- Send a letter home to parents/guardians with notification of the event.

- Opt to answer parent/guardian questions via telephone or written notice. Remember to refer to most recent memos when answering phone calls and questions.

- Offer the following resource information:

    - Warning signs for youth who may be suicidal.

    - Supportive services available to students at the school.

    - Community resources they may wish to utilize.

    - How to respond to students' questions about death.

    - Reminders about their child's special needs during this time.

Student Memorials and Funeral Arrangements

- Provide information about visiting hours and funeral arrangements to staff, students, parents/guardians, and community members.

- Follow procedures for onsite memorials created at school.

- No services should be held at school unless it is accepted community practice.

- Funeral attendance should be in accordance with the procedures for other deaths of students.

  – Arrange for students and staff to be excused from school to attend the funeral if necessary.

  – Avoid glamorizing the death; do not fly the school flag at half-mast.

• • •

The procedures outlined in this policy example are, of course, subject to variation in certain circumstances. The following issues, however, need to be addressed consistently:

- When a potential suicide risk is present, the parents or guardians are to be contacted and advised of the steps that need to be taken. Remember to remind them to remove access to lethal means, especially firearms and drugs.

- When confronted with an actual situation in which life-threatening behaviors or ideation is present, immediate mobilization of all appropriate resources is paramount.

LIFELINES PREVENTION **IMPLEMENTATION PROCEDURES**

As mentioned earlier, the number of referrals to school support staff will often increase after your school has become competent to address suicide prevention. Referrals usually come from students themselves, peers, and parents/guardians. Your school must be prepared to respond to the referrals that the program will generate. That's why the *Lifelines Prevention* implementation begins with a review of school policies and procedures by administrators and/or committees designated to develop such procedures. Some schools already have procedures in place, and this initial meeting will simply consist of a review and identification of contact persons in the local human services system.

After completion of the Readiness Survey (section 1), steps are taken as necessary to update school policies and protocols to best-practice levels and to formalize links between the school system and local or tribal prevention and crisis intervention services through memorandums of agreement. Meanwhile, suicide prevention education is provided to faculty, other school staff (section 2), and parents/guardians (section 3). There can be a variety of formats and content in these presentations, all of which would emphasize information that has practical implications for educators and parents/guardians. Presentations that contain clinical or mental health jargon or abstract statistics are generally not well received.

The student sessions are the core of the *Lifelines Prevention* program (section 4). When *Lifelines Prevention* was first published in 2009, the curriculum was designed to be presented to students in grades 8–12. However, in the intervening years, several things occurred that pointed to a need to begin suicide prevention earlier, in elementary and middle school, and to create a separate curriculum for eleventh- and twelfth-graders.

The need to provide suicide prevention information to fifth- and sixth-grade students stems from an increase in the attempt rate for ten- to fourteen-year-olds.[1]

Finally, the number of suicides in young members of the military (ages eighteen to twenty-four) has also raised the question about how to better prepare older youth (eleventh- and twelfth-graders) to cope with the life events that happen after graduation that could increase suicide risk.

For these reasons, the curriculum in this second edition of *Lifelines Prevention* includes lessons tailored to address three grade levels: grades 5–6 (four sessions), grades 7–10 (four sessions), and grades 11–12 (two sessions).

Program Evaluation

Because outcome measures have become an essential part of best-practice school programming, the program's digital files include an evaluation instrument—both pre-test and post-test—for use with all grades in the student curriculum. There is also both a pre-test and post-test for school staff to use before and after they receive training. Other ways to evaluate the program's impact include addressing the issues that surface through completion of the readiness assessment survey and collecting data on the number of adults in the school community who chose to identify themselves as "trusted adults" and the number of students who approach them in a given period of time. Finally, comparing the number of visits to school resource staff and their referral source prior to inception of the program to the number of visits after program implementation will give you a measure of the effectiveness of the curriculum's help-seeking component.

OVERVIEW OF *LIFELINES PREVENTION*

Overall Program Goal

The goal of *Lifelines Prevention* is to increase the likelihood that school administrators, faculty, staff, and students who encounter at-risk youth will more readily identify them, provide an appropriate initial response, know how to obtain help, and consistently take such action.

Features of the *Lifelines Prevention* Student Sessions

Several features have been incorporated into the *Lifelines Prevention* student sessions to make them easily adaptable to the realities of school systems.

Class Schedules
The sessions are organized into forty- or forty-five-minute lesson plans that can be incorporated into existing classes. They can be easily adapted to two ninety-minute sessions for schools that have block scheduling. No time outside of class is required for students or teachers, and no expansion of already overburdened school curricula is necessary. It should be noted that there is a high correlation between youth suicide and other behaviors that are often discussed as part of health curricula, such as substance use and addiction, mental health issues, and teen pregnancy. This can provide an opportunity for an educator to reinforce the key learning objectives of the suicide prevention curriculum in other classes as well.

Educational Focus

The lesson plans are based on sound educational principles of interactive teaching. They neither focus on mental health problems nor use mental health language. Instead, the sessions address issues that students are currently dealing with, such as keeping confidences. Activities and the use of videos promote participatory learning. Each session is limited to three or four basic points, which are reinforced in each session using different teaching techniques to increase the likelihood of their retention.

Teacher Provided

The sessions are designed for presentation by regular classroom teachers rather than external consultants. This is cost-effective and consistent with the goal of enhancing school-based student supports and making the program more sustainable. Research indicates that students are more likely to talk about their concerns with an adult who has demonstrated interest and expertise in that area. Therefore, when classroom teachers cover material on suicide, students may see them as concerned, responsive adults who are available during school hours.

Students have also reported that they perceive staff and faculty who take the time to interact with them outside of their office or classroom as helpful. Thus, presenting the curriculum can enhance the credibility of a teacher, but additional interaction with students may be necessary to increase the likelihood that students will see the teacher as a resource.

The curriculum is also designed to meet national academic standards, which are listed within each grade level's section.

Lifelines Prevention Components and Objectives

Program Components	Objectives
Part 1: **Administrative** **Perspective**	• Administrators will review and update policies and protocols on all issues related to suicide. • All faculty and staff will know school procedures for responding to suicidal situations. • School officials (administrators and other school personnel designated to respond to suicidal situations) will know community providers and referral procedures.
Part 2: **Training for School** **Faculty and Staff**	• All faculty and staff will know relevant suicide facts, indicators of at-risk students, and response guidelines, including referral procedures. • Faculty and staff will self-select to be identified as "trusted adults" for students.
Part 3: **Parent/Guardian** **Workshop**	• Parents/guardians will know how to identify at-risk youth, be familiar with resources, and support the school program.
Part 4: **Student Curriculum**	• Students will demonstrate positive attitudes about intervention and help-seeking for themselves and others. • Students will know relevant facts about suicide, including warning signs. • Students will know how to respond to troubled peers. • Students will know resources for help, be able to name one helpful adult, and know how resources will respond.

ADMINISTRATIVE PERSPECTIVE HANDOUTS

These handouts can be found in the Introduction to Hazelden Lifelines, Introduction to Youth Suicide, and Administrative Perspective packet of digital files.

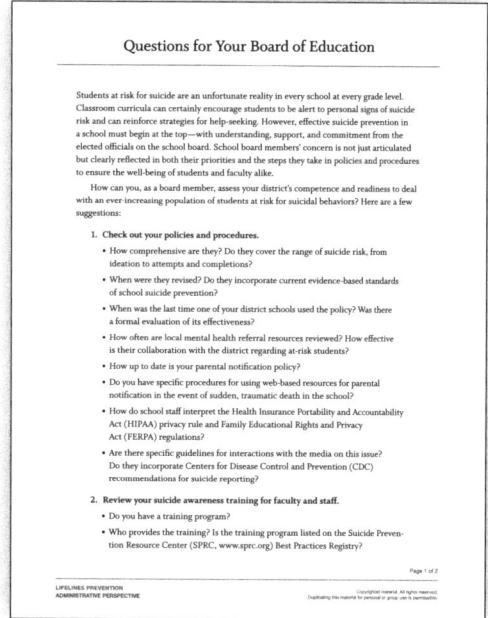

Questions for Your Board of Education

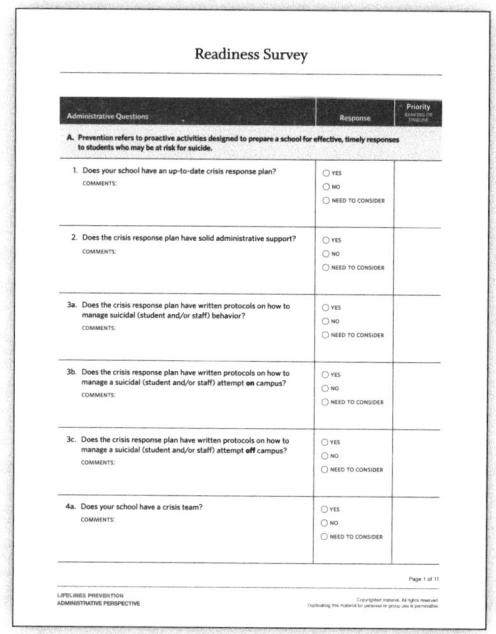

Readiness Survey

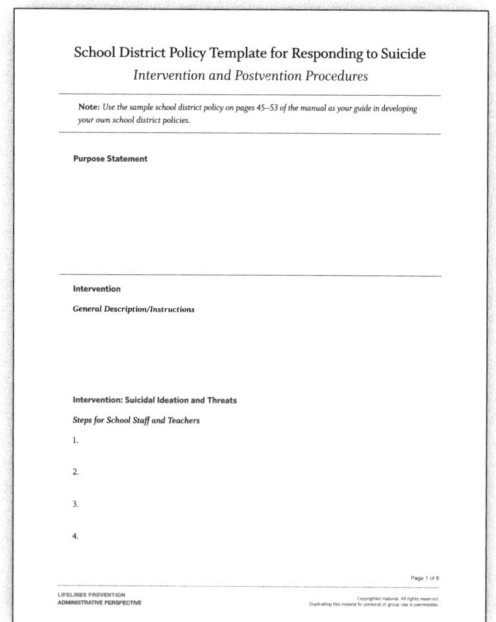

**School District Policy Template
for Responding to Suicide: Intervention
and Postvention Procedures**

Section 2

....

Faculty and Staff Training

Faculty and Staff Training

DESCRIPTION

It remains a reality that many people are afraid to discuss suicide; the topic is shrouded in stigma for a variety of reasons. Understandably, it is difficult for most people to comprehend the irrationality of the suicidal mind. We try to apply standards of logic to the decision to take one's life, and we fail miserably. It just doesn't make sense, and it can be very difficult to accept things we can't understand. We also tend to make the mistake of thinking that suicide is about wanting to die, which is also frightening when most of us are trying so hard to live. The definitions we have of suicide and the language we use to talk about suicide don't provide us with much insight. "Committing" suicide seems akin to committing a crime, an act that does not inspire empathy or compassion. Some people's lives have been directly touched by suicide, which they often keep secret because they fear the reactions of others. And some of the people who hold these values and attitudes are members of school faculty and staff. To avoid reinforcing this stigma, presenters should be aware of their word choice and use more appropriate phrases such as "died by suicide."

It's helpful to understand the stigma and fear surrounding suicide before making the following presentation. It may also be helpful to know that the content for the presentation, which is outlined in this section and in a training presentation slide show in the digital files, was created taking this type of thinking into consideration.

Everyone is entitled to their own attitudes about suicide, and a short presentation isn't likely to be a significant change agent. It presents suicide not simply as a product of mental illness, but from the perspective of impaired problem solving about a life problem, which can make the information a little less frightening and a little easier to hear. The presentation's primary objective is to help faculty and staff clearly recognize the things they can do to prevent suicide, and as we know from life experience, most people feel more positive and more engaged in a problem they think they can solve.

Time Allotted

Although many states have legislative mandates that require schools to provide a certain amount of time for staff professional development in suicide prevention, a lot of schools continue to find it challenging to allocate much time for these presentations. In the first edition of *Lifelines Prevention*, content was outlined for a presentation that could last as long as ninety minutes. Since that time, according to the hundreds of educators who have taken the *Lifelines Prevention* training nationwide, it has become clear that the most realistic amount of time to expect for a presentation of this type is between thirty and forty-five minutes. The following presentation reflects those time constraints. It is designed to provide the most relevant information to educators about their critical but limited role in suicide prevention. It reviews the reasons for the school's decision to address youth suicide prevention, introduces the *Lifelines Prevention* curriculum, clarifies the role that school faculty and staff play in the prevention process, and provides information about school and community resources.

Content Scope

In this content, some important topics are only touched on briefly; for example, risk factors. Presenters are certainly free to add more information if the school provides more time for a suicide prevention in-service.

Notice that the content does not include information about depression or other mental health disorders. The authors felt that it was not appropriate to discuss clinical issues in a short presentation that was broader in scope than just risk factors such as depression. They also firmly believe that diagnosis of emotional problems belongs in counseling settings, not classrooms.

Presenters

The program is usually conducted by a member of the school's crisis resource/ response team (such as a school social worker, psychologist, counselor, or nurse) or by a health teacher familiar with the content. The presentation should be scheduled after the review of policies and procedures by school administration and prior to the first lesson for students. It is usually provided as part of an in-service day or at an all-faculty and staff meeting. If you can't get all faculty and staff together at one time, you could give this training to smaller groups at the school at different times.

Because *Lifelines Prevention* is framed in the context of the "competent school community," it is extremely important to encourage attendance by all staff who interact with students, including administrative assistants, food service employees, and maintenance staff.

Notes for Effectiveness

Although both the content and format of this training are flexible and can be adjusted to the needs of individual schools, the emphasis should be on information that has practical implications for educators. Remember, the *Lifelines Prevention* program is designed to support the mission of the school to create a safe learning environment for all students.

Presentations that contain mental health jargon, theoretical concepts, or abstract statistics are generally not well received. Also, be careful using videos of people who either have attempted suicide or have survived the suicide of a family member. These can sometimes be upsetting, perhaps even retraumatizing, to participants who have had similar experiences. There are also guidelines for the safe use of media in suicide prevention at http://reportingonsuicide.org. You are encouraged to consult these guidelines before adding a media element.

For schools that require program evaluations, instruments can be found in section 2, Training for School Faculty and Staff; section 3, Parent/Guardian Workshop; and section 4, Student Curriculum. All pre-tests are to be administered at the beginning of the program or presentation. With faculty and staff, administering the post-test at a later date (for example, one to two months after the presentation) will provide a more accurate indication of presentation retention.

A detailed Presentation Outline follows. The presentation does include presentation slides; however, to be most effective, the delivery of this material should be adapted to the presenter's style. Please note, however, that slide content is written in a conversational tone that can be replicated verbatim, so presenters do not need to elaborate on any content if they are not comfortable doing so.

The following table summarizes each key part of this presentation. You'll find the presentation slide show, titled "Educators as Partners in Suicide Prevention," in the program's digital files.

FACULTY AND STAFF PRESENTATION OUTLINE

Content	Rationale	Slide Numbers
Lifelines Prevention Pre-test: Faculty and Staff	• Taking a pre-test before hearing the presenter helps faculty and staff assess their views and knowledge of suicide and/or suicide prevention, alerting them to areas/topics/aspects they may want to listen carefully for or ask questions about.	—
Part 1: **Why Talk about Youth Suicide?**	• Review workshop objectives. • Provide data to support your school's involvement in youth suicide prevention. • Explain why your school is addressing suicide prevention.	1–3
Part 2: **What Is the School's Role in Suicide Prevention?**	• Explain how everyone in the school will be involved in your school's suicide prevention effort; reinforce that the burden does not fall solely on the faculty but that the responsibility will be shared. • Briefly summarize your school's policies and protocols around suicide. • Review the list of commonly asked questions about suicide; this will enhance the information about why suicide is an important topic in a school. (**Note:** Some of these may be abbreviated in the interest of time.)	4–13
Part 3: **How Can Educators Address Their Role in Suicide Prevention?**	• Summarize staff roles. • Explain the risk factors, warning signs, and protective factors for suicide. • *Optional:* Show the *Suicide Risk and Warning Signs* video. • Use the Warning Signs of Suicide (FACTS) handout to point out what faculty should pay attention to. • Discuss the procedures for a warm handoff of a student. • *Optional:* Show the *Practicing the Warm Handoff* video. • Explain protective factors for suicide prevention.	14–24
Part 4: **What Will Our Students Learn?**	• Review how the *Lifelines Prevention* curriculum enhances protective factors. • Review program objectives for the grade level(s) that will be participating.	25–29
Part 5: **Do You Want to Be a Trusted Adult?**	• Discuss the role of the faculty and staff in protective factors. • Explain the role of a trusted adult and invite interested faculty and staff to pick up the Trusted Adult Card handout as they leave. • Review the key points of an educator's role.	30–31
Part 6: **Closure**	• Remind staff of the importance of supporting each other as members of the competent school community. • Provide a list of local, statewide, and online resources for at-risk students.	32
Lifelines Prevention Post-test: Faculty and Staff	• Taking a post-test a month or two after the training helps faculty and staff members assess what information they've gained from the presentation and from working with the program, and gauge their level of confidence in their roles in suicide prevention at the school.	—

Outcomes

By the end of the presentation, participants will be able to

- describe their role in your school's suicide prevention strategy
- identify students who may be at risk for suicide
- demonstrate an effective initial response to these students
- describe where and how to refer students for further help

Materials Needed

- *Optional:* Handouts on your school's policy and procedures, if desired
- Pens or pencils
- "Educators as Partners in Suicide Prevention" presentation slide show
- Handouts and materials from the Faculty and Staff Training packet:
  - *Lifelines Prevention* Pre-test: Faculty and Staff
  - "Educators as Partners in Suicide Prevention" Faculty and Staff Presentation Notes
  - Frequently Asked Questions about Youth Suicide
  - Trusted Adult Card
  - Warning Signs of Suicide (FACTS)
  - Resources for Suicide Prevention and Support
  - *Lifelines Prevention* Post-test: Faculty and Staff
- *Optional: Suicide Risk and Warning Signs* and *Practicing the Warm Handoff* videos ▶
- Video player, projector, and screen if the videos and presentation slides are to be used

Preparation Needed

- Review the presentation outline and adjust the content to the time constraints you have.
- Research state or local data on suicide to include with slide 3 of the presentation on national statistics.
- Review the presentation slides and practice delivering them.
- Use the Resources for Suicide Prevention and Support handout to create a list of resources that includes local organizations or individuals; make one copy of this handout for each participant.

- Print the Trusted Adult Card document and cut out and fold the cards so you have enough cards for each participant to have one. You may want to print these cards on a heavier paper stock.

- Photocopy the rest of the handouts, one copy of each per participant.

- *Optional:* Preview the videos. At certain points in the presentation, you will have the option to insert these short videos, which can provide a change of pace from the didactic information.

- Set up the video player, projector, screen, and any other needed equipment.

In one school, the counselor who was presenting this training anonymously surveyed faculty and staff before the meeting to find out who had previous experience with suicide. She created a heart sticker for each positive response and she handed these out randomly to faculty and staff as they entered the training. At the beginning of the presentation, she asked people who had received a heart to stand to demonstrate the number of participants who had personal experience with suicide. In this particular school, it was approximately 60 percent. "I had the attention of the entire room immediately," she reported.

Presentation Content

PART 1: WHY TALK ABOUT YOUTH SUICIDE?

1. As participants enter the meeting and you greet them, hand out the pre-test and a pen or pencil to each person, asking them to complete the short questionnaire before the presentation begins. Collect the pre-tests as people complete them.

2. Although it may seem counterintuitive, any program that touches on suicide should begin with an acknowledgment that the topic may be uncomfortable or upsetting for some members of the school community. Giving people permission to leave the room or not listen to what you are going to say is a respectful way to acknowledge that suicide may be personal for some of the school faculty and staff. Starting like this also conveys that you have some understanding of the topic.

   Note: If your school has experienced a suicide in the recent past, it's important to refer to that event in the beginning of this training. It isn't advisable to ask participants to share their recollections of the impact of that death, because this could retraumatize those who were seriously affected by the death.

3. Display slide 1, Educators as Partners in Suicide Prevention, and say: **Thank you for attending this workshop on the important topic of suicide prevention.**

4. Explain: **Some of you may know that, when measured in 2016, suicide was the second leading cause of death for youth ages ten through twenty-four.[1] Some of your lives may also have been personally touched by the tragedy of suicide. It may have been in your circle of friends, your community, or your family. Some of you may have struggled with your own thoughts of suicide. And the students in our school are no different than you. Some of them will also have been affected by another person's suicide or suicidal behavior.**

   That's one of the reasons why this training is so important—it acknowledges the personal reality of suicide and makes a statement that our school is committed to devoting time and resources to suicide prevention.

   Some of you in the room may find this topic hits too close to home. If the content makes you upset or uncomfortable at any time, please feel free to leave the room.

5. It's also always important to reinforce that faculty and staff are already providing support for at-risk students. Say: **Many of you already provide support to at-risk youth by making referrals to school resource staff, encouraging connections to the school, or using a curriculum that teaches life skills. What we'll share with you today—the *Lifelines Prevention* program— may be a new program for our school; however, it is built on the skills and experience of our school faculty and staff. And for many of you, it will simply be a reiteration of what you're already doing.**

Program Objectives

6. Show slide 2, What We'll Review. Program objectives are purposely simple and limited; faculty and staff in-service presentations can be difficult for even the most seasoned presenter, so the information you are presenting here is clear and concise.

7. Explain: **This *Lifelines Prevention* training has four simple objectives. By the end of the training, you should understand**

- **why we're talking about suicide**
- **what's important for us to know**
- **what we're going to teach our students**
- **what each of us can do to help in suicide prevention**

This training will help us understand why suicide prevention is an important topic for our school, clarify our critical but limited role in the prevention process, and help us understand what we can do to help our students.

The most important takeaway for all of us here is to understand what our students will be learning and what our role is in suicide prevention.

Pertinent Data

8. Show slide 3, Current National Data on Youth Suicide, and read this national data out loud to participants.

Note: If you are in a school that has recent experience with suicide(s) (within the past academic year), faculty and staff generally understand why suicide prevention is important. As a result, you don't usually need data to show the prevalence of suicide and the reasons for the school's concerns. What is of equal concern is the number of youth who admit to thinking about suicide or having made a plan.

9. Explain: **A review of the Centers for Disease Control and Prevention's Youth Risk Behavior Surveillance Survey data from 1999 to 2014 confirms that a consistent percentage of high school students—almost one-third of the students who are sitting in our high school classrooms—could be at risk for suicide, even if we don't recognize who they all are.**[2] **And as you know, students who are feeling sad or hopeless or who are thinking about suicide are not thinking about math or language arts or history—they are thinking about dying. What you also see is a significant discrepancy between the number of students who report making an attempt or attempts and those who receive medical help. What this tells us is that there are many more attempts than those documented in health care data. This is the type of information that has motivated many schools to implement a suicide prevention program.**

10. Share any state or local data that you were able to find on suicide. Conclude: **This data also makes it clear that suicide prevention falls within our school's mandate to educate and protect our students and staff.**

11. After you have presented data, you can also say to the group: **Raise your hands if you remember your last fire drill.** (It's likely that all hands will be raised.)

    Then say: **Raise your hand if you remember the last time you reviewed our school procedures for dealing with a student potentially at risk for suicide.** (There will be a startling difference in the number of hands raised!)

    Say: **We are well prepared for something that rarely happens—a school fire—yet at-risk students are currently sitting in every one of our classrooms every day.**

PART 2: WHAT IS THE SCHOOL'S ROLE IN SUICIDE PREVENTION?

1. Show slide 4, *Lifelines Prevention* Program, and explain: **Our school has chosen a program called *Lifelines Prevention* for our suicide prevention efforts. *Lifelines Prevention* is a comprehensive best-practices and evidence-based program that targets the entire school community to help everyone recognize when a student is at potential risk of suicide and how to access help. The goal of *Lifelines Prevention* is to develop the school-based expertise and supports for responding to the problem of suicidal behavior among youth.**

2. Say: **This doesn't mean we expect all of you to become mental health experts. Just as a mental health clinician wouldn't be the appropriate person to teach a calculus class, neither is an educator the right person to make a mental health diagnosis.**

3. Explain: **By focusing on students' specific, observable behaviors that may signal risk, we have the critical role to refer students to appropriate school staff who take the next steps, or we refer them to trained mental health professionals for more comprehensive assessments.**

4. Show slide 5, The Context for Prevention, and explain: **The overarching role of the school in the prevention of all student self-destructive behaviors is to maintain what is called a "competent community."**

    In a competent community, all members of the school are concerned about the welfare of each other and know how to come to each other's aid. Everyone, from the top administrator to the part-time bus driver, is committed to suicide prevention and engaged in activities to support this goal, which includes

    - **providing an effective initial response to at-risk students (not becoming professional counselors) and**

    - **knowing where in the school to refer them for further help**

5. Ask: **So what are the practical and specific ways our school can address these goals?** Allow several participants to respond.

6. Show slide 6, Your School's First Official Step: Policies and Procedures, and explain: **The first part of a competent community is leaders who are committed and engaged in suicide prevention. This is reflected in our school officials' development of policies and procedures for responding to completed suicides on and off campus, attempted suicides on and off campus, and students who are identified as possibly at risk for suicide attempts or completions.** The guidelines for crisis response are based on three key principles: support, control, and structure.

    We will make sure that these policies and procedures are disseminated to all school personnel and are reviewed and revised regularly. These policies help our school plan proactively so that there is ample structure and support to provide us with some degree of control in the event of a suicide crisis.

    This planning process also includes the creation of a crisis team that will take leadership roles in the crisis and assist all members of the school community in following the board-approved procedures.

    Note: Remind faculty and staff where they can locate these policies and procedures so they can review them in their entirety.

    Identify the resource staff to whom all referrals should be directed, even if you think everyone already knows this information. It can also be helpful to briefly explain the boundaries of confidentiality. Sometimes faculty and staff who have made referrals have expressed frustration at not getting any feedback on what happened when they referred a student. In writing your policies and procedures, you may want to consider a statement that explains these limits but provides an opportunity for resource staff to share, with student permission, suggestions to faculty and staff about things they can do to support the struggling student.

How Is Our School Addressing Its Role in Youth Suicide Prevention?

7. Show slide 7, *Lifelines Prevention* Program Objectives, and explain: **The objectives of the *Lifelines Prevention* program are to increase the probability that any of us who encounter potentially suicidal students**

    - can more readily identify them

    - know how to respond to them

    - know how to rapidly get help for them

    - will be consistently inclined to take such action

8. Show slide 8, Definition of Suicide, and read the definition out loud to participants.

    Note: Because this training is directed at people who do not usually have clinical backgrounds, *Lifelines Prevention* uses a behavioral definition of suicide that has been adapted from a clinical definition. Talking about suicide from this perspective avoids some of the personal and cultural issues that can arise when presenting a strictly mental-health-based definition of the term. It also emphasizes that something is happening in a person's life that is impairing his or her problem-solving ability. By asking, "What's going on in your life that makes you think about dying?" you have opened the door to the prevention process. This approach is covered in more detail in *Lifelines Intervention.*

....

Behavioral Definition of "Suicide"

Suicide is an attempt to solve a life problem with problem solving that is impaired by psycho-pathology or other skill deficits.[3]

—KALAFAT AND UNDERWOOD, 1989

Are School Programs That Discuss Suicide Safe?

9. Explain: **An initial step in the prevention process is to separate fact from fiction by answering some of the most commonly asked questions about youth suicide.**

10. Show slide 9 and say: **Yes, such programs are deemed safe. According to the Centers for Disease Control and Prevention (CDC), students do in fact benefit from programs that present suicide in a factual way.**[4]

Can Talking about Suicide Plant the Idea in the Minds of Vulnerable Youth?

11. Show slide 10 and explain: **This is one of the biggest myths in suicide prevention. If you were to go into any high school classroom and ask the students if they know anyone who has attempted or completed suicide, more than 75 percent of them would respond affirmatively. Suicide is a frequent topic in the media and one of the most significant public health problems of our time. Talking about suicide provides an opportunity to address stigma and correct misinformation.**

    The issue is not whether suicide should be talked about, but how it is treated as a topic for discussion. The *Lifelines Prevention* curriculum, which is based on research about the most effective classroom interventions, focuses on helping students recognize the signs of risk in peers, identify ways they can express their concerns, and talk to adults about their concerns. Because research has also shown that young people are often reluctant to talk with school-based adults about their concerns, the curriculum focuses on helping students realize that adults in their school can be resources, and it encourages them to identify at least one adult in the school to whom they would be willing to turn.

Is Talking about Suicide Just a Way for Someone to Get Attention?

12. Show slide 11 and address this question by explaining: **The answer is NO. Talking about suicide is something to take seriously! Sometimes the way students "talk" about suicide is indirectly, through their writing or artwork. Alert teachers should pay attention to these types of communications from their students. Ask the student about anything that gets your attention if it is out of the developmental norm or is especially violent. Not every inquiry will need follow-up—but if you get an answer that concerns you, keep your eyes open for other signs of suicide risk.**

    If a youth talks about suicide to get attention, then you're dealing with a student whose problem-solving skills are compromised. Suicide isn't a socially acceptable way to solve problems *or* get attention. Any student who talks about suicide, whether or not the threat is perceived as serious, should be referred to our school's resource staff for assessment.

Do You Need to Address Suicide in Middle or Elementary School?

13. Show slide 12 and read it out loud. Then show slide 13 and explain: **The answer is YES. Elementary school and middle school faculty and staff should address suicide prevention with their students. Although the number is very**

small, young children between the ages of five and twelve do take their lives. Because only a small percentage of suicidal children verbally disclose their suicidal thoughts or intentions, their parents or guardians are often unaware of the problem and may mistakenly identify suicide attempts as "accidents."

14. Explain: **The attempt rate for girls ages ten through fourteen increased 200 percent between 1999 and 2014, and there has been speculation that that is correlated with the decrease in the age of puberty for girls. Numerous studies have shown that girls with early puberty experience higher rates of depression and anxiety, which can be risk factors for suicidal behavior.[5] Finally, it's important to remember that suicide affects young children when they experience the suicide of a parent, sibling, peer, or another adult figure.**

PART 3: HOW CAN EDUCATORS ADDRESS THEIR ROLE IN SUICIDE PREVENTION?

Clarifying Faculty and Staff Responsibilities

1. Show slide 14 and ask: **How can educators address their role in suicide prevention?**

2. Then show slide 15 and explain: **The first step is clarifying the responsibilities that school faculty and staff have in the process. Your role is simple, critical, and limited in scope: to learn, identify, support and refer, and educate.**

Learning

3. Say: **To be able to identify and refer at-risk students to appropriate resources, it is important to learn the signs of escalating risk in students. We'll talk more about these signs next. For now, let's continue with the second aspect of your role.**

Identification

4. Say: **Educators spend more time with youth in a relatively structured environment than parents or guardians do, so you may be able to spot changes in a student that may indicate he or she is experiencing trouble. Likewise, the staff in our school—including the bus drivers, cafeteria workers, and janitors— see students at their most unguarded moments. You often have informal relationships with the students that might help you recognize the changes in a student that signal he or she may be in trouble.**

Support and Response

5. Continue: **Your contacts with students may enable all of you to have supportive relationships that make it easier for a student to ask for help. You don't have to be counselors to help students; all you need to do is make an initial helpful response and refer the student to the appropriate resources.**

Education

6. Say: **Another role of educators in the suicide prevention process is the same as it is in all school activities: to instruct. Students need to know how to respond to troubled peers and what resources are available. Troubled students need to know available resources, and parents and guardians need to learn what the school is doing and how to get help if they are concerned about their children.**

Identifying risk factors and warning signs

7. Display slide 16, Risk Factors and Warning Signs, and say: **The next step is to be able to identify risk factors, warning signs, and protective factors for youth suicide. One way to envision the differences in suicide risk factors and warning signs is to use the model of a traffic signal.**

8. Explain: **Consider the risk factors as the "yellow light" that tells us we need to slow down and pay attention. Think of the warning signs as the "red light" that signals we need to stop immediately. There is also a "green light" to consider—these are protective factors that buffer a person against suicide risk. Let's review each of these separately.**

9. *Optional:* At this point, if you prefer, show the video *Suicide Risk and Warning Signs.* Slide 17 provides a placeholder for the video. The video, which runs 5 minutes, simply and logically explains these signs.

Risk Factors (Yellow Lights)

10. When the video ends, move to slide 18, Risk Factors for Youth Suicide, and explain: **Please note that risk factors do not cause suicide, nor do they predict suicide. They simply place people at higher risk for suicide, the same way risk factors for heart disease don't mean someone will necessarily have a heart attack. They are just more at risk than those in the general population.**

    Risk factors can also be organized into biopsychosocial factors, access to lethal means, and a previous suicide attempt.

- Biopsychosocial factors include things like age, sex, race, stressful life events like being bullied, nonsuicidal self-injury—which is what we call cutting or burning behaviors—having an eating disorder, being exposed to the death of a peer, having emotional problems like alcohol or other drug use or depression and anxiety, and having a family history of suicide.

- Access to lethal means includes having easy access to firearms or dangerous prescription or over-the-counter drugs.

- Finally, a previous suicide attempt dramatically increases the risk of a future attempt, which is why addressing a student's reintegration into school after a suicide-related absence is so important.

11. Explain: **As you think about these risk factors, of course, you may recognize them in many of the students in our school. Many students enter our school with suicide risk factors and will leave with suicide risk factors without ever being suicidal. Unfortunately, risk factors are not uncommon. When we see an escalation to what we call "warning signs," we should start to worry.**

Warning Signs (Red Lights)

12. Show slide 19, Warning Signs: Feelings, Actions, Changes, Threats, Situations. At this point, give each participant a copy of the Warning Signs of Suicide (FACTS) handout and review it using the handout and the explanation below.

13. Say: **The "red light" on the traffic light is the warning signs—the things that make us stop in our tracks. The word "FACTS" provides a helpful acronym for identifying these red lights or warning signs.**

> **F**eelings
>
> **A**ctions
>
> **C**hanges
>
> **T**hreats
>
> **S**ituations

F stands for *feelings.* **Hopelessness, worthlessness, despair, emptiness, feeling anxious or trapped—these are examples of feelings that should concern us.**

A indicates *actions.* **Actions include trying to get access to a gun or pills, behaving recklessly, increasing alcohol or other drug use, or fighting. Looking online for ways to die also fits in this category. Self-harming behaviors and being bullied are also actions that can indicate elevated suicide risk.**

C indicates *changes*. This is a very important category because it means we're looking for changes from the student's previous attitude, moods, or behaviors. Students who were active may become withdrawn, quit athletic teams, stop paying attention to personal appearance, daydream or fall asleep in the classroom, or simply cut class. It would be impossible to list all the potential behaviors you might see, so concentrating on recognizing changes from previous behaviors is the real key to making assessments in this category.

T represents the *threats* that some students make or hint at. These can be specific, such as verbal statements of intent like "I'm tired of living" or "I'm thinking of killing myself," or they can be worrisome innuendos in writing or other class assignments. Whether specific or vague, these threats tell us the student is thinking about death or suicide, and that is what escalates our level of concern.

S refers to *situations* that may serve as triggers for the suicide. These include getting into trouble at home, in school, or with legal authorities; personal losses regarding relationships, opportunities, or even less tangible things like self-esteem or hopes for the future; or any type of life change for which the student feels overwhelmed or unprepared, such as moving or the transition after high school graduation. The most worrisome time is between the occurrence of the triggering situation and its resolution—in that period of uncertainty before the outcome is known.

14. Explain: **These FACTS—***feelings, actions, changes, threats,* **and** *situations*—**are "red lights" or warning signs, and usually lead to a referral for further evaluation of risk by a mental health professional.**

15. Show slide 20, The Perfect Storm, and explain: **This image reflects the way these risk factors must come together to escalate to a warning about an imminent suicide.**

    This metaphor came from a coach in Wisconsin who participated in one of these trainings. He explained that his son had died by suicide and that this was the easiest way for him to understand what had happened—that a set of factors, just like those that create a perfect storm, had come together to push his son over the edge.

    What is helpful about this analogy is that it also offers a clue for prevention: If we change the intensity of just one of those risk factors, the "perfect storm" of risk no longer exists, and we can get the person the help to stay out of harm's way.

And one of the most effective ways to lower risk is to recognize when students are at elevated risk and get them to a resource person who can assist them in developing more permanent risk reduction strategies.

16. Explain: **Remember, though, that these risk factors and warning signs are not a foolproof set of indicators for suicide. Except for the category of "threats," the other signs may just indicate that a student is troubled. However, troubled students are more likely to think about suicide. If you do come across a student who has made a threat, no matter how vague, or who gives you the sense through conversation, class work, or behavior that he or she is thinking about suicide, refer that student immediately to your resource staff member for additional assessment.**

Practicing the Warm Handoff

17. *Optional:* At this point in the presentation, if you prefer, show the video *Practicing the Warm Handoff,* which runs 4:30 minutes and simply, logically explains these steps. A placeholder for this video, slide 21, is included in the training presentation.

18. Ask: **What does an intervention and referral look like in real life? Consider the following scenario:**

    A student in your classroom—let's call her Jenny—hasn't been acting like herself for the past three weeks or so. Her grades are falling, and she looks like she hasn't slept in weeks. She used to come into your class chatting it up with a bunch of her friends, but now the other students seem to ignore her, and she seems pretty much alone. You just got a writing assignment back from her in which she talks about this dark fantasyland where the only way you live is to die.

    You're worried about Jenny. You notice some of those FACTS. There's been a change in her appearance, her social interactions, and her grades, and she's written something that describes dying. So what do you do?

    The best strategy is to make what's called a "warm handoff"—get her to talk to someone who can explore what's going on with her and figure out whether she needs some professional help or an immediate assessment for suicide. That's the "handoff" part. The "warm" part refers to the way you do it.

19. Explain: **So here are some guidelines for making a handoff warm:**

    • **First, know your referral source—the person or persons in our school who are responsible for handling these kinds of situations.** (Name these people if your audience doesn't already know.)

- **Approach Jenny with your concerns. The easiest and least threatening way to do this is to simply ask Jenny if you can speak with her a minute, and then tell her you've noticed some changes in her that have you concerned. Listen to what she says.**

- **Be prepared for Jenny to dismiss the seriousness of her situation. Expect an answer like "It's nothing" or "I don't know what you mean." If Jenny seems to question you, simply tell her the things you've observed that have you worried.**

- **Even if Jenny continues to insist nothing is wrong, reiterate that you're concerned and you'd like her to talk to someone at the school who is trained to talk with students when a faculty or staff member is concerned about them. If you phrase it this way, you're not suggesting that Jenny isn't telling the truth—you're putting the responsibility on yourself.**

- **If your schedule allows, you may want to walk Jenny to the office of the designated staff member. That way, you can take a minute or so to talk to the staff member and explain the reasons for your referral. This data is important—you want to show your concerns are rooted in the changes you've noticed in Jenny during the past several weeks. Observations that are rooted in facts have much more weight than those that are rooted in feelings.**

- **If you can't take Jenny personally, use the protocol our school has in place for making referrals like this.**

20. Continue: **Whatever strategy you use to get Jenny to our designated staff person, remember to follow up, both with Jenny and with the person to whom you made the referral. Give Jenny a few days and then ask her how she's doing. Make sure to check in with the person to whom you referred her and ask if there's anything you should know to be able to help Jenny. Even if you don't get an answer because of confidentiality, at least you asked.**

The *Lifelines Prevention* DVD ▶ includes two short videos, *Suicide Risk and Warning Signs* and *Practicing the Warm Handoff,* that can be used to help faculty and staff understand these steps and their roles.

21. Summarize: **So the bottom line is that when you notice things about students that concern you, you don't need to jump to questions about suicide. In fact, that may be the least helpful thing to do. Simply let the student know that you're concerned, explain the reasons for your concern, and let them know you're making a referral because you're worried about them.**

     If you don't have a sense of immediacy created by a specific threat or ideation, but you identify other warning signs in your students, what do you do? Share your concerns with colleagues. By comparing notes with other teachers, staff, or administrators, you may get a more complete picture that will either

calm your concerns or make a case for taking action. The action you take always involves going to the appropriate person designated in our school policy. Don't be afraid of making mistakes—overreacting is always better than underreacting.

Identifying Protective Factors (Green Lights)

22. Display slide 22, Risk Factors versus Protective Factors. Say: **What balances suicide risk is something we mentioned earlier as the "green lights," or protective factors. What are protective factors against suicide risk?**

23. Show slide 23, Protective Factors, and explain: **Protective factors are personal, behavioral, or situational characteristics that contribute to a student's resiliency and buffer him or her against factors that can increase risk. One of the most significant protective factors for youth is a caring relationship with a trusted adult. For many youth, that person is a teacher.**

Here are some other protective factors:

- **a sense of connection or participation in school**

- **positive self-esteem and good coping skills**

- **access to care for emotional or physical problems or for substance use disorders**

- **cultural or religious beliefs that discourage suicide and promote self-preservation**

24. Introduce slide 24, Fostering Protective Factors. Say: **A school that truly functions as a competent community is in the position to foster the development of protective factors in its student population. For example, students can be helped to identify trusted adults in their lives and encouraged to participate in school and community activities. They can also be taught, as some current school suicide prevention programs emphasize, that it's courageous to ask for help, a particularly important concept for boys.**

Students' efforts in school can be acknowledged; this is critical for students who are marginal performers. Lastly, and perhaps both the easiest and hardest thing for educators to do, is to be a good listener to both verbal and nonverbal student communication as often as possible. Even if a student approaches you multiple times with the same questions, try to be patient and consider that asking the same questions is a sign the student needs more help than you've already given.

How Is Our School Encouraging the Development of Protective Factors?

25. Explain: **The *Lifelines Prevention* curriculum, which is on the National Registry of Evidence-based Programs and Practices (NREPP), has been selected to help our school develop the expertise needed for responding to the problem of suicidal behavior and for fostering the development of protective factors in our students.**

PART 4: WHAT WILL OUR STUDENTS LEARN?

1. Explain: **Students in selected grades will be taught a unit that is correlated to national academic standards, covers basic facts about suicide, and outlines the student's role in suicide prevention. Students will also learn about the resources available in our school and the importance of having trusted adults in their lives, especially when they need help.**

2. Focus on the grade level(s) that will be taught in your school. Display slide(s) 25, 26, and/or 27, as appropriate, as you describe the program's objectives for grades 5–6, grades 7–10, and/or grades 11–12, depending on which students will participate in the *Lifelines Prevention* program. Explain:

Grades 5–6

For fifth- and sixth-grade students, these are the learning objectives of the four-session curriculum:

    1) To increase the probability that students who encounter potentially at-risk peers will inform a trusted adult regardless of whether this encounter is in person or online

    2) To make sure that troubled youth who are personally in need will ask an adult to help

Grades 7–10

These are the objectives of the four-session curriculum for seventh- through tenth-graders:

    1) To increase the probability that students who encounter potentially suicidal youth

        a) can more readily identify them

        b) know how to respond to them

        c) know how to rapidly obtain help for them

        d) will be consistently inclined to take such action

2) To make sure troubled youth are aware of and have access to **helping resources so that they are inclined to seek help as an alternative to suicide**

Grades 11–12

The challenge inherent in personal transition after high school, especially as it relates to unrealistic positive assumptions, is the focus of the two-session unit for grades 11 and 12. These are the objectives:

1) To increase the probability that students who have unrealistic expectations about their transition after high school will learn at least two of these three coping strategies:

   a) Own it.

   b) Change it.

   c) Share it.

3. Display slide 28, Student Curriculum, as you describe these features of the *Lifelines Prevention* program. **The *Lifelines Prevention* program**

   • **is taught in individual classroom settings during four sessions in grades 5–6 and 7–10 and two sessions in grades 11–12**

   • **includes detailed lesson plans correlated to national academic standards**

   • **uses audiovisual aids included with the program**

   • **reviews in-school and community resources**

   • **is designed to be taught by a school faculty member**

4. Show slide 29, So Here's Your Homework, and remind faculty and staff: **As we prepare to introduce this suicide prevention program to our students, remember the homework you have to do:**

   a. **Review our school's policies and procedures.**

   b. **Remember your role in the competent community.**

   c. **Review the curriculum for ways in which you can foster protective factors (resiliency).**

   d. **Become familiar with local resources.**

   e. **Be a trusted adult!**

   What does it mean to be a trusted adult? Let's talk about that.

PART 5: DO YOU WANT TO BE A TRUSTED ADULT?

Note: Not everyone in a school community needs to become a "trusted adult," and it's important to give faculty permission to decline that role. In the digital files you'll find an example of a Trusted Adult Card with the text "I am a trusted adult."

1. As you show slide 30, continue: **The *Lifelines Prevention* program talks a lot about students turning to a "trusted adult" if they're worried about themselves or a friend. But what does that mean? Here's how students describe trusted adults:**

   - **being nonjudgmental**

   - **making time to talk, even if your schedule is tight**

   - **taking me seriously**

   - **not telling me, "It will be better tomorrow"**

   - ***listening*—recognizing you probably can't fix what I'm worried about, but that just listening to me talk about it can really help**

   - **being someone who takes *action***

   - **being honest if you think you should tell someone else about my problem**

   - **remembering what we talked about and asking me about it later**

2. Continue showing slide 30, and if you like, hold up a printed, folded example of the Trusted Adult Card, and say: **On this Trusted Adult Card, you'll find the words, "I am a trusted adult."**

3. Explain that any faculty and staff who are comfortable doing so may pick up a Trusted Adult Card at the end of the training and post it in their classroom or work area to assure students they can approach them for help.

4. Reassure teachers and staff that being a trusted adult is more about listening and helping than about having answers, and explain: **If a student brings up a topic that you find really uncomfortable, know that it's totally okay to say something like this: "You know, I'm not sure I'm the best person to talk with you about this. But I know someone else who is a great listener." Your job then is to connect the student with this other resource.**

   Not everyone in our school must be a "trusted adult," but our students will benefit from having numerous trusted adults available. So ask yourself, "Do I want to be a trusted adult?"

5. Display slide 31, Staff Role Simplified, and remind faculty and staff:
   Whether or not you're comfortable displaying a Trusted Adult Card, we all have a role in suicide prevention. Let's recap.

   We all have a role in
   - **learning the signs of escalating risk in students**
   - **identifying at-risk students**
   - **referring students to appropriate resources**
   - **educating students on how to respond to troubled peers, how to get help for themselves, and what resources are available**

PART 6: CLOSURE

1. As you close the presentation, be sure to thank everyone for their attention during the workshop and their involvement in the school's suicide prevention efforts.

2. Showing slide 32 provides a thoughtful and appropriate final thought:
   We leave you with an Irish proverb that reminds us of why becoming a "competent community" for suicide prevention is so important, because "It's in the shelter of each other that we live."

3. In about a month or two, have all staff who attended this training complete the post-test and turn it in.

   Note: In this type of presentation, it works well to distribute materials at the end of the presentation. Have a stack of the Trusted Adult Cards by the exit and invite anyone who is interested to pick one up on the way out. If a teacher or staff member feels comfortable accepting that role, ask the person to display the card in a prominent place in the classroom or other work area.

   Have copies of the Frequently Asked Questions about Youth Suicide handout available nearby or hand them out to faculty as they leave the training.

   It's also important to have a handout with a list of local community resources available. One resource to feature is the National Suicide Prevention Lifeline, https://suicidepreventionlifeline.org, 1-800-273-TALK (8255). Additional resources are listed in School-Based Suicide Prevention Resources near the end of this manual.

FACULTY AND STAFF TRAINING HANDOUTS

These handouts can be found in the Faculty and Staff Training packet of digital files.

Lifelines Prevention Pre-test:
Faculty and Staff

"Educators as Partners in
Suicide Prevention" Faculty and Staff
Presentation Notes

Warning Signs of Suicide (FACTS)

Trusted Adult Card

FACULTY AND STAFF TRAINING HANDOUTS

These handouts can be found in the Faculty and Staff Training packet of digital files.

Frequently Asked Questions about Youth Suicide

Resources for Suicide Prevention and Support

Lifelines Prevention **Post-test: Faculty and Staff**

Section 3

....

Parent / Guardian Workshop

Parent/Guardian Workshop

DESCRIPTION

This forty-five- to sixty-minute presentation is designed to increase awareness of youth suicide for parents and guardians. If time allows for a discussion, the presentation may be extended, but it's wise to limit it to no more than ninety minutes. Even when delivered with the most upbeat presentation style, this is a heavy topic, and continuing too long can become overwhelming. Parents and guardians will be introduced to the *Lifelines Prevention* program and goals, and they will learn basic information about addressing the topic of suicide with their children.

OUTCOMES

By the end of the presentation, participants will be able to

- describe the prevalence of youth suicide

- explain the reasons for the school's decision to present a student unit on suicide prevention

- identify at least three topics covered in the *Lifelines Prevention* student curriculum

- explain how discussing suicide does not plant the idea in anyone's mind

- describe at least four guidelines for talking about suicide with their children

Note: For ease of reading, the term "parents" is used throughout the rest of this section to refer to the participants of this workshop. However, this term is meant to apply to anyone who is a caregiver for a child. This could include parents, grandparents, other family members, or foster parents.

WHAT ARE THE LOGISTICS OF THE PRESENTATION?

What Should the Presentation Be Called?

Unless you have had a recent suicide in your community, using the word "suicide" in the title of your presentation for parents will probably not encourage attendance. Although it seems more acceptable to use than it did twenty years ago, the word "suicide" still carries enough stigma to keep people away. Rather than fight an uphill battle, simply broaden the title to something like "Raising Children in Challenging Times" or "Parenting Resilient Children."

Who Should Present?

A member of the school's crisis team usually conducts this presentation. It can be helpful to have a member of your local mental health community there as well. Questions may arise from worried parents about individual students, and having the ability to arrange an immediate consultation with a professional takes the school off the hook and demonstrates the partnership the school has made with these resources. School administrators should attend the meeting as well.

A question that often comes up is whether to invite parents who have lost a child to suicide (in the field, they are called "survivors") or those who have personally recovered from a suicide attempt (they are described as "having lived experience") to be part of this presentation. Here are some things to keep in mind if you decide to invite a presenter who has been personally affected by suicide:

- **Make sure the presenter is aware of "safe messaging" guidelines.** The Suicide Prevention Resource Center provides such information at www.sprc.org. These guidelines are *very* clear that the method of either a suicide or an attempt should *not* be discussed. If this happens in a presentation to youth, there is concern that it could inspire vulnerable students to imitate or copy the method. With both youth and their parents, there is a chance that a participant might be retraumatized by hearing a story that touches on their own personal history.

- **Ask whether the speaker plans to focus primarily on the suicide or the attempt rather than on prevention or intervention strategies.** Although personal stories will probably be dramatic, emphasize that what's important to communicate are the ways in which these situations could have been prevented.

- **Stay clear of religious or even spiritual explanations of the consequences of suicide,** unless the speaker makes very clear that these are personal beliefs and may not apply to others. People can be offended and stop listening if they hear something that is very different from their own moral perspective.

- **Find out whether this person has presented before.** If the person has, ask for an outline of that presentation. This is the easiest way to make sure the content is going to reinforce your prevention message rather than detract from it.

When and How Should the Presentation Be Held?

This presentation should be held prior to implementing the student curriculum. It is usually provided in conjunction with a school's parent-teacher organization or another community organization or group that can engage parent participation. Because parental attendance is often challenging, you may need to be creative in figuring out how to encourage participation. Some schools have given students incentives (like ice cream or a pizza party) to get their parents to come; in other schools this type of reward is prohibited. Schools have provided pizza for the parents (which does not seem to be prohibited!) or held presentations prior to other all-school events (like sports events). Do the best you can!

Before the presentation, use the Sample Letter for Parents/Guardians Introducing *Lifelines Prevention* Implementation (found in the digital files) to create and send a letter to alert parents to the program's use in their children's classes, to answer basic questions about the program, and to let them know about the presentation where program details will be shared and more of their questions can be addressed. The letter also provides an opportunity to request permission for the children to participate in the program, should it be needed. Parents are asked to bring the completed permission slips with them to the presentation, where the forms will be collected.

For the fifth- and sixth-grade curriculum, also check the digital files for the Sample Letter for Parents/Guardians Regarding *Lifelines Prevention* Lessons, Grades 5–6, a take-home letter to parents. Students are asked to bring this home after their first session to keep parents aware of the classroom activities and encourage them to ask questions.

The program's digital files also includes a pre-test and post-test for the parent workshop. The pre-test, *Lifelines Prevention* Pre-test: Parents and Guardians, is to be administered at the beginning of the presentation. It may be hard to catch up with parents at a later date, so it is advised to ask them to complete the post-test at the conclusion of the presentation.

The Presentation Outline that follows suggests one way of organizing and presenting the material to parents. Both the content and format of the meeting, however, are flexible and can be adjusted to the needs of individual schools.

Before the presentation, you should use the Resources for Suicide Prevention and Support handout to create a list of local mental health resources to distribute.

PARENT/GUARDIAN PRESENTATION OUTLINE

Content	Details and Rationale	Slide Numbers
Lifelines Prevention Pre-test: Parents and Guardians	• Taking a pre-test before hearing the presenter helps parents assess their views and knowledge of suicide and/or suicide prevention, alerting them to aspects they may want to listen carefully for or ask questions about.	—
Part 1: The Context for Parents: Raising Resilient Children in Challenging Times	• Beginning the presentation with an activity that addresses some of the challenges presented to parents by today's culture provides an opportunity to start the presentation on a topic about which everyone in the audience can agree.	1–4
Part 2: Why Should We Talk about Youth Suicide?	• Providing accurate information about suicide, answering common questions about youth suicide, and outlining risk factors and warning signs creates a shared understanding for discussion.	5–12
Part 3: What Is Our School Doing about Suicide Prevention?	• The *Lifelines Prevention* program, especially the student curriculum, is explained. If the parents' children are participating in the program for grades 7–10, the presenter could show the curriculum video *One Life Saved* to demonstrate the ways in which students have responded to the curriculum. • The curriculum also introduces the idea of "protective factors" that can buffer against some levels of suicide risk.	13–19
Part 4: How Can Parents Foster Protective Factors for Their Children?	• Providing parents with concrete suggestions to promote protective factors in their children translates the concept of protection into a reality.	20–22
Part 5: Should You Worry about Your Child?	• Because some of the parents attending the program may be concerned about their children, it can be helpful to provide a very brief review of mental health resources and the assessment process to empower them with actions to address their concerns.	23–26
Part 6: Becoming Partners in Prevention	• The program ends with an encouraging reminder to parents of the importance of becoming partners in the prevention process.	27–28
Part 7: Closure	• Before parents leave, they should be encouraged to access local resources for themselves and their children and reach out to designated resources in the school if they have concerns about their child's well-being.	29
Lifelines Prevention Post-test: Parents and Guardians	• Taking a post-test after hearing the presenter helps parents assess the information they've gained from the presentation and their level of confidence in their role in suicide prevention.	—

Materials Needed

- *Optional:* Name tags

- Pens for pre-/post-test and permission form

- "Raising Resilient Children in Challenging Times" presentation slide show

- Handouts and materials from the Parent/Guardian Workshop packet:

    – Sample Letter for Parents/Guardians Introducing *Lifelines Prevention* Implementation (SP)

    – Sample Letter for Parents/Guardians Regarding *Lifelines Prevention* Lessons, Grades 5–6 (SP)

    Note: These two letters should be sent out before the presentation, as applicable.

    – *Lifelines Prevention* Pre-test: Parents and Guardians (SP)

    – Resources for Suicide Prevention and Support (SP)

    – "Raising Resilient Children in Challenging Times" Parent Workshop Presentation Notes (SP)

    – Frequently Asked Questions for Parents (SP)

    – Warning Signs of Suicide (FACTS) (SP)

    – Starting the Conversation (SP)

    – Addressing Behaviors That Concern You (SP)

    – *Lifelines Prevention* Post-test: Parents and Guardians (SP)

- *One Life Saved* video ▶

- Video player, projector, and screen if the video and presentation slides are to be used

Preparation Needed

- Decide on the venue. Consider the anticipated attendance when you select a location. For a small group, a classroom or library generally facilitates more participation than a larger space like an auditorium or cafeteria.

- Complete the Resources for Suicide Prevention and Support handout to include a list of local mental health resources. This list should include private practitioners, public agencies, and hospitals that provide suicide risk assessment and counseling services. Make enough copies to provide one for each participant you anticipate will attend the parent workshop.

- Review the presentation outline. Incorporate the slides and video, if desired.
- Photocopy the *Lifelines Prevention* Pre-test: Parents and Guardians and *Lifelines Prevention* Post-test: Parents and Guardians handouts, one for each participant you anticipate will attend the parent workshop. Place them near the entrance for easy distribution to attendees.
- Photocopy the other handouts, one for each participant.
- Preview the *One Life Saved* video.
- Set up the video player, projector, screen, and any other needed equipment.
- Have slide 1, showing the title of the presentation, displayed as parents begin to arrive.

Presentation Content

PART 1: THE CONTEXT FOR PARENTS: RAISING RESILIENT CHILDREN IN CHALLENGING TIMES

1. As parents arrive, greet them, hand them a copy of the pre-test, and offer them a pen. Ask them to complete the questionnaire as they wait for the presentation to begin. Collect the pre-tests as people complete them. After pre-tests are collected, give each person a copy of the "Raising Resilient Children in Challenging Times" Parent Workshop Presentation Notes

    Optional: Have each parent fill out a name tag and wear it.

2. Continue displaying slide 1 and say: **Thank you for coming to this presentation. Parenting children today is difficult. The world has become different and more complex, and with the technological revolution, it seems to change almost daily. A lot of these changes have been positive; however, many of them have placed additional stress on simply surviving, let alone parenting.**

3. Ask: **How has the world changed? Let's review some of the ways in which life is definitely not the same as we remember it was when we were children. Here are just a few of the significant cultural shifts.**

4. Show slide 2, Growing Up in the 21st Century, and briefly acknowledge some of the issues that young people face today. You need not mention every item in these lists; highlight those you deem likely to resonate with your community.

Culture of Violence

- violence and destruction in video games and media
- angry street slang that has become commonplace language
- music and music videos advocating alcohol and other drug use, containing explicit sexual lyrics, and presenting and encouraging suicide or homicide as a solution to problems
- a level of hostility more blatant in students than it was even ten years ago

Reality of Terrorism

- the climate of life changed forever on September 11, 2001

- reminders that the world is no longer the safe place most of us knew growing up

- daily news showing terrifying images of unpredictable violence

- increasing numbers of mass shootings in schools, malls, movie theaters, churches (for example, Columbine High School in 1999, Sandy Hook Elementary School in 2012, South Carolina church in 2015, a Las Vegas outdoor concert in 2017)

Change in Family Structure

- an increase in two-income families, often economically necessary

- grandparents pressed into parenting responsibilities

- codes of discipline becoming modified

- role models for family life coming from reality stars in Hollywood

- increasing acceptance of cohabitation, serial monogamy, and parenthood without marriage

A Competitive Climate as the Norm

- children working on "résumés" as early as elementary school

- sometimes competitive application processes to get into preschool

- pressure to compete resulting in "Starbucks Generation" youth who gulp down caffeinated drinks for energy

Earlier Sexual Development

- prior to 2005, puberty before age eight occurred in only 5 percent of girls; since 2005, it occurs in 27 percent of eight-year-old girls and 15 percent of seven-year-old girls (no similar study has been done for boys)[1]

- hypotheses about causes include environmental exposure to chemicals that mimic estrogen in the body, the use of antibiotics in food, obesity, and stress

- earlier maturity in girls resulting in higher levels of anxiety and depression, earlier sexual activity, and earlier substance use than peers[2]

Fantasyland of Cyberspace

- social media providing opportunity to create a new identity or to be anonymous

- social media's digital responses serving as a measure of social worth, spurring young people's anxieties, attempts for attention, and preoccupation with electronic communication

- impact of often anonymous cyberbullying on vulnerable youth anywhere at any time

5. Show slide 3, Another Complicating Factor: Adolescent Brain Development, and say, **Complicating matters further, young people's brains are a work in progress, especially in the frontal lobe from the ages of ten through twenty. The frontal lobe is the portion of the brain that allows reasoned decision making, cognitive flexibility, and executive functions like strategizing, organizing, and assessing the consequences of behaviors. Researchers have found that when adults process emotions, they generally do so in the frontal lobe. When young people process emotions, they do so in the amygdala—the brain's region that controls fight or flight.**

6. Continue: **So when emotions are involved—and for many young people that is all the time!—they are less likely to engage in good reasoning about a situation. They do not** *think*—**they** *feel* **and** *act*. **People learn to make good choices by paying attention to the consequences of their actions. However, it's much harder to figure out the consequences of actions online, in the fantasyland of cyberspace.**

7. Show slide 4, Suicide Is Also a Concern, and say, **Also of concern is that in yearly mortality studies, suicide ranks as either the second or third leading cause of death in children between the ages of ten and twenty-four.**[3] **What is of even greater concern is that the age of deaths or attempts by the youngest group, youth ages ten through fourteen, has increased dramatically in the past several years.**[4] **While suicide was rarely discussed in classrooms, as curricula content has expanded to include more real-life issues like substance use or self-harm, suicide prevention strategies have become an important focus of teaching life skills to children beginning in late elementary school.**

PART 2: WHY SHOULD WE TALK ABOUT YOUTH SUICIDE?

1. Show slide 5, Why Talk about Youth Suicide? and read: **We teach our children about seat-belt safety; to stop, drop, and roll in case of fire; about the dangers of alcohol and other drug use; and about safe sex practices. We practice fire safety drills in most of our schools once a month even though there have been no reported fatalities from fires in the last fifteen years. Yet we often do not address the second leading cause of death in our youth— suicide.**

2. Continue by sharing some more suicide statistics, either local information you've researched or some of the following information.

3. Say: **Youth suicide is a secret that takes the lives of more than 5,000 youth in the United States each year. But 5,000 is a large number that in some ways masks the more personal impact of a death by suicide. Let's break that number down into figures that are easier to understand:**

    - **Every year, 13 youth suicides occur for every 100,000 youth.**

    - **Every day, approximately 12 youth suicides happen.**

    - **Every 2 hours and 11 minutes, a person under the age of 25 completes suicide.[5]**

4. Continue: **These numbers tell only part of the story. Experts estimate that for every youth suicide death, between 50 and 200 attempts occur. Why is there such a difference in these estimates? One reason is that there is still so much social stigma about reporting a death as a suicide that it is often recorded as accidental.[6]**

5. Say: **These numbers are what experts tell us. What do our young people tell us? Every year the Centers for Disease Control and Prevention conducts a Youth Risk Behavior Surveillance Survey (YRBSS) in which high school students are asked several health-related questions. Let's look at what children reported about suicide in 2013:[7]**

    - **17 percent of high school students reported suicidal thoughts or ideation in the past twelve months.**

    - **8 percent of students reported one or more suicide attempts in the past year.**

6. When presenting these figures, you may also incorporate your state's statistics about youth suicide. You can find this information at www.sprc.org or from the Youth Risk Behavior Surveillance Survey at www.cdc.gov. Just

remember, current numbers are generally not available, because there is often a delay of as much as two years in data analysis.

7. Say: **What we take away from these statistics is that our young people are challenged by thoughts and feelings about suicide. And we as their parents, educators, and caregivers need to be better prepared to deal with this disturbing reality. Because young people spend the greatest amount of their time in school, one of the easiest ways to integrate learning about suicide prevention into the lives of our children is in the educational setting.**

8. Show slide 6, Answering Common Questions, and ask: **So, given this reality, what do you want to know to help you better understand suicide? Here are some of the most common questions raised by parents around the country. Let's see if they address some of your questions, too.**

    Inform parents that a Frequently Asked Questions handout with additional questions and answers will be made available for them at the end of the meeting.

If you are in a school district that has experienced a suicide in the past academic year, you do not need to review these numbers. You can simply make the point that suicide is not a statistic in your community but a tragic reality.

Can Talking about Suicide Plant the Idea in the Minds of Vulnerable Students?

9. Show slide 7 and answer: **No. Whether we like to admit it, as the earlier statistics have demonstrated, suicide is a tragic reality in the lives of our students.**

10. Explain: **If you were to go into any high school classroom and ask the students if they know anyone who has attempted or completed suicide, more than 75 percent of them would respond affirmatively. Suicide is a frequent topic in the media and one of the most significant public health problems of our time. Talking about suicide provides an opportunity to address stigma and correct misinformation. The issue is not whether suicide should be talked about, but *how* it is treated as a topic for discussion.**

11. Continue: **The *Lifelines Prevention* curriculum, the program we will be using at our school, which is based on research about the most effective classroom interventions, focuses on helping students recognize the signs of risk in peers, identify ways they can express their concerns, and talk to adults about their concerns. Because research has also shown that adolescents are often reluctant to talk with school-based adults about their concerns, the curriculum focuses on helping students realize that adults in their school can be resources and encourages them to identify at least one adult in the school to whom they would be willing to turn.**

Is Talking about Suicide Just a Way for Someone to Get Attention?

12. Show slide 8 and respond: **If you think your child is talking about suicide to get attention, then your child is really challenged by something in his or her life that is so overwhelming, there does not seem to be another way out. For most students and adults, suicide isn't a socially acceptable way to solve problems or get attention. Don't make assumptions about your child's degree of seriousness based on how often or how casually suicide threats are made. Every threat should be taken seriously. If your child says or does anything that relates to suicide, take it seriously! Consult with a professional if you need to form a more objective opinion of what's going on; just don't ignore these behaviors.**

How Do Young People Talk about Suicide?

13. Explain: **Here are some of the expressions that should alert your parent radar: "Nothing has any meaning anymore," "I'm so tired of my life," "I wish I could go back in time to when life was easier," "I have no future," "I want to be dead," "I'm done," "I can't take any more," "No one would miss me if I died," "I'm tired of being such a burden to everyone," or "There's no way out for me."**

14. Add: **Remember, not all of these expressions indicate that your child is suicidal. What all of them do tell you, however, is that your child is struggling with something right now and needs some adult help.**

What Puts a Youth at Risk for Suicide?

15. Show slide 9 and answer: **To be aware of what puts a youth at risk for suicide, we must identify risk factors, warning signs, and protective factors for youth suicide. One way to envision the differences in suicide risk factors and warning signs is to use the model of a traffic signal.**

16. Show slide 10 and continue: **Risk factors for suicide are like the yellow lights on a traffic signal. They remind us to slow down and pay attention. They include a variety of factors that can increase the risk for suicide. These include having a family history of suicide, being diagnosed with some type of mental health disorder, having made a previous attempt, and, for youth, being exposed to a peer's death through any circumstance, not just suicide. The death of another often makes us think about our own death or mortality. For preteens, teens, and young adults who are struggling to find their own identities and place in life, being confronted with mortality can be very unsettling emotionally, and some young people who are already vulnerable in one way or another may think about dying themselves.**

17. Explain: **What's important to remember about these risk factors, however, is that they are simply factors that put someone at risk. Just as risk factors for a heart attack do not predict that someone will experience a heart attack, these risk factors do not mean for certain that a person will die by suicide.**

18. Show slide 11, Warning Signs (FACTS), and say: **When the traffic light turns** *red,* **that's our signal to** *stop* **and pay immediate attention. Although warning signs can certainly be individual, some have been documented by research. The** *Lifelines Prevention* **program organizes these warning signs using the acronym FACTS.**

19. At this point pass out and review the Warning Signs of Suicide (FACTS) handout, or simply refer to the screen and mention that handouts with this information will be available to the parents as they leave. Share the following:

    F **stands for FEELINGS. Hopelessness, worthlessness, despair, emptiness, feeling anxious or trapped—these are examples of feelings that should concern us.**

    A **indicates ACTIONS, such as trying to get access to a gun or pills, behaving recklessly, increasing alcohol or other drug use, fighting, looking online for ways to die, behaving self-destructively, or being involved in bullying.**

    C **indicates CHANGES. This is a very important category because it means we're looking for** *changes* **from the student's previous attitude, moods, or behaviors. Students who were active may become withdrawn, quit athletic teams, stop paying attention to personal appearance, daydream or fall asleep in the classroom, or simply cut class. It would be impossible to list all the potential behaviors you might see, so concentrating on recognition of changes from previous behaviors is the real key to making assessments in this category.**

    T **represents THREATS. Some students make or intimate threats. These can be specific verbal statements of intent such as "I'm tired of living" or "I'm thinking of killing myself." Or they may be worrisome innuendos in writing or other class assignments. Whether specific or vague, these threats tell us the student is thinking about death or suicide, and that is what escalates our level of concern.**

    S **refers to SITUATIONS that may serve as triggers for the suicide. These include events like getting into trouble at home, in school, or with legal authorities; personal losses regarding relationships, opportunities, or even of less tangible things like self-esteem or hopes for the future; or any type**

of life change for which the student feels overwhelmed or unprepared, like moving or the transition after high school graduation. The most worrisome time is between the occurrence of the triggering situation and its resolution—in that period of uncertainly before the outcome is known.

20. Show slide 12 and say: **A suicidal crisis can occur when risk factors and warning signs come together to create a situation that resembles a "perfect storm." Just as a perfect weather storm like a major hurricane depends on the precise and rare combination of circumstances like a cold front, high and low weather pressure systems, water temperature, and wind speed, so, too, does a suicide attempt depend on the coming together of certain variables in a precise combination. One of the most effective ways to lower the risk of the "perfect storm of suicidality" is to recognize when students are at elevated risk and get them to a resource person. The intervention of that resource person alters those variables just enough so the perfect storm no longer exists. The student can then be assisted in developing more permanent risk-reduction strategies.**

PART 3: WHAT IS OUR SCHOOL DOING ABOUT SUICIDE PREVENTION?

1. Show slide 13 and say: **Our school has chosen the *Lifelines Prevention* program as a way of engaging the entire school community in suicide prevention.** Show slide 14. **The first objective of the *Lifelines Prevention* program is to increase the likelihood that those who encounter potentially suicidal youth can take these steps:**

   - **readily identify them**
   - **know how to respond**
   - **know how to quickly get help**
   - **always be ready to take such action**

2. Explain. **The *Lifelines Prevention* student curriculum will be delivered to students in** (specify) **grades. It is a** (specify two or four sessions, depending on grade levels) **unit that is evidence-based, correlated to national curriculum standards, covers basic facts about suicide, and outlines the student's role in suicide prevention. Students will also learn about the resources available in the school and the importance of having trusted adults in their lives, especially when they need help.**

3. Say: *Lifelines Prevention* is designed to involve everyone in the school community—including administrators, faculty, staff, students, and you as parents—in these prevention efforts.

4. Explain: **You play a key role in the prevention process. This workshop is designed to help you understand why our school has decided to address this important topic and to provide you with guidelines and resources for addressing suicide risk with your own children.**

5. Show slide 15 and address the program's staff training and instructional objectives: **Students in** (*specify grade*) **will participate in a unit that will be taught by one of their regular teachers who has received training in the curriculum implementation. Teacher and staff training is an important feature of the *Lifelines Prevention* program, which is designed to increase both the capacity of school staff to respond to students at risk of suicide and the perception of students that staff members are approachable if they need help. The curriculum, which includes activities and videos, teaches students these topics, among others:**

   - **recognize the threat of suicidal thoughts and behavior and take troubled peers seriously**
   - **know relevant facts about suicide, including warning signs**
   - **demonstrate positive attitudes about intervention and help-seeking behavior**
   - **know how to respond to troubled peers**
   - **know resources: be able to name one helpful adult and understand how resources will respond**

Adjust this part of the presentation to the appropriate grade-level curriculum that you will be using. Review the "What Will Our Students Learn?" section of the faculty/staff presentation for brief summaries that you can incorporate here.

6. At this point, if you wish, show the video *One Life Saved*, which will be used in the grades 7–10 curriculum. Slide 16 provides a placeholder for the video. The video, which runs about 7 minutes, will provide a change of pace from the didactic information and provide an example of the impact the program can have.

7. If you use it, be sure to introduce the video. Say: **Because it is often easier to see something in action than just talk about it, here is a short video that is part of the third session of the *Lifelines Prevention* unit for students in grades 7–10. In it you will see three young boys from Maine who participated in the *Lifelines Prevention* curriculum. The video shows how the boys took what they learned and applied it in a real situation with one of their friends who may have been suicidal. These boys, with the help of caring adults in their school, may have just saved a life!**

8. Show slide 17 and ask: **Are there other things that can protect young people from suicide risk?**

9. Answer: **Yes, there are. Although the *Lifelines Prevention* curriculum has been designed to emphasize skills that can protect our students from risk and help them identify trusted adults in their lives whom they can turn to for support, the good news is that you, as parents, also have an important role to play in building their resilience.**

10. Show slide 18 and continue: **You have the capacity to help your children develop what are called "protective factors." We can think of protective factors as cushioning the stresses of life and contributing to personal resiliency. In simpler terms, we can think about protective factors like the bumpers on a car. If we have an accident or bump into something, these protective factors help absorb the shock.**

11. Show slide 19, Protective Factors for Youth, and say: **Protective factors can include**
    - **contact with a caring adult**
    - **a sense of connection—at school or in the community**
    - **positive self-esteem and good coping skills**
    - **access to care for emotional and physical problems or for alcohol or other drug use**
    - **cultural or religious beliefs that discourage suicide and promote self-preservation**

Protective factors can include

- contact with a caring adult

- a sense of connection at school or in the community

- positive self-esteem and good coping skills

- access to care for emotional and physical problems or substance use

- cultural or religious beliefs that discourage suicide and promote self-preservation

PART 4: HOW CAN PARENTS FOSTER PROTECTIVE FACTORS FOR THEIR CHILDREN?

1. Show slide 20 and say: **Parents can help their children build resilience and protective factors in a variety of ways. To start, of course, it's helpful for you to understand what our school is doing for suicide prevention. Our school is here as your partner in prevention. The more you understand our approach to prevention, the more you'll be able to take advantage of our resources. Here are other things you can do:**

Encourage children to ask for help

2. Show slide 21 and read: **Teach your children it's okay to ask for help.** Explain: **We may think it's intuitive to ask for help when we need it, but for youth who are beginning to separate from their parents as a normal developmental task, asking for help may be perceived as a sign of failure or weakness. So be clear with your children that sometimes we all need a little help to deal with life.**

Help children identify trusted adults

3. Read: **Help children identify trusted adults.** Remind the parents and guardians: **Try to not take it personally if you're not at the top of your child's list of "go to" trusted adults. As young people age, their normal developmental tasks take them farther away from the family as the first place to go to for support. As long as they feel that at least one adult has their back, that's good.**

Encourage participation in school and community activities

4. Read: **Encourage participation in school and community activities.** Explain: **One of the things that has been very clear from research in the past few years is the value of connection in keeping us healthy. The importance of having at least one thing in your life that helps you feel a sense of connection and belonging to something outside of yourself is essential to keep us—children and adults included—grounded. And who knows, we just might learn something in the process!**

Acknowledge your child's efforts

5. Read: **Acknowledge your child's efforts.** And explain: **What's critical in acknowledging your child's efforts is to remember to recognize the things that are important to your child, not just important to you. Although grades and school performance may be at the top of your list, they could be close to the bottom of your child's. Be honest in your acknowledgment—young people are quick to pick up on something that doesn't sound quite true.**

Be a good listener, as often as you can

6. Continue: **Then there's that listening part. We have all shared the experience of having our children ask us the same questions or tell us the same stories again and again. After the first time, most of us tune out or remind our children we've heard it before. But if you put yourself in your child's shoes, you know when *you* tell the same story over and over, you have a reason for doing it. So does your child. After the third time, perhaps you want to point out that you've discussed this topic before and it's clear your response isn't helping your child. Then see if you both can't approach the subject in a different way. Pay attention to what your children tell you—and what they don't. Most children know how to push parental buttons, so be attentive to the message under the message. And if words ("I'm okay") and behavior (for example, moping around the house) don't fit, ask again.**

Give children permission to talk about suicide

7. Say: **Talking with your children about suicide is essential. It is as important as talking about alcohol, other drugs, and safe driving.** Explain: **As we mentioned before, a common and unfortunate myth about suicide is that talking about it can plant the idea in someone's mind. Not only is this false, but it is also dangerous. Keeping thoughts and feelings about suicide a secret does nothing to address their dangerousness or root out the reason behind them.**

8. Explain: **Giving your children permission to talk about suicide opens an important area of communication. Suicide is, in fact, often referred to as a "crisis of communication." People who struggle with thoughts or feelings about suicide report that often they are afraid to bring up the subject. By opening the conversation, you model how suicide can be talked about and reinforce your availability as a supportive resource when your child is having a hard time.**

9. Distribute the Starting the Conversation handout, or tell parents that it will be available as they leave.

10. Show slide 22 and say: **So how do parents talk with their children about suicide? Here are some suggestions:**

    - **Pick a good time.** You want your child's full attention, so choose a time with minimal distractions and a reasonable degree of privacy.

    - **Be conversational.** Remember that your goal is to have a conversation with your child, not to deliver a lecture. It always helps to have a "reference point," such as an event or a news story, or the school's *Lifelines Prevention* classes, to start the conversation.

      Example: **"I was reading in the newspaper that the rate of suicide for teens has increased . . ." or "I noticed on the school's website that the school is having a suicide prevention workshop for the teachers . . ."**

    - **Be honest.** If this is a difficult subject for you to talk about, acknowledge it. By acknowledging your discomfort, you give your child permission to acknowledge his or her discomfort, too.

      Example: **"You know, I never thought I'd be talking with you about suicide. It's a topic I've never been really comfortable with . . ."**

    - **Be direct.** Ask open-ended questions to clarify your child's responses.

      Examples: **"Tell me how you feel talking about suicide," "What do you think about suicide?" or "What have you learned about suicide in school?"**

    - **Listen to what your child has to say.** You've brought up the topic. You're interested in his or her responses, so simply listen to your child's answers. Don't interrupt or interject your opinion unless asked.

    - **Ask Questions.** If you hear something that worries you, ask for more information.

      Example: **"You say that one of your friends has talked about suicide. Tell me more."**

    - **Open the door to revisit the conversation.** Suicide isn't a onetime discussion topic. Once you've made it okay to talk about, it should be easier to bring up again. If you've heard something that concerns you, make sure to ask about it again.

PART 5: SHOULD YOU WORRY ABOUT YOUR CHILD?

1. Show slide 23 and say: **Experts have identified warning signs of suicide that might indicate a child is at risk. These are organized under the FACTS acronym we talked about earlier: Feelings, Actions, Changes, Threats, Situations.**

2. At this point, mention that parents can pick up an Addressing Behaviors That Concern You handout as they leave.

3. Continue: **If certain behaviors concern you, it's important to take these concerns seriously. Here are guidelines to follow when addressing behaviors that concern you:**

    - **Don't worry about overreacting. Sit with your child and let him or her know about your concerns.**

      Examples: **"You said something that worries me" or "You don't seem to be yourself lately."**

    - **Be specific about your concerns.**

      Examples: **"I've noticed you aren't spending as much time with your friends and you seem annoyed when they call you" or "You spend hours doing your homework, but every time I check on you, you're just staring into space" or "Your teacher called and said you're failing English because you're late to class almost every day."**

    - **Expect your child to minimize your concerns.**

      Examples: **Your child might say, "All the kids are having trouble getting homework finished" or "My friends are annoying" or "That teacher fails everybody."**

      Explain that you're not concerned about everybody in the class. You are concerned about your child. Be prepared to offer more than one example; the more evidence you have, the harder it will be for your child to minimize your examples.

4. Show slide 24, What Happens If You Need to Get Help? and continue:

    - **If your child says anything that even hints at thoughts of suicide, ask about it.** For example, statements like **"Sometimes I'm not sure life is worth living" or "I just can't take it much more" must be explored further. You cannot plant the idea of suicide in your child's mind by asking about it. In asking about thoughts of suicide, you open the lines of communication, and you introduce the idea of help-seeking by asking to hear more about your child's distressing thoughts.**

5. Show slide 25, What Is a "Mental Health Evaluation"? and continue:

    • **Act immediately if you have concerns about suicide. Get your child to a mental health professional as soon as possible for an evaluation. If you are worried about your child's safety, take your child to the nearest emergency resource immediately.**

6. Say: **Getting help for your child may not be as easy as it sounds, so let's review a couple of key points.**

7. Explain: **If you have been in contact with the school, you can ask for a list of community resources that address your concerns about your child. The school administrators may ask you to sign a form to indicate you will be taking their recommendation and/or to ask for limited information back from the mental health resource you're going to see. The** *only* **information they want is to understand what they can do to create a safety net in the school to add to your child's resources. If you read the form closely, this is the way the request for information should be worded. You should take this form with you when you go to that resource.**

8. Add: **It is certainly your right to refuse to let the school have any information, although it is usually helpful for your child, so think about this carefully.**

9. Distribute the list of local resources you have generated and review them with the parents briefly. This list should include the local mental health providers and agencies the school works with. Also include a list of national helplines (see the Resources for Suicide Prevention and Support handout in the digital files).

10. Say: **Whatever resource you choose, indicate the urgency of the situation. Make sure to use the phrase "at risk for suicide." (For example, "I'm concerned that my son may be at risk for suicide and I'd like to schedule an evaluation as soon as possible.") Although the evaluation might determine that your child is not at immediate risk for suicide, this is an assessment you'd like to have made quickly, and it is a decision that is best left to a trained mental health professional.**

11. Show slide 26 and say: **Be an educated consumer! Here are some of the questions you may consider asking the professional who is completing your child's evaluation. If it helps you remember, write them down so you get the information you need to be a partner in your child's recovery:**

    • **Have you determined whether my child is at risk for suicide?**

- **What factors did you consider in making that determination?**
- **What appear to be the reasons for my child's risk?**
- **Are you helping my child create a safety plan?**
- **What type of follow-up are you recommending?**
- **How can I help make a safe environment for my child?**
- **What can the school do to be part of my child's safety net?**

12. If you wish, at this point you may add: **An excellent video titled** *Not My Kid* **demonstrates some of the questions you might want to ask a mental health professional and how to ask those questions. The** *Not My Kid* **video was created by the Society for the Prevention of Teen Suicide and is available for free online at www.sptsusa.org.** Be sure that your local resource handout lists this video and website, too.

13. Explain: **It's also important to recognize that psychiatric hospitalization isn't the primary treatment for youth who may be suicidal. Mental health evaluations for suicide risk determine what's called "the least restrictive" option for treatment. Many times, this least restrictive option will be community-based treatment. If hospitalization is recommended, it is because the professional making the evaluation feels that it's necessary to keep your child in a safe, protected environment for a few days to determine the most effective treatment plan.**

PART 6: BECOMING PARTNERS IN PREVENTION

1. Show slide 27 and remind attendees: **As parents, you play a crucial role in suicide prevention. You know your child's moods and behaviors better than anyone else. If you see behavior that concerns you, ask your child about it.**

2. Show slide 28, How Can You Be a Partner in Prevention? and say: **Be sure your child knows that he or she can feel comfortable coming to you for help. Reiterate that you are there to listen, not to judge, and that you are there for your child, no matter what he or she has to say.**

3. Add: **Here are a few specific ways you can play an active role in the prevention process:**

   - **Be an advocate for your child!**
   - **Become educated about youth suicide.**

- **Be alert to what's going on with young people in your community.**
- **Be nosy—ask about rumors or gossip—and monitor the Internet.**
- **Monitor behavior, especially alcohol or other drug use.**
- **Know your resources.**
- **If your child needs mental health services, be an educated consumer.**
- **Stay concerned.**

PART 7: CLOSURE

1. Show slide 29 and pass out the *Lifelines Prevention* Post-test: Parents and Guardians. Ask the parents to complete the post-test before they leave, to fill out and drop off the permission form if your school requires one, and to pick up the additional handouts as they leave the room. Have a table set up where parents can leave the forms or, even better, have someone available to take the completed forms and offer handouts.

2. After the presentation, the primary message for parents is that they can be empowered to have a role in the suicide prevention process. Thank them for attending and remind them: **As members of our school's competent community, you are vital partners in enhancing the protections that can help all youth feel safe.**

    Encourage them to access resources for themselves and their children in the local community and to reach out to the designated resources in the school if they have concerns about their child's well-being.

PARENT/GUARDIAN WORKSHOP HANDOUTS

These handouts can be found in the Parent/Guardian Workshop packet of digital files.

(SP) **Sample Letter for Parents/Guardians Introducing *Lifelines Prevention* Implementation**

(SP) **Sample Letter for Parents/Guardians Regarding *Lifelines Prevention* Lessons, Grades 5–6**

(SP) ***Lifelines Prevention* Pre-test: Parents and Guardians**

(SP) **Resources for Suicide Prevention and Support**

PARENT/GUARDIAN WORKSHOP HANDOUTS

These handouts can be found in the Parent/Guardian Workshop packet of digital files.

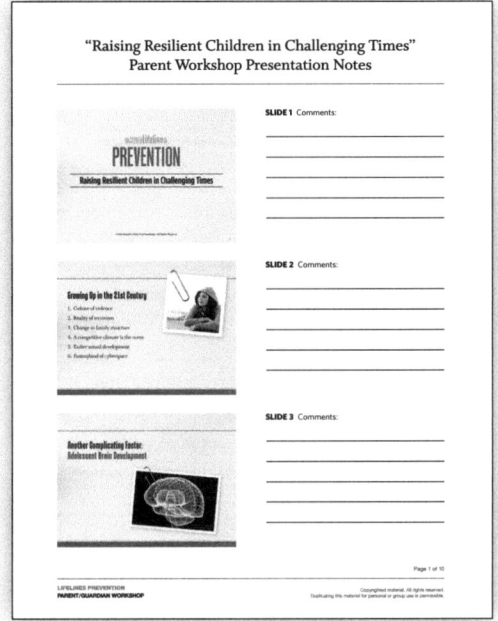

(SP) **"Raising Resilient Children
in Challenging Times"
Parent Workshop Presentation Notes**

(SP) **Frequently Asked Questions
for Parents**

(SP) **Warning Signs of Suicide (FACTS)**

(SP) **Starting the Conversation**

PARENT/GUARDIAN WORKSHOP HANDOUTS

These handouts can be found in the Parent/Guardian Workshop packet of digital files.

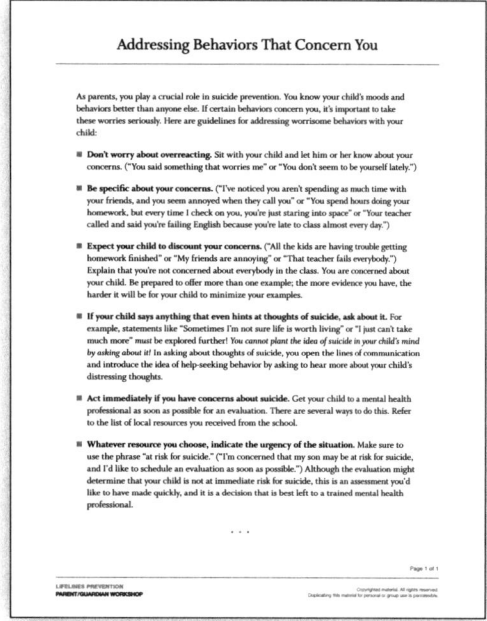

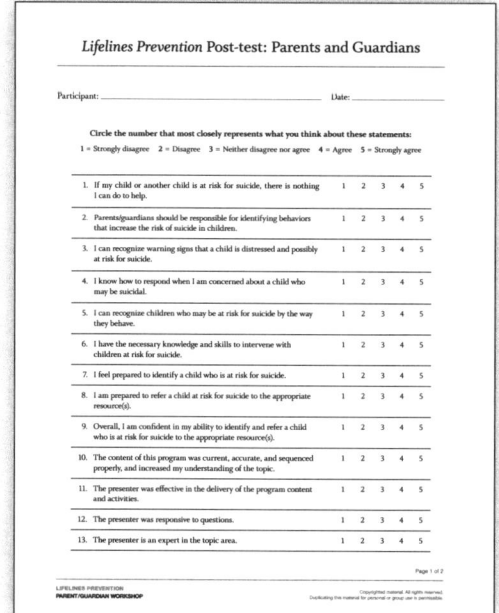

(SP) **Addressing Behaviors
That Concern You**

(SP) *Lifelines Prevention* **Post-test:
Parents and Guardians**

Section 4

Grades 5–6 Student Curriculum
Grades 7–10 Student Curriculum
Grades 11–12 Student Curriculum

Grades 5–6 Curriculum

When the *Lifelines* model was first conceived in the 1980s, there was no perceived need to address suicide prevention in classroom settings below seventh grade. Unfortunately, recently released data from the National Center for Health Statistics, a part of the Centers for Disease Control and Prevention (CDC), show that suicide attempt rates for girls ages ten to fourteen have tripled during the past fifteen years—the biggest increase among any population subset covered in the study.[1] A CDC behavioral scientist stressed that schools can play a role in suicide prevention by educating people about suicide risk factors, decreasing stigma, and reducing the availability of lethal means to people who are at risk.

A review of middle-grade literature confirmed that more serious issues like suicide are being covered in younger grades, perhaps as a response to the social and cultural changes young people in these grades are facing. While a majority of the books that address suicide for this younger age group are well done, some do not follow guidelines for safe messaging about suicide. In such books, the method of the suicide or attempt is presented in detail, and the theme of getting help for a suicidal friend is often reduced to feeling guilty for missing signs after the person has died. Turning to a trusted adult for help seems like the last option, rather than the first.

In addition, suicide has become a frequent online topic. Blogs by middle schoolers and young teens reflected conversations in which peers responded to the suicide of someone they knew. They asked each other the unanswerable question "why" or shared stories about the people they personally knew who had died by suicide.

The question for this curriculum then became not whether to talk about suicide with children in late elementary school, but how to present the topic in a way that was safe, helpful, accurate, and not anxiety provoking.

Because the initial grades 7–10 curriculum is grounded in theoretical knowledge, educational objectives, national curriculum standards, and safe messaging guidelines for talking about suicide, this curriculum for grades 5–6 follows that same model, with appropriate adaptations for this younger developmental level. It also includes content related to social media, which is becoming the most prevalent communication medium for youth in this age group.

Session 1 reflects the tendency of children (and adults!) to make fun of things that frighten or scare them. This first session, entitled "Suicide Isn't Silly," sets the foundation for continuing classroom discussions of suicide by acknowledging the anxiety that may come with these lessons. Basic information about suicide is reviewed by engaging the students in discussion and by clarifying myths and misinformation.

Session 2, "Friends Help Friends," begins to present the dilemma of knowing something is not right with a friend but not knowing what to do about it. Focusing on helping a friend rather than going for help for oneself is designed to open up the topic of help-seeking in a nonthreatening way.

Session 3, "Asking for Help Takes Courage," builds on that theme and redefines asking for help as a character strength rather than a weakness. Video scenes in the last session, session 4: "Practicing What We've Learned," acknowledge that asking for help for a friend might not be easy but demonstrate the benefits of doing so. The session concludes with a personalization of the content by asking students to sign a help-seeking pledge and name a trusted adult.

Some schools may choose to do an evaluation of the program. A pre-test and post-test are included for that purpose. The pre-test may be completed in class before this unit begins, rather than in the unit itself, or it can be done quickly at the beginning of the first session. For the best measure of program retention, it is advised that the post-test be completed at least one month after the unit has been completed. Both the pre-test and post-test can be found in the accompanying digital files.

Scope and Sequence

By the end of each session, students will be able to do the following:

Session 1: Suicide Isn't Silly	Session 2: Friends Help Friends	Session 3: Asking for Help Takes Courage	Session 4: Practicing What We've Learned
• Explain the reasons for a unit on suicide • Explain the way the assumptions we make about suicide affect our problem-solving • Identify basic facts about suicide • Identify types of helpful versus unhelpful problem-solving	• Identify the reasons for not keeping suicide a secret • Describe the difference in reactions to online posts or texts versus in-person interactions • Explain why a person should take any communication about suicide—whether in person or online—seriously • Explain the importance of involving a trusted adult in the help-seeking process	• Identify caring behaviors • Interpret help-seeking as a courageous act • Describe the characteristics of helpful people • Identify in-school support resources	• Identify at least one trusted adult • Demonstrate willingness to help themselves or a peer by signing a help-seeking pledge • Explain the purpose of the Lifelines Card

Related National Academic Standards*

Grade 5

Students will

- Describe the relationship between healthy behaviors and personal health

- Identify examples of emotional, intellectual, physical, and social health

- Describe ways in which safe and healthy school and community environments can promote personal health

- Describe ways to prevent common childhood injuries and health problems

- Identify how peers can influence healthy and unhealthy behaviors

- Describe how the school and community can support personal health practices and behaviors

- Locate resources from home, school, and community that provide valid health information

- Demonstrate effective verbal and nonverbal communication skills to enhance health

- Demonstrate refusal skills that avoid or reduce health risks

- Demonstrate nonviolent strategies to manage or resolve conflict

- Demonstrate how to ask for assistance to enhance personal health

- Identify health-related situations that might require a thoughtful decision

- Analyze when assistance is needed in making a health-related decision

- List healthy options to health-related issues or problems

- Predict the potential outcomes of each option when making a health-related decision

- Choose a healthy option when making a decision

- Describe the outcomes of a health-related decision

- Demonstrate a variety of healthy practices and behaviors to maintain or improve personal health

- Demonstrate a variety of behaviors to avoid or reduce health risks

- Encourage others to make positive health choices

---

* Source: *National Health Education Standards—Achieving Excellence,* Joint Commission on National Health Education Standards, 2004, www.cdc.gov/healthyschools/sher/standards/index.htm.

Grade 6

Students will

- Analyze the relationship between healthy behaviors and personal health

- Describe the interrelationships of emotional, intellectual, physical, and social health in adolescence

- Describe ways to reduce or prevent injuries and other adolescent health problems

- Examine the likelihood of injury or illness if engaging in unhealthy behaviors

- Examine the potential seriousness of injury or illness if engaging in unhealthy behaviors

- Describe how peers influence healthy and unhealthy behaviors

- Analyze how the school and community can affect personal health practices and behaviors

- Determine the accessibility of products that enhance health

- Describe situations that may require professional health services

- Locate valid and reliable health products and services

- Apply effective verbal and nonverbal communication skills to enhance health

- Demonstrate refusal or negotiation skills that avoid or reduce health risks

- Demonstrate effective conflict management or resolution strategies

- Demonstrate how to ask for assistance to enhance the health of self or others

- Identify circumstances that can help or hinder healthy decision-making

- Determine when health-related situations require the application of a thoughtful decision-making process

- Distinguish when individual or collaborative decision- making is appropriate

- Distinguish between healthy and unhealthy alternatives to health-related issues or problems

- Predict the potential short-term impact of each alternative on self or others

- Analyze the outcomes of a health-related decision

- Demonstrate a variety of healthy practices and behaviors that will maintain or improve personal health

- Demonstrate a variety of behaviors to avoid or reduce health risks

- State a health-enhancing position on a topic and support it with accurate information

- Demonstrate how to influence and support others to make positive health choices

- Work cooperatively to advocate for healthy individuals, families, and schools

Session Descriptions and Preparation

Session Title	Session Description	Materials Needed	Preparation Needed
Lifelines Prevention Pre-test: Students	Taking a pre-test before beginning the sessions helps students assess their views and knowledge of suicide and/or suicide prevention, alerting them to aspects they may want to listen carefully for or ask questions about.	• *Lifelines Prevention* Pre-test: Students 📄 • Pens or pencils	• Photocopy the pre-test.

Session 1: Suicide Isn't Silly	The session begins with a discussion about the seriousness of suicide. It continues with an exercise that links the assumptions we make about suicide to our understanding of it.
	
	Relevant basic information about suicide is provided with a focus on help-seeking and helpful versus unhelpful problem solving.
		• Pens or pencils
		
		• Handouts from the Student Curriculum Grades 5–6 packet 📄
		  – *Lifelines Prevention* Pre-test: Students (if not completed before this session)
		  – What Do You Know?
		  – The Thinking Tunnel
		• Poster board and marker
		• Masking tape
		• Whiteboard or flip chart and markers
			• Read the session outline.
			
			• Photocopy the handouts, one copy for each student.
			
			• Using poster board and a marker, list the ground rules or "norms" you would like students to follow when discussing this sensitive topic. Post this list where all students can see it.
			
			• Set up the whiteboard or flip chart and place a marker within reach.
			
			• If you didn't administer the pre-test before this session, photocopy it and administer it at the beginning of this session.

continued

Session Title	Session Description	Materials Needed	Preparation Needed

Session 2: Friends Help Friends	The session begins by reinforcing the message that concerns about a peer's suicidality should never be kept a secret.
	
	By viewing short video scenes, students have an opportunity to see the differences between in-person communication and communication through text or online messaging, especially when it concerns potential suicide risk. The concept of going to a trusted adult with concerns about suicidality is reinforced.
		• Pens or pencils
		
		• Handouts from the Student Curriculum Grades 5–6 packet 📄
		  – What Would You Do?
		  – The Thinking Tunnel (from session 1)
		
		• Grades 5–6 video scenes 1–4 and a video player, projector, and screen ▶
		
		• Norms poster from session 1
		
		• Masking tape
		
		• Whiteboard or flip chart and markers
			• Read the session outline.
			
			• Photocopy the handouts, one copy for each student.
			
			• Set up a video player, projector, and screen for showing the video scenes.
			
			• Preview the video scenes.
			
			• Post the Norms poster from session 1, if it isn't still up.
			
			• Set up the whiteboard or flip chart and place a marker within reach.

continued

Session Title	Session Description	Materials Needed	Preparation Needed

Session 3: Asking for Help Takes Courage	An activity introduces the concept of "courage" into the help-seeking process to put a positive spin on the importance of reaching out to trusted adults.
	
	Students describe the qualities of helpful people and are asked to apply those qualities to people in their own lives. The resources provided by the school for students who may be concerned about the safety of themselves or a friend are reviewed.
		• Pens or pencils
		
		• Handouts from the Student Curriculum Grades 5–6 packet 📄
		  – Courage Is ...
		  – The Qualities of Helpful People
		  – What Does It Mean to Be a Trusted Adult?
		  – Trusted Adult Card
		
		• Large sheets of paper and markers
		
		• Norms poster from session 1
		
		• Masking tape
		
		• Whiteboard or flip chart and markers
			• Read the session outline.
			
			• Photocopy the first two handouts, one copy for each student.
			
			• Make one copy of the What Does It Mean to Be a Trusted Adult? handout and read through it.
			
			• If you don't already have one, print out the Trusted Adult Card.
			
			• Select and prepare discussion questions for use in part 3, the Looking for Help activity. See the Preparation Needed section at the beginning of session 3 for more details.
			
			• Post the Norms poster from session 1, if it isn't still up.
			
			• Set up the whiteboard or flip chart and place a marker within reach.

continued

Session Title	Session Description	Materials Needed	Preparation Needed

Session 4: Practicing What We've Learned	This session presents students with the key curriculum messages in short video scenes that demonstrate how to show you care and have the courage to ask a trusted adult for help if you're worried about yourself or a friend.
	
	After viewing these video scenes, students sign a help-seeking pledge and receive a small card on which to write the names and contact information for their trusted adults.
		• Pens or pencils
		
		• Handouts from the Student Curriculum Grades 5–6 packet 📄
		  – Help-Seeking Pledge
		  – Lifelines Card
		  – *Optional: Lifelines Prevention Post-test: Students*
		
		• Scissors
		
		• Grades 5–6 video scenes 5–9 and a video player, projector, and screen ▶
		
		• Norms poster from session 1
		
		• Masking tape
		
		• Whiteboard or flip chart and markers
			• Read the session outline.
			
			• Photocopy the Help-Seeking Pledge hand-out and the post-test, one copy for each student.
			
			• Print the Lifelines Card handout and cut the cards apart. Make enough cards for all students. It is recommended that you print these cards on a heavier paper stock.
			
			• Set up a video player, projector, and screen for showing the video scenes.
			
			• Preview the video scenes.
			
			• Post the Norms poster from session 1, if it isn't still up.
			
			• Set up the whiteboard or flip chart and place a marker within reach.

Lifelines Prevention Post-test: Students	Taking a post-test after completing the sessions reminds students of the actions they can take to help a troubled or suicidal peer and gauges whether and how their confidence about their role in suicide prevention has changed through the program.	• *Lifelines Prevention Post-test: Students* 📄 • Pens or pencils	• Photocopy one copy of the post-test for each student.

Session 1: Suicide Isn't Silly

....

DESCRIPTION

Although most students have heard about suicide, the word still carries a mysterious and somewhat scary meaning because it deals with intentional death. It's not unusual, therefore, that many younger students joke about it. Like adults, youth often make assumptions about suicide that have an impact on their responses to someone who might be suicidal. To address this, the session begins with an interactive classroom activity that demonstrates how the assumptions we make about something can influence both our ability to understand it and how we solve problems related to it. Relevant basic information about suicide is provided with a focus on help-seeking and helpful versus unhelpful problem-solving.

LEARNER OUTCOMES

By the end of the session, students will be able to

- explain the reasons for a unit on suicide
- explain the way the assumptions we make about suicide affect our problem-solving
- identify basic facts about suicide
- identify types of helpful versus unhelpful problem-solving

MATERIALS NEEDED

- Pens or pencils
- Handouts from the Student Curriculum Grades 5–6 packet
    - *Lifelines Prevention* Pre-test: Students (if not completed before this session)
    - What Do You Know?
    - The Thinking Tunnel
- Poster board and marker
- Masking tape
- Whiteboard or flip chart and markers

PREPARATION NEEDED

- Read the session outline.
- Photocopy the handouts, one copy of each per student.
- Using poster board and a marker, list the ground rules or "norms" that you would like students to follow when discussing this sensitive topic. In this *Lifelines Prevention* program, we refer to them as "norms" because teachers reported that students perceived "ground rules" as punitive, and we want to set an example of being sensitive to language. Post this list where all students can see it. Here are some sample norms:
    - Maintain Confidentiality: what is said here, stays here.
    - Track the Speaker: listen when someone is talking— no side conversations.
    - Show Respect: no joking around, use respectful language, no criticism of others' ideas.
- Set up the whiteboard or flip chart and place a marker within reach.
- If you didn't administer the pre-test before this session, photocopy it and administer it at the beginning of this session.

Session 1 Outline

PART 1
10 minutes

DEFINE THE REASONS FOR A UNIT ON SUICIDE

The purpose of part 1 is to introduce the *Lifelines Prevention* program and to establish a safe atmosphere for discussion. The session's content is directed at helping students identify their current assumptions about suicide and understand how these can affect their response to suicidality in themselves or a friend. Basic information about suicide that considers the developmental level of the students is reviewed, and a working definition of "suicide prevention" is introduced that emphasizes telling a trusted adult about personal or peer concerns.

Note: It's important to spend adequate time establishing norms and introducing the topic of suicide in a calm, nonjudgmental way. If you are anxious about teaching this unit, the students may pick up on your feelings, which could influence their reactions to the topic.

Regarding setting class norms with students in this age group, it might work better to tell them what they *can* do rather than telling them what they *cannot* do. For example, rather than saying, "No talking when someone else is speaking," suggest that students "Listen to each other."

1. Explain: **In our next four class sessions, we'll be talking about the topic of suicide. Because our lessons may include some questions about your personal feelings, I want to make sure before we start that we're all very clear about the norms we'll be using for our discussions.**

2. Point to the poster you've displayed in the classroom and say: **Here are some of the ideas I have for our norms.** Read the following guidelines out loud.

   We're going to

   - *Maintain Confidentiality:* **What happens in our class stays in our class. This is how we describe "confidentiality."**

   - *Track the Speaker:* **Look at the speaker. Keep your mouth closed and your eyes and ears open.**

   - *Show Respect:* **Consider the reactions and feelings of others. Follow the guideline "How would I feel if someone said the same thing to me?"**

- *Tell Personal Stories Privately:* **If something we talk about reminds you of an experience in your own life or upsets you in some way, tell me after class so we can be sure to address it in private.**

3. Ask: **Does anyone want to add any other norms for our discussion today?**

    If suggestions fit within these four guidelines, point that out; if any students offer an additional idea, add it to the poster if appropriate. Now you're ready to introduce the topic.

4. Ask: **How many of you have heard the word "suicide" before? Raise your hands.**

5. Pause for a moment to consider the number of raised hands. Usually, between 50 and 60 percent of students answer affirmatively. If the number is smaller, you can make a comment like this: **It looks like some of you are familiar with the word, and for others, what we're going to be talking about in the next four sessions may be new information.**

    Then ask: **What do you think the word "suicide" means?**

    Possible answers include

    - It's when somebody kills themselves.

    - I've never heard the word.

    - Doing something that causes you to die.

    If students are reluctant to respond or don't mention ideas similar to those listed, you may choose to prompt them or describe one meaning of the word.

6. Say: **It sounds like you are familiar with the word "suicide." You're right when you say it means that a person decides to take his or her life.**

    I know some of you have heard people talk about suicide, or you've read about it in books or seen stories about it on TV. Maybe it's even happened to someone in your family or to someone you know. Please know that you won't be asked to share any personal experiences with this topic. As I said, if there is something we talk about that upsets you, please see me at the end of the class, and I'll give you an alternate assignment for this unit if it's appropriate.

7. Ask: **What are some of the things you've heard people say about suicide?**

    Possible responses may include

    - It's a crazy thing to do.

    - It's a sin.

- It's very sad.

- It's a waste.

- It's dumb and stupid.

- I don't understand why he or she did it.

Note: One of the expressions that people often use when they talk about suicide is that "It's a permanent solution to a temporary problem." While this may be true, this saying is, in fact, a cliché that minimizes the feelings of the person who is experiencing the problem. Especially when our perception of a student's problem is that it's pretty minor in the larger scheme of things, we can't forget to recognize that the perspective of the student is probably different. For example, getting one F in a semester might not be a big deal to us, but a student may view it to mean he or she is stupid and might as well give up on the class. It's critical to validate what we hear students expressing rather than making what might feel like a discounting judgment to them.

8. Say: **I bet you've even heard people joke about suicide. We see that a lot on television shows, and you may even see it here in school when someone gets upset or frustrated and says something like "I think I'll just kill myself" or some students make a gesture like they're hanging themselves or shooting themselves. Why do you think people joke about suicide?**

    Possible responses may include
    - They think it's funny.
    - They mean it.
    - They don't really understand how painful it is to feel suicidal.

9. Say: **All those answers may be correct. It may also be because it can be a scary thing to think about, and we sometimes make jokes and laugh about the things that frighten us or that we don't understand. That's why these next classes are so important. We'll all learn some things about suicide that will help us understand it better and, more importantly, know what to do if we ever know someone who might be suicidal or if, at some point in our lives, we think about suicide ourselves. And even though suicide is something we usually don't address until upper grades, here at our school we believe that the sooner you can learn help-seeking skills, the better you'll be able to help both yourselves and your peers.**

<table>
<tr><td>

PART 2
7 minutes

</td><td>

HOW ASSUMPTIONS AFFECT YOUR PROBLEM-SOLVING: STORIES WITH HOLES

</td></tr>
</table>

The purpose of part 2 is to demonstrate that sometimes we are unaware of the assumptions we are making about situations and the ways in which these mistaken assumptions compromise our problem-solving skills.

1. Say: **Before we talk more about suicide prevention, let's do a brief activity to sharpen our minds. I'm going to read a short situation to you, and I want you to figure out what happened. We'll go around the classroom, and you'll each take a turn asking me a "yes or no" question about the situation. When you think you know what happened, raise your hand. Remember, you can only ask "yes or no" questions. If you've heard this story before, please skip your turn, because we don't want to spoil it for others.**

2. Read: **A man is running away from home. A second man is running after him. The second man is wearing a mask. Who are they and where are they going?**

    (Answer: The men are playing baseball. The first man is the batter, who is running from home to first base, and the catcher is chasing him, trying to tag him out.)

3. Allow students to ask "yes or no" questions and continue until someone gets the right answer or the entire class seems stumped. At that point, provide the answer. Then continue:

    One of the things that often starts our problem-solving about this situation in the wrong direction is the assumptions we make about the facts. Can someone tell me what the word "assumption" means?

4. After the students share their ideas about the meaning of "assumption" write the following definition on the whiteboard or flip chart and read it aloud:

    Assumption: A fact or a statement that is taken for granted or the belief that something is true.

5. Explain: **For example, I bet there are times when your parents/guardians make assumptions about you or what you're doing that aren't true. Have there been times when they assumed you couldn't possibly be studying because you were sitting at your computer or listening to music? That's an example of an assumption.**

6. Say: **In our baseball riddle, most of you started making the assumption that the man was leaving his house because when we hear the word "home" we usually think about where somebody lives. So that was the first assumption.**

   The second assumption you made was based on the fact that someone was running after the man.

7. Ask: **What assumption did you make there?** If needed, prompt the students by asking: **What are some of the reasons people run after someone else?**

   Possible answers include

   - They are trying to do something bad to them.

   - The first person is the one who did something bad, and the second person is trying to stop him.

   - Whatever is going to happen isn't going to be good.

8. Say: **That's right. And what was the third assumption you made?**

   Give the students a moment to respond and then provide the answer: **Anyone who is wearing a mask is up to no good.**

9. Say: **So what happened is that, based on this series of wrong or faulty assumptions, you came up with what turned out to be the wrong answer.**

   Continue: **Your problem-solving of the other facts in the situation continued to build on your first assumption.**

   So if we were more open-minded in the beginning, we could probably have solved the situation more accurately. Can you see how the assumptions we make about things can lead us to conclusions that aren't right? Ask the class to comment.

   Note: If someone did ask a question that helped them get the right answer, ask how they changed their thinking—how "home" became a baseball position instead of a place to live. It's unusual, though, for someone to think in this direction.

<table>
<tr><td>

PART 3
20 minutes

</td><td>

BASIC INFORMATION ABOUT SUICIDE

</td></tr>
</table>

The purpose of part 3 is to present accurate information about suicide that is appropriate to the developmental levels of fifth- and sixth-graders. As we noted earlier, because the topic of suicide is often treated as a joke by students in this age group, it's important to re-emphasize this attitude in the first session and underscore how knowledge about suicide and help-seeking can change these perceptions. Students begin by completing a short questionnaire about suicide that includes not just facts but also behaviors in response to a suicidal peer. The questions leave room for classroom discussion if your class chooses to go in that direction.

This part concludes with a short exercise that introduces the topic of The Thinking Tunnel of helpful and unhelpful choices. This activity reinforces how reaching out to a trusted adult can interrupt even unhelpful or poor choices in problem-solving and help get a student back on the right track.

1. Say: **So in that last activity, we experienced that when we make assumptions about things, we can be very wrong. When we *don't* make assumptions about things, our problem-solving skills can be better because we're open to all possibilities. We can figure out the answer to what seems like a complicated problem much more quickly and accurately.**

    Suicide is one of the things people often make assumptions about. Some of the words to describe suicide we listed earlier in the lesson are like assumptions. Remind students of some of those words: that suicide is "crazy," "a sin," or "stupid."

    Those descriptions are judgments we make without having all the knowledge or information we need to make a good decision. So, for the next part of our class, we're going to review some facts about suicide to help us look at some of our assumptions and understand suicide a little better.

2. Distribute the What Do You Know? handout and a pen or pencil to each student and explain: **This isn't a test or a quiz. It's just a questionnaire to find out what knowledge you already have about suicide and what information you need to learn. You don't have to know the right answers, because afterward, I'm going to give them to you.**

3. Give the class about two minutes to answer "true" or "false" to each question on the handout. When students seem finished, ask for volunteers to read each question and take a show of hands for answers. Read aloud or summarize the answers given here.

    • ***A person who is thinking about suicide is using poor problem-solving skills. True.***

Read aloud or summarize the following: **Thinking that taking your life will solve problems you're having in life doesn't really make any sense. It shows that the person is not thinking clearly, even though they might not realize it themselves. That's why it's so important that if we hear someone talk about suicide, we tell an adult we trust who can help that person figure out a better way to deal with what's going on in his or her life.**

- *Asking someone about suicide can make the person think about doing it.* ***False.***

Read aloud or summarize the following: **Many people who have thoughts about suicide keep those thoughts to themselves, because they're afraid of how people might react if they talk about them. Think about a time in your life when you were really upset about something, and you felt like you had to keep it to yourself because no one would really understand. If you shared those worries with someone else, my guess is that you probably felt a lot better. In fact, talking about feelings can help prevent a person from acting on them, giving them a chance to come up with better ideas for handling what's getting them upset.**

- *People make jokes about suicide because they don't know any better.* ***True.***

Read aloud or summarize the following: **Most people try not to say things that will hurt or offend someone else. And as we said before, when we joke about suicide, we don't stop to think that it isn't funny to laugh about someone taking his or her own life. It's sad to think someone would feel so terrible that he or she would want to die. It's our school policy that we never make jokes about killing someone else in our school—if anyone does, you know that has very serious consequences.**

We send the message that other people's lives are so important that we don't joke about killing them. So why don't we send the same message to every student in the school who is thinking of suicide? We could send the message that threatening to take your own life is as serious as a threat against someone else's life, and it's something our school takes very seriously. All our lives are important!

- *People who talk about suicide just want attention.* ***False.***

Read aloud or summarize the following: **It may be easy to think that someone who talks about suicide is just looking for attention, especially if that person talks about it a lot. It's important to remember, however, that if people are so desperate for attention that the only way they can think of getting it is to threaten to kill themselves, then they really do need attention! But they need attention from someone who can truly help them figure out what's going on in their lives and what to do about it. All talk about suicide, threats, and attempts must be taken seriously and shared with an adult who can help.**

- *If you are thinking about suicide, you should keep those thoughts to yourself. **False.***

Read aloud or summarize the following: **This question brings up a very important point about keeping secrets about suicide—our own thoughts about suicide or those that a friend may share with us and ask us to promise not to tell anyone else. Let's look first at keeping a secret about your own thoughts or feelings about suicide. What are some of the reasons we don't tell other people what we're thinking?**

At this point, you can ask the class for feedback or continue.

Just as we said before, we might be afraid that people will make fun of us or call us mean names, especially if we tell them about suicide. That's why it's so important for us to identify trusted adults in our lives with whom we can talk about anything that bothers us. If we feel like we can talk to that person about anything that's going wrong in our lives, then we might not ever get to the point of thinking about suicide at all. It's kind of like what can happen in class. If you see your grades are dropping and you're afraid you might fail, you know that we tell you to talk to your teacher to get some help at the first sign of trouble, before things get out of hand. This is the same idea.

- *Suicide is not a solution to problems we are hav ing in life. **True.***

Read aloud or summarize the following: **While it's true that sometimes problems in life can seem overwhelming, dying doesn't fix anything. Suicide is simply a desperate attempt to do something—anything!—to try to make the pain and upset being caused by our problems go away. Think about a time in your life when you had a bad day, or even a bad week. When you're in the middle of a bad time, it can feel like it's never going to end. But if you wait a day or a week, things do change—change is one of the things we can count on in life—and you can find yourself thinking about things in life that make you feel good instead of sad and upset. If that doesn't happen, if those upset feelings** last longer than a week or so, it's important to talk to an adult you trust to get some help in sorting out what's going on in your life.

- *If a friend tells you to keep his or her suicidal feelings a secret, that's okay. **False.***

Read aloud or summarize the following: **This can be hard sometimes, especially if your friend says you'll be a snitch if you tell. Yet it's important to remember that there can't be secrets when it comes to life and death. If you did keep the secret and your friend did something to harm or even kill himself, you'd feel terrible that you kept the secret. It may sound like it could be a choice between being a snitch or having a dead friend—and sometimes it is. So don't take the chance. Be up front with your friend that you don't keep secrets that could hurt someone. And then tell a trusted adult what's going on right away.**

- *If someone talks to you about suicide, you must tell that to a person you trust. **True.***

Read aloud or summarize the following: **Even if you think that person is joking, you want to let a trusted adult in on what's going on. Leave it to this adult to figure out how serious this person is—that part is not your job. It would be like a friend coming to you saying she thinks she broke her arm. You'd need a doctor— a trusted adult—to figure out whether she did break it and what treatment she needs. You do have an important role to play, which is getting that trusted adult involved. Then your job is to turn the situation over to someone who can take the next step.**

If you have students who say they would never tell an adult anything, validate them by acknowledging that we all run across adults in our lives at one time or another who may not be helpful. But as we move through these lessons, we're going to be talking about help-seeking in different ways. Tell these students that you'd like to check in with them at the end of the unit to see if they have identified an adult they can trust. Then remember to catch up with them again!

4. Say: **You did a great job answering these questions, and it looks like you already know a lot about suicide. And while some of these answers seem simple, suicide is a complicated thing. People who die by suicide aren't thinking logically or clearly. They have so many things going on in their lives that cause problems for them that they aren't able to solve problems very well. Let's look at a handout to help us understand this better.**

5. Give each student a copy of the handout The Thinking Tunnel.

6. Explain: **What you see on this handout is a picture of an upside-down triangle that we are calling "The Thinking Tunnel." You'll notice that the top section of the tunnel is called "Helpful Thinking" while the middle section is labeled "Unhelpful Thinking." Since we think about something before we take action, "Helpful Thinking" means the things that we think about and do that can make our problems better—or at least *not* make them worse. "Unhelpful Thinking" leads us to do things that can make our problems worse, at which point we feel "The walls close in!"**

7. Explain: **I'm going to read you a story about a boy named Joseph. Listen to the story, and then I'll ask you some questions. I want you to write down your answers in either the helpful or unhelpful section of The Thinking Tunnel diagram.**

   Joseph is a sixth-grade student who had been doing pretty well in school. His grades had been A's and B's, he was on the school's football team, and he was a popular member of his class. Recently, though, his grades have begun to slip. He's especially worried about his math grade because he's close to failing. He's missed several assignments, and his grade is so low that he's close to getting kicked off the football team and, if he does, he could be in a lot of trouble with his parents. Yeah, he worries about math, but he's more worried about being kicked off the football team. He hasn't told anyone what's going on, but he thinks his parents suspect he's in some kind of trouble.

8. When you've finished reading, ask the students this question: **What are the things in Joseph's life that are causing him problems right now?**

   Possible answers include

   - His grades are getting worse.
   - He's not keeping up with assignments.
   - He may be failing math.
   - He may get in trouble with his parents.
   - He may get kicked off the football team.

9. Explain: **Write down some helpful things in The Thinking Tunnel that Joseph can do in his situation. What thoughts or actions would help him?**

   Here is an example to get students started: Joseph could think about asking his math teacher for help.

10. Give the students a few minutes to write their responses on the handout. Then ask: **Would some of you volunteer to tell us what you wrote?**

Possible responses include

- Tell his math teacher.

- Try to get a tutor.

- Make up the assignments he missed.

- Tell his parents.

- Ask for an extra assignment to complete.

11. Say: **Okay. Let's say Joseph tries all those things, and they just don't work. Listen to the rest of the story. As I read, I want you to write down the *unhelpful* ways Joseph begins to try to solve his problems.**

12. Read: **Joseph did try to talk to his math teacher, but she always seemed to be busy with other students. The only time she could meet with him was after school, when he had football practice. He couldn't miss that! He found another student in the class who understood what was going on, so he asked to borrow this student's homework, and he copied it. His parents began to ask him if there was something going on, and he lied and told them everything was fine. He reassured them that his math grades were good, and he asked if he could go on a camping trip the weekend before the math final. "Sure," they said. So instead of studying, he left with his friends. He knew he could copy the test answers from his friend because the teacher usually left the classroom when they were taking tests. But Joseph got caught. He still can't figure out how his teacher knew he was cheating, but she did. And the principal just told him he's been kicked off the football team for violating the school's code of ethics.**

13. Allow students a few minutes to write down the unhelpful thinking that Joseph did. Then ask: **Can I get some volunteers to tell me the unhelpful things Joseph did that got him to the point that the walls of the tunnel felt like they were closing in on him?**

Possible responses include

- copied another student's assignments

- stopped trying to talk to his teacher

- lied to his parents

- cheated on the test

14. Ask: **So, what could Joseph have done differently that might have changed the outcome?**

Possible answers include

- been honest with his parents
- told his coach he might have to miss practice to pass math
- told his math teacher how lost he was
- not gone camping and studied instead

15. Say: **Yes, those are all better solutions. And as we can see from this tunnel diagram, even when Joseph started doing unhelpful things, he could have always reversed direction and returned to helpful solutions. Most of the solutions you suggested as helpful had Joseph turning to a trusted adult for help. I want you to keep this diagram in your head. We're going to look at it again in some of the upcoming sessions, because it's a visual way to remind us that even when we make unhelpful choices in our lives, the simple step of turning to a trusted adult brings us back to helpful problem-solving again.**

PART 4
3 minutes

WRAP-UP

1. Say: **So today we began to learn what the word "suicide" actually means and how the assumptions we may have made about it can affect the way we respond to someone who may be thinking about suicide.**

2. Ask: **What are some of the other important things we just learned today?**

If students do not include these possible answers among their replies, be sure to mention these key ideas yourself:

- **Suicide is not a joke.**
- **Even if people talk about suicide to get attention, we need to tell an adult we trust.**
- **We don't make jokes about killing other people, so we shouldn't make jokes about people killing themselves.**
- **Suicide isn't a secret we can keep.**
- **We can come up with helpful and unhelpful ways of thinking about problems.**

3. Remind students that if they have personal stories related to suicide, you have time for them to talk with you privately after class. And remember to tell them that if they or any of their friends may be having a hard time, like Joseph was, they should talk to a trusted adult.

4. Say: **In our next session, we'll look at our reactions to things we read online and our reactions to hearing the same things in person. You'll also learn ways to help your friends.**

Session 2:
Friends Help Friends

··

DESCRIPTION

The session begins by reinforcing the message that concerns about a peer's suicidality should never be kept a secret. By viewing short video scenes, students have an opportunity to see the differences between in-person communication and communication through text or online messaging, especially when it concerns potential suicide risk. The concept of going to a trusted adult with concerns about suicidality is reinforced.

LEARNER OUTCOMES

By the end of the session, students will be able to

- identify the reasons for not keeping suicide a secret

- describe the difference in reactions to online posts or texts versus in-person interactions

- explain why a person should take any communication about suicide—whether in person or online—seriously

- explain the importance of involving a trusted adult in the help-seeking process

MATERIALS NEEDED

- Pens or pencils
- Handouts from the Student Curriculum Grades 5–6 packet 📄
  - What Would You Do?
  - The Thinking Tunnel (from session 1)
- Grades 5–6 video scenes 1–4, a video player, projector, and screen ▶
- Norms poster from session 1
- Masking tape
- Whiteboard or flip chart and markers

PREPARATION NEEDED

- Read the session outline.
- Photocopy the handouts, one copy of each per student.
- Set up a video player, projector, and screen for showing the video scenes.
- Preview the video scenes, so you are familiar with their content.
- Post the Norms poster from session 1, if it isn't still up.
- Set up the whiteboard or flip chart and place a marker within reach.

Session 2 Outline

<table>
<tr><td>

PART 1

15 minutes

</td><td>

KEEPING SECRETS

The purpose of part 1 is to help students identify the differences in their responses to in-person communication and communication through text or online messaging. Because of the increasing use of social media, especially to express feelings that might be uncomfortable to say in person, it's important to review the instruction about not keeping secrets that was covered in the previous class: suicide should never be kept secret, regardless of the way in which it is communicated.

</td></tr>
</table>

1. Ask students to pull out The Thinking Tunnel handout from the first session, so they can refer to it later in this session. Explain to the students: **This is our second session on suicide prevention. Can anyone tell me some of the things we talked about in our first session?**

   Possible answers include

   - Suicide is not a joke.
   - Even if people talk about suicide to get attention, we need to tell an adult we trust.
   - We don't make jokes about people killing other people, so we shouldn't make jokes about people killing themselves.
   - Suicide isn't a secret we can keep.

   If students don't cover these possible answers when they reply, be sure to remind them of these key ideas yourself.

2. Say: **We also talked about how we're going to conduct ourselves during these sessions. Remember our norms?** Briefly review the Norms poster that you and the students developed during the first session.
   - *Maintain Confidentiality:* **What happens in our class stays in our class. This is how we describe "confidentiality."**
   - *Track the Speaker:* **Look at the speaker. Keep your mouth closed and your eyes and ears open.**
   - *Show Respect:* **Consider the reactions and feelings of others. Follow the guideline "How would I feel if someone said the same thing to me?"**

• *Tell Personal Stories Privately:* **If something we talk about reminds you of an experience in your own life or upsets you in some way, tell me after class so we can be sure to address it in private.**

3. Say: **Now we're going to watch a short video scene of a boy who is talking about suicide. He is sending this message via text. I'm going to give you a handout that reviews what the boy is saying and some questions to answer about this.**

4. Give a copy of the handout What Would You Do? to each student along with a pen or pencil.

5. Say: **You can follow along with the written text if you'd like, or just watch the video scene.**

6. Start the grades 5–6 video scene 1. On camera, a boy is reading a message on his phone. The words of the message appear on the screen:

"I'm so done! I can't do anything right. My grades suck. I don't understand my homework so obviously I'm going to fail my tests. My mom says I don't try hard enough. I don't even want to run track anymore. I hate the kids on my team and the coach is always yelling at me. I know a lot of kids but none of them are my friends except you. I tried to talk to my mom but she just yells at me too. I don't know.......I wish I was dead. Don't tell anyone I said that. Last thing I need is more trouble."

7. Say: **Take a few minutes to answer the questions on your handout, and then we'll discuss your responses.** Have students write their answers to these questions individually.

8. Watch the class to see when students seem to have completed the task. Usually, allowing two to three minutes is sufficient. When the students have completed their answers, discuss the questions one at a time. During this discussion, write student responses to the questions on the board, and then go back and address each response separately. Leave answers to all questions on the board without erasing so you can refer to them later in the lesson. The most common (and relevant) responses are listed on the following pages. If your students miss important points, feel free to add them. Preface these remarks by saying something like this: **Other students who have taken these classes have also said . . .**

9. Discuss the first question: **If you got a message like this from a friend, how do you think you'd feel?**

    Possible responses include

    - shocked

    - worried

    - dejected for my friend

    - sad for the friend

    - nothing, this person says it all the time

    - creeped out

    - I don't know

10. Say: **So, what you're saying is that you might have a lot of different feelings, most of which don't make you feel very good. Some of you may not even feel anything, because sometimes you have friends you don't take too seriously, or you may have friends who threaten things like suicide so often you simply tune them out. And sometimes you may even ignore what someone is saying because you don't know what to say or do.**

11. Discuss the second question: **What do you think you would do or say?**
    Write the students' answers on the board.

    Possible answers include

    - I would immediately tell an adult and show him or her the text.

    - I would write back and ask my friend if he or she was okay.

    - I would show it to another friend.

    - I'd write back and say that it's really not that bad.

    - I'd call my friend's mom.

    - I'd say he or she was being stupid.

    - I'd send it to other students so my friend could get some attention.

    - Do nothing. I've got a lot going on myself.

    - I would just hope my friend told someone else.

    - Keep the secret.

12. Ask students to look again at The Thinking Tunnel handout from the first session.

a. Say: **Take out your handout from the last session, the one on the Thinking Tunnel. Look at some of your responses to this message, and let's see where they might fit in the tunnel—whether they are helpful or unhelpful.**

b. Ask: **How about telling this boy that sending this message was a dumb idea or a stupid thing to do? How do you think he'd feel if you told him that it was a dumb or stupid thing to say?**

Possible answers include

- more isolated and alone than ever

- like you don't understand

- that you aren't listening or you don't care

- maybe he'd think that nobody cares

- angry at you

- like you're not really his friend

c. Say: **Judging by your answers, this would probably go in the unhelpful part of the tunnel, since this kind of response might make a suicidal person feel worse. And even though each of us is responsible for our own lives, and these kinds of comments won't cause a suicide, these comments don't help.**

d. Say: **Think for a second about how you'd feel if someone said one of these things to you:**

- **"Don't talk like that—you're upset over nothing!"**

- **"You wouldn't kill yourself over that, would you? That's crazy!"**

- **"Don't be so dramatic! Here's what you ought to do ..."**

e. Ask: **How would you react if someone made comments to you like those we just discussed?**

Possible responses include

- I would feel mad.

- I would think that my friend didn't care about me.

- I would feel stupid or embarrassed.

- I would feel like nobody understands me.

13. a. Say: **So, when people are telling you something that really upsets them, it's not very helpful to tell them our feelings—like we think they're stupid—or tell them how to solve their problems. What we need to do to be helpful is to simply listen!**

b. Say: **Another suggestion in the list was to do nothing. Why might someone choose this option?**

Possible answers include

• You would want someone to keep your secret if you asked them.

• Your friend is always saying things to get attention, and if you did something every time he threatened, you'd be overreacting!

• Because you didn't know what to do and were afraid to make a mistake.

c. Ask the class for input: **So where would you put this option on The Thinking Tunnel?**

d. Give several students a chance to reply. Then say: **This answer would probably fall on the line between being helpful and unhelpful, wouldn't it? It might be a bit closer to unhelpful, because usually we tell people things when we are looking for their help.**

14. a. Ask: **What about keeping your friend's secret because you want him to trust you? I know that keeping a secret is important. But are all secrets the same? What are some of the things that are okay to keep secret?**

Possible responses include

• a party that's a surprise

• a present you got for somebody

• somebody telling you they like someone

• your answers on a test

b. Say: **Those are all great examples of things that are okay to keep secret. But keeping a secret about something that may make the difference between life and death seems to be a special category. Not keeping a secret about suicide is not being disloyal or untrustworthy.**

c. Emphasize: *Keeping this kind of secret doesn't help your friend at all!*

d. Continue: **You break this secret because you're loyal to your friend. You care about his life. Your friend may be angry with you if you tell, but after the crisis has passed, the anger will most likely pass, too. Even if it doesn't, it's a lot easier to live with someone being angry at you than feeling guilty about a friend who is dead or seriously injured because you did nothing to help.**

e. Write this phrase on the board as you say it: **Losing a friendship is better than losing a friend.**

15. a. Say: **There's one more suggestion you made that I'd like to talk about—your decision to tell some other person, such as another friend or an adult such as a parent or teacher. Why do you think someone might decide to try this?**

Possible answers include

- to share the responsibility

- adults are good at solving big problems

- because you need help figuring out what to do

- because you're scared

- because you don't know what else to do

b. When several students have answered, continue: **Given what you've just said, where would you put this on the Thinking Tunnel? It's much closer to being helpful for both you and your friend, isn't it?**

Note: Usually, most students will acknowledge and agree. If not, indicate that you think it's more helpful. Then say: **How do you pick the adult you decide to tell?**

Possible answers include

- The adult knows your friend and is in a good position to understand.

- You have talked to this person about other important things in the past.

- You have seen how this person responds to other students and he or she seems okay.

- You tell this adult everything already, so this is no different.

- Your parents are helpful in situations like this.

- Your friend's parents seem okay to you, and you think they ought to know.

c. Say: **No matter whom you pick, telling someone else does help both you and your friend. You get the advice and opinion of someone you trust, and you don't have to feel like your friend's life is in your hands. And your friend gets the benefit of another person's help.**

d. Say: **One of the best people to tell is a parent or an adult in our school who you know will listen and take you seriously. All the adults in our school have been trained to know what to do in a situation like this. It's important to help your friend get some adult help!**

PART 2
20 minutes

HOW TO HELP A FRIEND

The purpose of part 2 is to demonstrate the differences in responses when receiving a text message about suicide compared to hearing that same message in person. The objectives are to demonstrate that it can be easy to minimize the seriousness of a situation when the only information available is electronic and how important it is to take *all* communication about suicide seriously.

1. Say: **Now let's look at what you do when you get a message from an upset friend. Let's watch a short video of a text message exchange between two girls named Stephanie and Lily.**

Play grades 5–6 video scene 2.

Here are the text exchanges:

Lily: Hey, what's up?

Stephanie: Just got a text from Amanda. She's not OK.

Lily: What do you mean?

Stephanie: She is really upset crying and stuff. She wanted to die.

Lily: What?

Stephanie: I couldn't believe it. It really freaked me out.

Lily: She hasn't been herself lately. I bet not making the team really messed her up. . .

Stephanie: She didn't make the team? I didn't know that. What should we do?

Lily: Leave it. She's fine.

Stephanie: OK, I guess you're right.

Lily: Duh, I always am. She's just being dramatic.

Stephanie: Got to go. Bye!

2. a. Ask: **How do you feel when you read these texts?**

   Possible responses include

   - worried for Amanda
   - sad that her friends don't help her
   - nothing; it's Amanda's responsibility to ask for help
   - like they are really bad friends!
   - I know students who send stuff like that every day

   b. Say: **It looks like you had a wide range of responses, which is pretty common because we give our own meaning to what we read in a text.**

3. Continue: **Now let's listen to Stephanie and Lily's conversation when they're talking in person. What we want to pay attention to is how the girls feel and react when they hear the words via text versus in person.**

   Play the grades 5–6 video scene 3.

4. a. Ask: **How was the reaction of Lily and Stephanie different when they met in person to talk about Amanda?**

   Possible responses include

   - They're showing emotion.
   - They took it more seriously.
   - They feel like they need to help her.
   - They seemed to pay more attention to Amanda's problem.
   - They tried to think of a way to make her feel better.

   b. Ask: **What do you think Stephanie meant when she told Lily, "You're better at this stuff"?**

   c. Encourage students' responses and validate them. Then reinforce this idea: **Lily seems to be better than Stephanie at handling tough situations like this.**

   d. Say: **Good observations.**

5. Continue: **Now let's watch Lily and Stephanie video-chatting with their friend Amanda.** Play the grades 5–6 video scene 4.

6. a. Ask students to consider: **How was this different from what you saw before?**

   Possible answers include

   • Stephanie and Lily took Amanda more seriously.

   • They came up with a way to get an adult involved.

   • They told her they'd check back with her.

   • They told Amanda they care about her.

   b. Say: **The girls seemed to be more understanding toward their friend when they talked over video-chat.**

   c. Ask: **Why do you think that made such a difference?**

   Possible answers include

   • It's easier to be nicer to someone when you are looking at them.

   • Because they could see Amanda, they knew how bad she was feeling.

   • They could ask questions so they had a better understanding of how Amanda was feeling.

   • It was like they were all together in person.

7. a. Ask: **How did the girls tell Amanda that they cared about her?** Give the students time to volunteer responses.

   Possible answers include

   • Lily and Stephanie told Amanda that she was their BFF.

   • They told her they didn't want anything to happen to her.

   • They said they loved her.

   • They were going to get her help.

   b. Say: **You're right. And if you remember, the girls didn't do that when they were just texting. It seems like the girls took Amanda more seriously when they could see her. They weren't very caring or helpful when she was just texting. Do you think Amanda was equally upset when she was sending a text message and when she was video-chatting?**

Classes generally answer affirmatively. If students respond that they didn't see a difference, point out tone of voice and body language as the clues that can tell us someone is calming down.

c. Ask: **So, what you're telling me is that an upset person is still upset when they're texting or messaging but may not get the help they need because that type of communication is less personal than talking face-to-face?**

8. a. Pause for students to think and/or react. Then ask: **What's the message you take away from this?**

Possible responses include

- We need to take messages sent online or through text seriously.

- When people are upset, we need to believe them no matter how they tell us.

- We need to tell a trusted adult when someone tells us something that sounds like suicide.

b. Explain: **That is the lesson these three girls are teaching us when someone tells us they're upset, or even if what they're saying sounds upsetting to us: we need to take them seriously, believe what they're saying, and if they seem to be talking about suicide, tell a trusted adult.**

PART 3
5 minutes

WRAP-UP

1. Explain: **We've talked about a lot of important things in our class today. I'd like you to turn to your elbow partner** (a person sitting next to you) **and tell them one of the messages you're taking away from this class.**

Give students about one minute to share their messages with each other.

2. Ask: **Can I get a show of hands for how many of you are going to remember these things?** Say each statement below and ask for a show of hands after each one.

- **You should never keep a secret about suicide.**

- **Take a friend seriously, even if they tell you something about suicide in a text or online message.**

- **Telling a friend you care about them is important.**

3. Say: **It's important to tell a trusted adult if someone talks about suicide. For your homework assignment, I'd like you to listen to what people around you are saying. See if you can find at least one example of somebody saying or doing a caring thing for someone else. We'll talk about what you observed during our next session. We'll also be talking about the courage it can take to ask for help.**

Session 3:
Asking for Help Takes Courage

....

DESCRIPTION

The focus of session 3 is on help-seeking. The session 2 idea of telling a friend you care about them is expanded to include the idea of showing someone you care, even if you don't know them very well. The concept of "courage" is introduced into the help-seeking process to put a positive spin on the importance of reaching out to trusted adults. Students describe the qualities of helpful people and are asked to apply those qualities to people in their own lives. The resources provided by the school for students who may be concerned about the safety of themselves or a friend are reviewed.

LEARNER OUTCOMES

By the end of the session, students will be able to

- identify caring behaviors
- interpret help-seeking as a courageous act
- describe the characteristics of helpful people
- identify in-school support resources

MATERIALS NEEDED

- Pens or pencils
- Handouts from the Student Curriculum Grades 5–6 packet
  - Courage Is
  - The Qualities of Helpful People
  - What Does It Mean to Be a Trusted Adult?
  - Trusted Adult Card
- Large sheets of paper and markers
- Norms poster from session 1
- Masking tape
- Whiteboard or flip chart and markers

PREPARATION NEEDED

- Read the session outline.
- Photocopy the first two handouts, one copy of each per student.
- Make one copy of the What Does It Mean to Be a Trusted Adult? handout. Read through the handout and keep it in a place where you can easily refer to it as needed, especially for part 3.
- If you don't already have one on your desk, print out the Trusted Adult Card and have it ready to show as an example in this session.
- Select and prepare discussion questions for use in part 3, the Looking for Help activity. You will be dividing the class into groups of three or four and assigning each group two to three of these questions to answer.

Choose your questions from the list that immediately follows. These questions lend themselves to small-group work. They are designed to empower students to seek help from adults and/or be helpful to others. Pick questions that will work best for your groups or write your own. It can be interesting to give each group one question that is the same. If you choose to present in this way, one question that works really well is this: **What can you do personally to make it more likely that people will turn to you for help?**

Here are some possible discussion questions:

- If you were on a committee to hire a new counselor at our school whose only responsibility would be to help students, what characteristics would you look for in this person?

- In your experience, what qualities make a person trustworthy?

- In your experience, what qualities make a person helpful?

- If you were looking for help, how would you check out a person to find out whether or not he or she would be a good person to approach?

- What can you do personally to make it more likely that people will turn to you for help?

- What makes it hard to get help from adults in our school?

- What do you suggest should be done to improve helpful resources for students?

Using the large sheets of paper, write one question at the top of each sheet of paper, making sure to have two or three sheets of paper per group. You will be distributing these to the groups to record their answers. Cut strips of masking tape so completed answer sheets can be posted in the front of the room to facilitate discussion.

- Post the Norms poster from session 1, if it isn't still up.

- Set up the whiteboard or flip chart and place a marker within reach.

Session 3 Outline

HOW PEOPLE CAN BE CARING

The purpose of part 1 is to demonstrate through student observations the variety of ways in which people can be caring. Expanding the definition of "caring" can help students reimagine the ways in which they can care about themselves and their peers, as well as be cared for by trusted adults.

1. Explain to the students: **When we ended our last session, you were given the assignment to look for people around you who did a caring thing for someone else. Let's talk about what you observed. Did anyone observe someone around your own age doing something caring? If so, would someone share a behavior you noticed?** Allow several students to answer.

    Possible answers include
    - opening a door for someone else
    - picking up something someone dropped in the cafeteria
    - helping a little kid tie her shoe
    - carrying groceries for someone
    - sharing a snack

2. Ask: **Those are all good examples of people your age helping and caring for each other. Did any of you see an adult behaving in a caring way? What did you notice adults doing?**

    Possible answers to this include
    - The crossing guard told me to have a nice day.
    - The lady in the cafeteria told me I look nice.
    - A stranger opened a door for me.
    - My mom made my favorite dessert.
    - My dad came to my game.

3. Say: **So, what you've seen is that people often show each other they care by what they do, like helping someone carry groceries or opening a door. Sometimes people show us they care by what they say to us, like telling us to have a nice day—and really meaning it!—or asking us if we need help with something. In our last session, we talked about how you can show a friend you care about them, especially if they need help with a problem in their lives. In this session, we'll talk about what you do when you need help for yourself.**

PART 2
15 minutes

BEING COURAGEOUS

The purpose of part 2 is to acknowledge that asking for help may sometimes take personal courage. By identifying other life situations for students that commonly require courage, it may be easier for students to understand that they *do* have the courage they need to ask for help for themselves.

1. Explain: **For many of us, asking for help for ourselves can be hard. It really can take courage. Courage can sound like something that requires special skills or talents, but it really is something most of you display in one way or another almost every day. Let's start by defining what we mean by courage.**

2. Ask: **What do you think the word "courage" means?** Give students time to volunteer answers and validate them.

3. After class input is done, write the following definition on the board:

    Courage is doing what you're afraid to do.
    There can be no courage unless you're scared.

    —Edward Vernon Rickenbacker

4. Say: **What's important for us to recognize in this definition is that it acknowledges that lots of things in life scare us, but we still have to do them. That's where courage comes in. The first things we want to look at are some of the things in life that can take courage. I'm going to hand out a list of situations that other students have identified as things that require courage, and I want you to pick out just one. Then write in the blank space below it why you think it requires courage. You'll have a few minutes to do this.**

5. Give each student a copy of the Courage Is handout and a pen or pencil. These are the courageous acts listed on the handout:

    - standing up for a friend when someone tells lies about him or her
    - staying in the game even when the coach just yelled at you
    - going to the dentist
    - saying I'm sorry to someone who is really angry at you
    - being nice to someone even if you don't like the person
    - telling an adult how you feel
    - telling an adult if you see students doing things to upset another student
    - telling your parent(s) the truth even if you're afraid they're going to overreact

6. Allow three to four minutes for students to write their answers. Then go over each statement quickly and ask: **Why could it be difficult to do this? Why would you need courage to take this action?**

    Encourage students to share their ideas. Write their responses on the whiteboard or flip chart to create a list of the reasons these activities may be hard or require courage.

    Possible answers may include

    - Your friends might make fun of you.

    - You're afraid the coach will yell at you again.

    - You know dental work might hurt.

    - You might make the person even angrier.

    - The person who is mean to you might get even meaner.

    - The adult might tell you you're stupid or too sensitive.

    - You might be called a snitch.

    - It's so much easier to lie.

7. Say: **Now we're going to look at another question: Why does it take courage to ask for help?**

    Possible answers include

    - People might say no.

    - When you ask for help, you might feel weak.

    - People might laugh at you.

    - Maybe your parents have told you no one should ask for help.

    - You might lose a friend.

    - You might ask the wrong person.

8. Say: **Let's look at the answer "You might ask the wrong person." That's a good point, because this worry can keep even adults from asking for help. There may be a lot of reasons why adults may not seem approachable when you need help. But I'm sure there are also many reasons to talk to an adult when you have a problem. That's what we're going to explore next. We're going to do that by looking at what qualities make someone a good person to ask for help.**

<table>
<tr><td>

PART 3
15 minutes

</td><td>

LOOKING FOR HELP

The purpose of part 3 is to help students define the qualities of people they find helpful. Because the perception of helpfulness is so individual, this topic creates the opportunity for interesting classroom discussion.

</td></tr>
</table>

1. Ask: **How many of you have ever helped someone else at some point in your life? Let's see a show of hands.**

   How many of you have ever needed help from somebody else? Raise your hand if you have.

2. Say: **Everyone needs help at some point in life. Our school system has planned how adults can and will be helpful whenever students need support.**

3. Divide the class into groups of three or four. Use your knowledge of the students to create functional work groups. Distribute a marker and two to three large sheets of paper with the prepared discussion questions on them to each group.

This activity usually takes about three minutes to complete. When it extends beyond that time, students tend to go off topic, so the curriculum design intentionally keeps the small-group time short.

4. Explain: **I gave each small group two or three questions to answer about the qualities of helpful people. Your questions are written on these large sheets of paper. I also gave each group a marker so you can write your answers on the paper to share with the rest of the class. You will have a couple of minutes to complete the assignment.**

   Note: It can be interesting to give each group one question that is the same. A question that works well if you choose to present in this way is **What can you do personally to make it more likely that people will turn to you for help?** When the groups have finished answering their questions, tell them to post their responses to this question in the front of the room to facilitate discussion.

5. When the small groups are done writing their answers, have the whole class come back together. Have the groups take turns reading their questions and answers. Try to have as many groups read their questions and answers as time allows.

6. Say: **There's an interesting pattern in your responses: What we look for in helpful people is the same thing people want from us when they're looking for help. Not all the answers are identical, though, are they? So, what one person finds helpful may not be what another person finds helpful. We should think about the people in our lives we find helpful and what it is about them personally that makes us trust them.**

7. Give each student a copy of The Qualities of Helpful People handout. Take turns reading this handout out loud as a whole group. Encourage students to take this handout with them and refer to it as needed when anyone asks for help.

<table>
<tr><td>

PART 4

3 minutes

</td></tr>
</table>

RESOURCES AVAILABLE FOR STUDENTS IN SCHOOL

The purpose of part 4 is to assure your students that the adults in the school have received training so they will know how to respond to situations involving suicidal behavior. Use your preparation from reading the handout What Does It Mean to Find a Trusted Adult? to inform your explanations. Students are reminded that not every member of the staff may demonstrate the qualities they personally find helpful. So if students are not satisfied with the response from the first adult, they should immediately find another trusted adult. They can also check for the Trusted Adult Card that many of the faculty and staff members have placed in their classrooms or offices to indicate they're prepared to assume that role. The school's response when a potentially suicidal student is identified is explained briefly.

1. Explain: **The question of whom students can approach to get help is so crucial that all the adults in our school have received training so we know what to do if one of you approaches us with a concern about another student's well-being. We're especially taught what to do if that concern has anything to do with suicide risk. It's also important to remember what we just learned in our activity today about the different qualities of helpful people: how what one person finds helpful may be very unhelpful to someone else. So, if you go to a teacher to ask for help and the response isn't something that helps you, go find another teacher or staff member to talk to.**

2. Say: **You may have already noticed that some of the faculty and staff have placed cards in their rooms that read "I am a trusted adult."** Show the sample card to the class. **These adults agree about the qualities that make an adult helpful and are willing to be approached by anyone who needs someone to listen to them in a nonjudgmental, trustworthy way.**

3. Next, students should be told exactly what the school's procedure is when there is concern about a student's well-being. For example, explain: **The Trusted Adult Cards are only one part of our formal school policy. Here's the procedure we follow:**

Read the following statement or adapt it to describe your school's policy, if it is different. Consider also writing the names of your school's resource staff on the board:

> **When a student has been called to the attention of any adult in the school, that adult will contact one of the school personnel who has been trained and designated to respond to this kind of situation. In our school those people are** (name the individuals)**. One of these individuals will talk privately with the student to find out what is bothering him or her. If the adult is concerned about this person being at risk for suicide, the parents/ guardians will be contacted, and the student will be referred for help. You may contact any adult in the school on your own if you are worried about someone else, and, if you wish, your name will not be revealed.**

4. Explain: **Sometimes students worry that their parents or guardians will be angry or upset with them if the school contacts them. And while there's no guarantee that this won't happen, remember that the resource person is there to explain to parents and guardians the reasons for the school's concerns and how important it is for the student to get help.**

PART 5
2 minutes

WRAP-UP

1. Say: **What we talked about today reminded us that sometimes we need to get help for ourselves, and it can take a bit of courage to do that. Can anybody tell me how we defined "courage"?**

2. Pause for a moment for one or more students to volunteer the answer. Then validate, paraphrasing the earlier definition:

   Courage is doing what you know is right even if you're afraid.

3. Say: **And while it can take courage to ask for help, that process can be easier if we identify the traits of the people we find helpful and then look for the trusted adults in our lives who meet those criteria.**

   We also learned that everyone in our school has been trained in what it takes to be a trusted adult. The people who feel they can meet those responsibilities have a Trusted Adult Card in their classrooms or offices.

   In our next session, we'll put into practice some of the things we've learned.

Session 4:
Practicing What We've Learned

··

DESCRIPTION

This session presents students with the key curriculum messages in short video scenes that demonstrate how to show you care and have the courage to ask a trusted adult for help if you're worried about yourself or a friend. After viewing these video scenes, students sign a help-seeking pledge and receive a small card on which to write the names and contact information for their trusted adults.

LEARNING OBJECTIVES

By the end of the session, students will be able to

- identify at least one trusted adult

- demonstrate willingness to help themselves or a peer by signing a help-seeking pledge

- explain the purpose of the Lifelines Card

MATERIALS NEEDED

- Pens or pencils
- Handouts from the Student Curriculum Grades 5–6 packet 📄
    - Help-Seeking Pledge
    - Lifelines Card
    - *Optional: Lifelines Prevention* Post-test: Students

- Scissors
- Grades 5–6 video scenes 5–9 and a video player, projector, and screen ▶
- Norms poster from session 1
- Masking tape
- Whiteboard or flip chart and markers

PREPARATION NEEDED

- Read the session outline.
- Photocopy the Help-Seeking Pledge handout and the post-test, one copy of each per student.
- Photocopy the Lifelines Card handout and cut the cards apart. Make enough so every student will have a Lifelines Card. These cards are designed to be carried by the students at all times. They should, therefore, be printed on sufficiently strong stock to stand up to use; 8-point white-coated cover stock is recommended. Students won't want to advertise the fact that they are carrying a card with help-seeking information, so use an unobtrusive color. Alternatively, you can create your own Lifelines Cards. Use an easy-to-read font and print them on heavy paper stock.
- Set up a video player, projector, and screen for showing the video segments.
- Preview the video scenes, so you are familiar with their content.
- Post the Norms poster from session 1, if it isn't still up.
- Set up the whiteboard or flip chart and place a marker within reach.

Session 4 Outline

HOW FRIENDS CAN HELP FRIENDS

The purpose of part 1 is to illustrate situations that demonstrate the key learning principles covered in this curriculum. Using short video scenes dramatizes the process of identifying a troubled peer, showing you care, and going to a trusted adult for help. Although the characters are not talking about a real-life experience, the content is drawn from discussions with real fifth- and sixth-grade students.

1. Explain: **We're going to start this session by looking at some short video scenes that illustrate important information we've been learning in this program. We'll observe some late elementary grade students who receive a disturbing text message from one of their friends. Then we'll listen to them talk about what to do about it. We'll stop between the video scenes so we can discuss what we've seen. The students we're going to see are named Caitlyn, Lea, and DeShon. They are reading a text from their friend Mattias.**

2. Show the grades 5–6 video scene 5. After the scene ends, ask the following questions: **Caitlyn, Lea, and DeShon are responding differently to Mattias's text message. Is one approach better than another? Why?**

    Possible answers include

    • Caitlyn is taking what Mattias says seriously.

    • Lea understands that sometimes students write things that are weird, and she's not overreacting. She'll wait to see if it happens again; she doesn't want to get him in trouble by telling an adult.

    • DeShon doesn't know Mattias well, but when Mattias has talked to him, he didn't mention the way he was feeling. When he texts Mattias to ask him about the text, Mattias says it's no big deal. That's enough to make DeShon feel it's okay not to do anything.

3. Ask the students: **How many "signs" from a friend do you think are enough to warrant telling an adult?**

    Possible answers include

    • One would make me scared.

    • I'd have to see a few more things before I would get really concerned.

- I'm not sure, especially if I don't know the student well.

- I tell my mom everything, so I'd probably tell her about a text like this.

4. Ask: **Is texting the best way to ask someone if he needs help?**

    Possible answers include

    - Yes, because it's easier to be honest.

    - If you text, they can go back and look at it later.

    - No, I need to see someone's face when I ask something this important.

    - Sometimes it's the only way you can do it.

5. Show the grades 5–6 video scene 6. When the scenes ends, ask the following questions:

    Here we see DeShon talking about Mattias to his friend, Jonathan. Why doesn't either boy want to be the person to tell somebody about what's happening with Mattias?

    Possible answers include

    - They'd be snitching.

    - He'd be angry at them.

    - They're making something out of nothing.

    - Maybe someone else knows Mattias better.

    - Maybe they don't like Mattias.

    - Maybe Mattias was mean to them, and they don't feel like helping him.

6. Ask: **So, what I hear you saying is that there might be a lot of reasons these students don't want to be the one to tell the teacher. What if we made this question a little more personal: Would you take it seriously if one of your friends sent a text like the one Mattias sent?**

    Possible answers include

    - I'd be more worried, because I know my friend doesn't joke about things like that.

    - I'd find it easier to ask him about it.

    - Since my mom knows my friend, I'd tell her about it right away.

7. Ask: **How many concerning texts or online messages are enough to get help?**

    Possible answers include

    - It depends on what they say.
    - It depends on which friend is writing them.
    - I'd tell my mom even if it was just one message.

8. Say: **So, there are a variety of factors that many of you would consider— although some of you would talk to someone you trust, like your mom, right away. That's what Caitlyn decides to do, so let's look at the next scene of Caitlyn talking with her mom.**

9. Show the grades 5–6 video scene 7. When the scene ends, ask: **How did talking to her mom help shape Caitlyn's plan?**

    Possible answers include

    - Her mom asked her questions about what's going on.
    - Her mom listened to the answers.
    - She made suggestions about what to do.
    - She offered to call the teacher for Caitlyn.

10. Ask: **How do you think Caitlyn felt after talking with her mother?**

    Possible answers include

    - Like maybe there was something to be concerned about—maybe she wasn't overreacting.
    - Not so confused—she had a plan.
    - Happy that her mother listened to her.
    - Glad that her mother was going to check in with her afterward.

11. Ask: **What other options do you think Caitlyn and her mom have to help Mattias?**

    Possible answers include

    - They could call Mattias's mom.
    - Caitlyn's mom could talk to the school counselor and tell him or her what's going on.

12. Say: **It sounds like you can think of a couple of other things that may have been helpful responses to Mattias's problems. Now let's see what happens when Caitlyn talks to the teacher, Mrs. Washington, the next day.**

13. Show the grades 5–6 video scene 8. When the scene ends, ask: **Why was Mrs. Washington a good trusted adult for Caitlyn to tell?**

Possible answers include

- She understood how hard it was for Caitlyn to tell her.
- She explained why this isn't really a secret, which makes Caitlyn feel better.
- She is going to go to the school counselor for his advice.
- She told Caitlyn she did the right thing.
- She recognized it took courage for Caitlyn to tell.

14. Say: **That's what we talked about in the last session, wasn't it—the courage it can take to ask for help? Even when you know it's the right thing to do.**

15. Ask: **Do you think it took courage for Caitlyn to do what she did?**

Possible answers include

- Yes, because Mattias isn't a close friend of hers, and she was afraid that she might lose her close friends by talking with an adult. She was risking her real friendships for a student she hardly knew.
- It's such a big deal today to mind your own business and people can get really upset if you don't.
- Mattias could freak out on her if he finds out she told.
- Mrs. Washington might not have taken her seriously.
- Her friends might have gotten angry at her.

16. Ask: **Why do you think Caitlyn was worried that her friends might be mad at her?**

Possible answers include

- They might think she can never be trusted with a secret.
- She blabbed to an adult, and some students don't respect that.
- They may feel that it wasn't that teacher's business.

17. Say: **You've listed several good reasons for Caitlyn to worry about how her friends might react if they found out she talked to an adult. Let's go back to the video. What's happening now is that DeShon has had some time to think about what he and Caitlyn have been talking about. He looks for Caitlyn and finds her in a classroom. Let's see the conversation they have.**

18. Show the grades 5–6 video scene 9. When the scene ends, ask: **In our second class, we had a conversation about how friends can show that they care about each other. How does DeShon show Caitlyn he cares about her?**

    Possible answers include

    - He tells her he thinks she was right to tell Mrs. Washington.

    - He says he felt bad that he tried to talk her out of it.

    - He admitted he felt guilty about not doing anything about it himself.

19. Ask: **Even though Caitlyn isn't a really good friend of Mattias's, how does she show she cares about him?**

    Possible answers include

    - She risks getting her friends angry at her by trying to get him some help.

    - She tells Mrs. Washington, because Mattias is in one of her classes and Mrs. Washington is easy to talk to.

    - She started by talking with her mom about Mattias's texts.

20. Say: **You're right. What these things show us is that you don't have to be good friends with someone to show that you care about them. Caitlyn did all these things without even talking with Mattias about her worries. Especially because her worries about Mattias were so serious, going to that trusted adult right away was the best thing that Caitlyn could have done. She realized it wasn't her job to find out why he was upset or to try to talk him into getting help. She left that up to Mrs. Washington to figure out. This is something that's really important to remember.**

PART 2
5 minutes

While you will find a handout with a copy of the help-seeking pledge in the Student Curriculum Grades 5–6 packet in the 📄 digital files, feel free to use your creativity to make this activity more interesting.

For example, several teachers have created puzzle pieces with the help-seeking pledge printed on it. After students have signed their pledge, they are asked to put their pieces together. Another teacher created a tree and made the help-seeking pledges into the shape of leaves.

If you choose to add a creative dimension to this activity, you will need to allocate more time.

THE HELP-SEEKING PLEDGE

The purpose of part 2 is to invite students to formally commit to the idea of seeking help for themselves or a friend. Created by students, this simple pledge is designed to encourage the identification of helpful adults.

1. Explain: **In the last part of our session today, we're going to talk about making a help-seeking pledge.**

2. Ask: **Can anyone tell me the meaning of a pledge?** Solicit responses from students until you get the answer that a pledge is a promise.

3. Explain: **The promise I'm going to ask you to make today is a promise to yourself. In these** *Lifelines Prevention* **sessions, you've learned to pay attention to your friends and peers if they say things online or in person that worry you. We also talked about going to a trusted adult for help. The promise you're making to yourself is that if you see or hear things that make you worry about someone else, or if you find yourself thinking or worrying about things that upset you, you'll get help from a trusted adult. This help-seeking pledge was created by real students as a way to formally commit to the idea of seeking help for yourself or for a friend.**

4. Give each student a copy of the Help-Seeking Pledge handout and a pen or pencil.

5. Explain: **On this pledge, you'll see that you're asked to identify three people you'd turn to if you needed help for yourself or someone else. I'd like you to write in the names of three adults you trust, and if you have their contact information, add that, too. If you have a cell phone, you can put your trusted adult's phone number in your contact list, too.**

   If there is anybody who can't think of even one name to put on the list, you certainly can add my name or come see me at the end of the session.

   Note: While you'll rarely have a student who can't name even one trusted adult, it does happen sometimes. If the student is open enough to share this information with you, set up a brief meeting to learn more about what's going on. Most likely, this is a student who could benefit from a consultation with your school's resource staff.

PART 3
5 minutes

WRAP-UP

1. Explain: **We've learned a lot about suicide prevention in these four sessions. It's the kind of information that you'll be able to use for the rest of your lives. What are some of the things you remember from these four sessions?**

    Possible responses include

    - Tell a trusted adult when you or someone else needs help.
    - You can show you care about someone even if they're not your friend.
    - Our school has trained all staff members to be trusted adults.
    - It takes courage to ask for help.
    - Don't keep a secret about suicide.

2. Say: **Although we've had a lot of thoughtful and interesting discussions, there are some *key points* that are important for you to remember. This information has been printed for you on a small card that you can keep in your wallet or in another safe, easily accessible place.**

3. Give each student a Lifelines Card.

4. Explain: **This small card summarizes all the information we've covered in these sessions on suicide prevention and help-seeking. Most important, it reinforces the fact that the first thing to do if you're worried about yourself or a friend is to tell a trusted adult. It even gives you room to write down the names and phone numbers of the adults you know you can go to if you need help. If you have a cell phone, add these phone numbers to your contact list so you have them with you at all times.**

    Remember these three key points:

    - **Show a friend you care.**
    - **It takes courage to ask for help.**
    - **Get help from a trusted adult!**

5. Conclude: **I'd like to make one last important point: We've been talking a lot about what our school is doing to take youth suicide prevention more seriously. Yet as we've talked over the last four sessions, you've made it very clear that you feel you're also in a great position to help each other. Be like Caitlyn, the student, we saw in the video: show that you care about other students, even if you don't know them very well, and know the trusted adults you can go to for help!**

6. *Optional:* Have students take the post-test one month after you end this session.

GRADES 5–6 CURRICULUM HANDOUTS

These handouts can be found in the Student Curriculum Grades 5–6 packet of digital files.

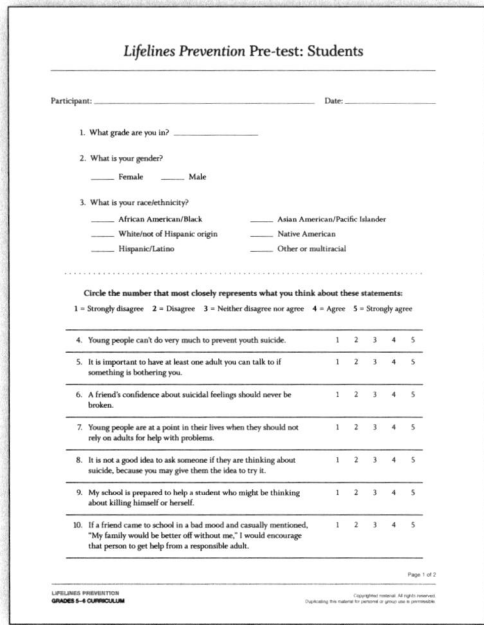

Lifelines Prevention Pre-test: Students

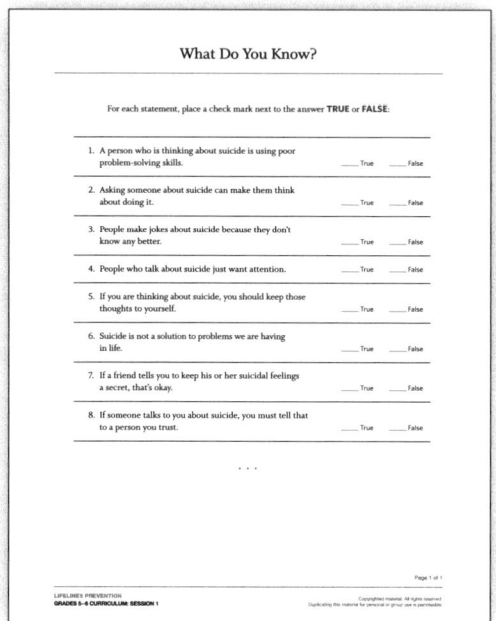

Session 1: What Do You Know?

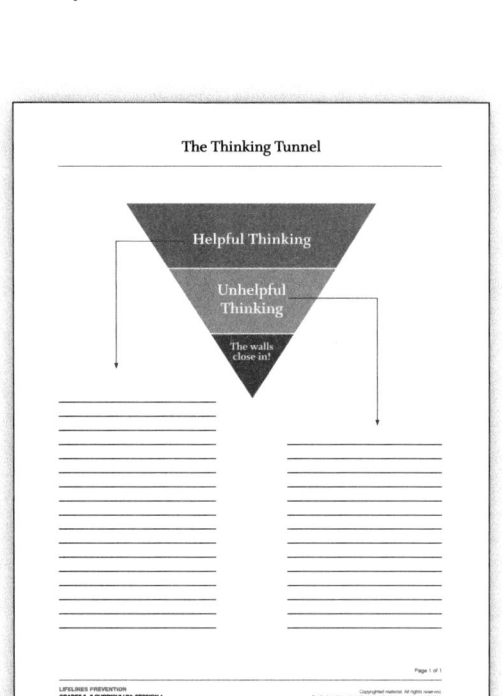

Session 1: The Thinking Tunnel

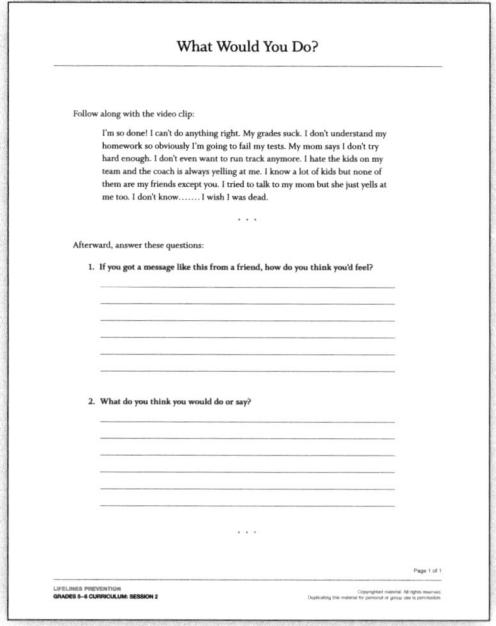

Session 2: What Would You Do?

GRADES 5-6 CURRICULUM HANDOUTS

These handouts can be found in the Student Curriculum Grades 5–6 packet of digital files.

Session 3: Courage Is

Session 3: The Qualities of Helpful People

Session 3: What Does It Mean to Find a Trusted Adult?

Session 3: Trusted Adult Card

GRADES 5–6 CURRICULUM HANDOUTS

These handouts can be found in the Student Curriculum Grades 5–6 packet of digital files.

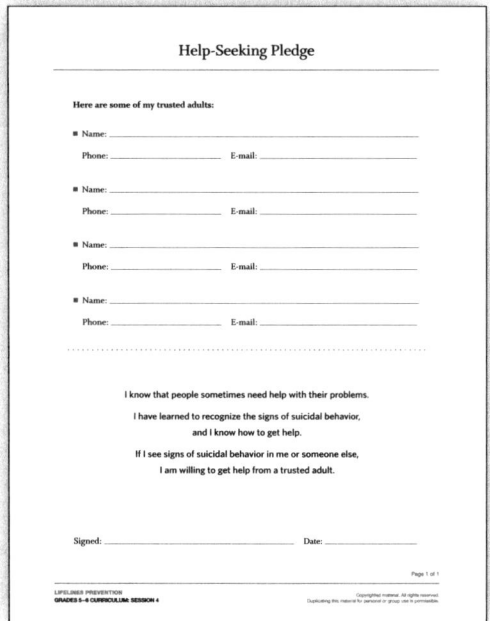

Session 4: Help-Seeking Pledge

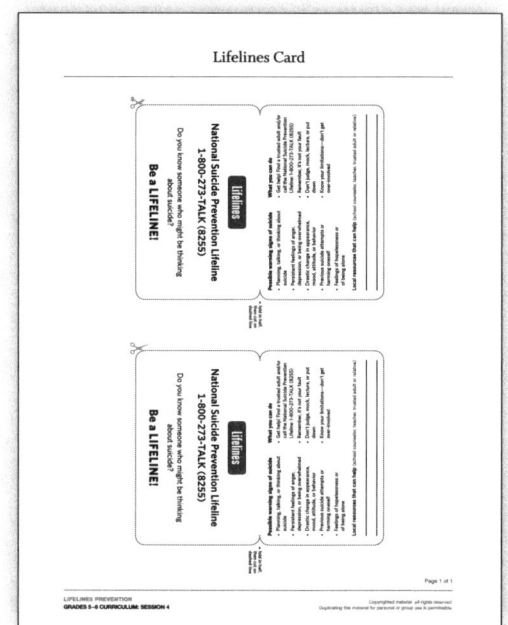

Session 4: Lifelines Card

Lifelines Prevention Post-test: Students

Grades 7–10 Curriculum

....

t child-development experts have known for a long time is that the peer group begins to take prominence over parents as youth move into adolescence. The same message that comes from a peer's lips will go unheeded if an adult is saying it. While the role models of childhood were often superheroes or celebrities, this gradually morphs into admiration for upper-class students, whose exploits are easier targets of aspiration. Peers become the new measuring sticks for respectability, sociability, coolness, and independence. Honor is thick in adolescence; teens will go out of their way to protect another's confidence, even if the secret is a matter of life and death.

And experts also know that death, especially death by suicide, has become more of an unfortunate reality for youth in these grades. According to the Centers for Disease Control and Prevention (CDC), suicide is now the second leading cause of death for youth ages twelve through eighteen.[1]

These were some of the variables that were taken into consideration in the construction of these curriculum sessions for grades 7–10. While the content is meant to apply to both youth themselves and their peers, the sessions begin with a question that is a little less personal than asking, "When are you in trouble?" by focusing the question on a friend ("When Is a Friend in Trouble?"). It may seem like a small thing, but it can defuse the intensity of the topic for vulnerable students and allow them to ease into the discussion. This first session is also designed to register at a more intellectual than emotional level, encouraging class discussion about keeping a suicidal confidence and correcting misinformation about suicide.

The second session moves into action, asking, "How Do I Help a Friend?" Recognizing the importance of peer role models, the content focuses on a video, hosted by two older teens, that presents a series of scenarios to demonstrate how to identify and respond to a troubled friend. Simple intervention steps are reviewed, with an intentional emphasis on not trying to solve a friend's problem but getting help for that person from a trusted adult.

The third session's topic is "Where Can I Go to Get Help?" A short video tells the true story of three eighth-grade boys who used what they learned in the *Lifelines Prevention* curriculum to help a friend. The youthful appearance of these boys does not seem to undermine their credibility with older students, who often remark, "If they could do it, I can do it." The voice of students is encouraged in an exercise that asks them to identify the qualities of helpful adults. The session concludes with a review of school resources.

The final session, "How Can I Use What I've Learned?" helps students apply the curriculum to real-life situations. Scripted role plays are used to dramatize situations in which a friend needs help. The scripting is an important aspect of role-play design; the authors of *Lifelines Prevention* felt strongly that unscripted role plays could go off track and might in fact be dangerous for vulnerable students. Such role plays would also make it hard to maintain the program's fidelity. The conclusion of the session engages students in making a help-seeking pledge and identifying trusted adults.

Some schools may choose to do an evaluation of the program. A pre-test and post-test are included for that purpose. The pre-test may be completed in the class before this unit begins rather than in the unit itself, or it can be done quickly at the beginning of the first session. For best measurement of program retention, it is advised that the post-test be completed at least one month after the unit has been completed. Both the pre-test and post-test can be found in the accompanying digital files.

Scope and Sequence

By the end of each session, students will be able to do the following:

Session 1: When Is a Friend in Trouble?	Session 2: How Do I Help a Friend?	Session 3: Where Can I Go to Get Help?	Session 4: How Can I Use What I've Learned?
• Explain the reasons for participating in a unit on suicide • Identify possible personal reactions to a situation involving a peer's suicidal behavior • Explain the ways in which our feelings about suicide influence our actions • Identify basic facts about suicide	• Identify specific warning signs of suicide in themselves and others • Organize warning signs around the FACTS acronym • Explain the three basic suicide intervention steps • Describe how to ask someone about suicide	• Describe how to implement the steps of a successful peer intervention • Define traits of helpful people • Identify school resources and procedures for responding to suicidal students	• Demonstrate the ability to help a troubled friend through scripted role plays • Demonstrate a willingness to help themselves or a troubled friend by signing a help-seeking pledge • Explain the purpose of the Lifelines Card

Related National Academic Standards[*]

Grades 6–8

Students will

- Analyze the relationship between healthy behaviors and personal health

- Describe the interrelationships of emotional, intellectual, physical, and social health in adolescence

- Describe ways to reduce or prevent injuries and other adolescent health problems

- Examine the likelihood of injury or illness if engaging in unhealthy behaviors

- Examine the potential seriousness of injury or illness if engaging in unhealthy behaviors

- Describe how peers influence healthy and unhealthy behaviors

- Analyze how the school and community can affect personal health practices and behaviors

- Determine the accessibility of products that enhance health

- Describe situations that may require professional health services

- Locate valid and reliable health products and services

- Apply effective verbal and nonverbal communication skills to enhance health

- Demonstrate refusal or negotiation skills that avoid or reduce health risks

- Demonstrate effective conflict management or resolution strategies

- Demonstrate how to ask for assistance to enhance the health of self or others

- Identify circumstances that can help or hinder healthy decision-making

- Determine when health-related situations require the application of a thoughtful decision-making process

- Distinguish when individual or collaborative decision-making is appropriate

- Distinguish between healthy and unhealthy alternatives to health-related issues or problems

- Predict the potential short-term impact of each alternative on self or others

- Analyze the outcomes of a health-related decision

- Demonstrate a variety of healthy practices and behaviors that will maintain or improve personal health

---

[*] Source: *National Health Education Standards—Achieving Excellence,* Joint Commission on National Health Education Standards, 2004, www.cdc.gov/healthyschools/sher/standards/index.htm.

- Demonstrate a variety of behaviors to avoid or reduce health risks
- State a health-enhancing position on a topic and support it with accurate information
- Demonstrate how to influence and support others to make positive health choices
- Work cooperatively to advocate for healthy individuals, families, and schools

Grades 9–10

Students will

- Predict how healthy behaviors can affect health status
- Describe the interrelationships of emotional, intellectual, physical, and social health
- Propose ways to reduce or prevent injuries and health problems
- Analyze personal susceptibility to injury, illness, or death if engaging in unhealthy behaviors
- Analyze the potential severity of injury or illness if engaging in unhealthy behaviors
- Analyze how peers influence healthy and unhealthy behaviors
- Analyze the influence of technology on personal and family health
- Evaluate how the school and community can affect personal health practice and behaviors
- Use resources from home, school, and community that provide valid health information
- Determine when professional health services may be required
- Access valid and reliable health products and services
- Use skills for communicating effectively with family, peers, and others to enhance health
- Demonstrate refusal, negotiation, and collaboration skills to enhance health and avoid or reduce health risks
- Demonstrate strategies to prevent, manage, or resolve interpersonal conflicts without harming self or others
- Demonstrate how to ask for and offer assistance to enhance the health of self and others
- Examine barriers that can hinder healthy decision-making
- Determine the value of applying a thoughtful decision-making process in health-related situations
- Justify when individual or collaborative decision-making is appropriate
- Generate alternatives to health-related issues or problems
- Predict the potential short-term and long-term impact of each alternative on self and others

- Defend the healthy choice when making decisions
- Evaluate the effectiveness of health-related decisions
- Demonstrate a variety of healthy practices and behaviors that will maintain or improve the health of self and others
- Demonstrate a variety of behaviors to avoid or reduce health risks to self and others
- Demonstrate how to influence and support others to make positive health choices

Session Descriptions and Preparation

Session Title	Session Description	Materials Needed	Preparation Needed
Lifelines Prevention **Pre-test: Students**	Taking a pre-test before beginning the sessions helps students assess their views and knowledge of suicide and/or suicide prevention, alerting them to aspects they may want to listen carefully for or ask questions about.	• *Lifelines Prevention* Pre-test: Students 📄 • Pens or pencils	• Photocopy the pre-test, one copy for each student.

Session 1: When Is a Friend in Trouble?	Through classroom discussion, a brief quiz, and a true-or-false questionnaire, students will learn accurate and relevant information about youth suicide. An exercise that explores feelings about responding to a suicidal friend introduces the concept of help-seeking and the danger of keeping suicidal confidences.	• Pens or pencils
		
		• Handouts from the Student Curriculum Grades 7–10 packet 📄
		  – What Would You Do?
		  – Questionnaire: True or False?
		  – *Optional: Lifelines Prevention* Pre-test: Students
		
		• Poster board and markers
		
		• Masking tape
		
		• Whiteboard or flip chart and markers
			• Read the session outline.
			
			• Photocopy the handouts, one copy of each per student.
			
			• Using poster board and a marker, list the "norms" (ground rules) you would like students to follow when discussing this sensitive topic. Post this list where all students can see it.
			
			• Set up the whiteboard or flip chart and place a marker within reach.
			
			• If you didn't administer the pre-test before this session, photocopy it and administer it at the beginning of this session.

continued

Session Title	Session Description	Materials Needed	Preparation Needed

Session 2: How Do I Help a Friend?	Through a discussion guided by a handout and video scenarios, students will begin to explore specific intervention steps to use when responding to suicidal friends. An additional handout will help them identify suicide warning signs.	• Pens or pencils
		
		• Handouts from the Student Curriculum Grades 7–10 packet 📄
		  – Warning Signs of Suicide (FACTS)
		  – *A Teen's Guide to Suicide Prevention* Discussion Guidelines
		  – Helpful Steps to Prevent Suicide
		
		• *A Teen's Guide to Suicide Prevention* video, a video player, projector, and screen ▶
		
		• Norms poster from session 1
		
		• Masking tape
		
		• Whiteboard or flip chart and markers
			• Read the session outline.
			
			• Photocopy the handouts, one copy for each student.
			
			• Set up a video player, projector, and screen for showing the video.
			
			• Preview the video *A Teen's Guide to Suicide Prevention.*
			
			• Hang the Norms poster from session 1, if it isn't still up.
			
			• Set up the whiteboard or flip chart and place a marker within reach.

Session 3: Where Can I Go to Get Help?	Students will view the dramatization of a real-life suicide intervention undertaken by three students in Maine, using the skills they learned in the *Lifelines Prevention* curriculum. Through a classroom activity, students will identify the qualities of helpful people. A discussion will also review in-school and community resources.	• Pens or pencils
		
		• Handouts from the Student Curriculum Grades 7–10 packet 📄
		  – Warning Signs of Suicide (FACTS) (from session 2)
		  – *One Life Saved* Discussion Questions
		  – The Qualities of Helpful People
		  – Trusted Adult Card (to print if you don't already have a sample available)
		  – Role-play scenarios (to hand out to selected students to study for homework)
		  – *Optional:* Help-Seeking Pledge (located in handouts for session 4)
			• Read the session outline.
			
			• Select discussion questions for the part 2 activity, The Qualities of Helpful People. Using the chart paper, write one question at the top of each sheet of paper, making sure to have two or three sheets of paper per group. Cut strips of masking tape to hang the paper. See the Preparation Needed section at the beginning of session 3 for more details.
			
			• Photocopy the *One Life Saved* Discussion Questions and The Qualities of Helpful People handouts, one copy of each per student.

continued

Session Title	Session Description	Materials Needed	Preparation Needed
Session 3: Where Can I Go to Get Help *continued*		• *Optional:* Handout on school procedure for responding to suicidal students (must be created) • *One Life Saved: The Story of a Suicide Intervention* video, a video player, projector, and screen ▶ • Norms poster from session 1 • Chart paper • Masking tape • Whiteboard or flip chart and markers	• Set up a video player and screen for showing the video. • Preview the video *One Life Saved: The Story of a Suicide Intervention.* • Post the Norms poster from session 1, if it isn't still up. • Make a handout describing your school's policy on handling suicide situations and make copies, one for each student. • Make preparations for session 4: Read the role plays for session 4 and select two or three for class discussion. Print out three copies of each role play you selected. Each role play will require two actors and a moderator. Choose three students for each role play. • Set up the whiteboard or flip chart and place a marker within reach.

continued

Session Title	Session Description	Materials Needed	Preparation Needed
Session 4: How Can I Use What I've Learned?	Session 4 uses scripted role plays to practice intervening in suicidal behavior. A help-seeking pledge further commits students to taking action for themselves and others, and clarifies the limits of their responsibility. A Lifelines Card serves as a review and a resource.	• Pens or pencils • Scissors • Handouts from the Student Curriculum Grades 7–10 packet 📄 – Role-play scenarios (for actors and moderators) – Role-Play Discussion handouts for the role plays you selected – Warning Signs of Suicide (FACTS) (from session 2) – Help-Seeking Pledge – Lifelines Card – *Optional: Lifelines Prevention* Post-test: Students • Norms poster (from session 1) • Masking tape • Whiteboard or flip chart and markers	• Prior to class, check in with the students you selected to participate in the role plays to make sure they are prepared. Make extra copies of the role plays in case they have forgotten to bring the copies you gave them at the last class session. If one of the actors is absent, the teacher should be prepared to step into that role. • Review the instructions for the role plays. • Photocopy the Role-Play Discussion and Help-Seeking Pledge handouts, one copy of each per student. • Print the Lifelines Card handout and cut the cards apart. Make enough cards for all students. It is recommended that you print these cards on a heavier paper stock. • Post the Norms poster from session 1, if it isn't still up. • Set up the whiteboard or flip chart and place a marker within reach.

continued

Session Title	Session Description	Materials Needed	Preparation Needed
Lifelines Prevention Post-test: Students	Taking a post-test after completing the sessions reminds students of some of the actions they can take to help a troubled or suicidal peer. It also gauges whether and how their confidence has changed through the program regarding their role in suicide prevention.	• *Lifelines Prevention Post-test: Students* 📄 • Pens or pencils	

Session 1:
When Is a Friend in Trouble?

DESCRIPTION

Through classroom discussion, a brief quiz, and a true-or-false questionnaire, students will learn accurate and relevant information about youth suicide. An exercise that explores feelings about responding to a suicidal friend introduces the concept of help-seeking and the danger of keeping suicidal confidences.

LEARNER OUTCOMES

By the end of the session, students will be able to

- explain the reasons for participating in a unit on suicide

- identify possible personal reactions to a situation involving a peer's suicidal behavior

- examine the ways in which our feelings about suicide influence our actions

- identify basic facts about suicide

MATERIALS NEEDED

- Pens or pencils

- Handouts from the Student Curriculum Grades 7–10 packet

    – What Would You Do?

    – Questionnaire: True or False?

    – *Optional: Lifelines Prevention* Pre-test: Students

- Poster board and markers

- Masking tape

- Whiteboard or flip chart and markers

PREPARATION NEEDED

- Read the session outline.

- Photocopy the handouts, one copy of each per student.

- Using poster board and a marker, list the ground rules or "norms" you would like students to follow when discussing this sensitive topic. In this *Lifelines Prevention* program, we refer to them as "norms" because teachers reported that students perceived "ground rules" as punitive, and we want to set an example of being sensitive to language. Post this list where all students can see it. Here are some sample norms:

  – Maintain confidentiality: what is said here, stays here

  – Listen when someone is talking, no side conversations

  – No joking around, use respectful language, no criticism of others' ideas

  – One person talks at a time, no sharing of personal stories

- Set up the whiteboard or flip chart and place a marker within reach.

- If you didn't administer the pre-test before this session, photocopy it and administer it at the beginning of this session.

Session 1 Outline

Note: Please note that there is an alternative part 1 for this session (starting on page 195) to be used by schools that have recently experienced a suicide or other tragic death.

<hr>

PART 1
5 minutes

<hr>

Confidentiality in a classroom setting is hard to enforce, so be prepared for some pushback if you decide to include this as one of your classroom norms. It can be helpful to pair confidentiality with the sharing of personal stories to illustrate why students may talk with you after class to share any information they want to remain private.

INTRODUCING THE *LIFELINES PREVENTION* PROGRAM TO STUDENTS

The purpose of part 1 is to introduce the *Lifelines Prevention* program and to establish a safe atmosphere for discussion.

You will be asking students about their experiences related to either hearing about suicide or knowing someone who has completed suicide. This discussion helps students connect the classroom information to their own lives.

If you don't normally teach these students, or if you are co-teaching with someone new to the class, make introductions. Include some reference to your experience in counseling youth. Talking about your experiences working with young people will engage students more effectively than a recitation of your professional or academic credentials.

1. *Optional:* Give each student a copy of the pre-test and a pen or pencil. Allow a few minutes for students to fill it out, and then collect the pre-test.

2. Say: **The subject of suicide is sometimes difficult to talk about. Because suicide can be a scary and confusing subject and involves extremely personal feelings, it's important to create some guidelines or norms that our entire class can agree on so we can all feel safe in our discussions during the next four sessions.**

3. Point to the poster you've displayed in the classroom and read the norms that you'd like to follow when discussing this sensitive topic. Explain each norm. Then ask students if they have any other norms that should be added. Add those to the poster. Here are some sample norms:

   - Maintain confidentiality (what is said here, stays here).
   - Listen when someone is talking/no side conversations.
   - No joking around, use respectful language, no criticism of others' ideas.
   - One person talks at a time.
   - No sharing of personal stories.

A practical alternate assignment for students who prefer not to participate may be a library project that asks them to compile a list of books and resources that encourage the development of resiliency.

4. Say: **While I realize that the first thing on this list is confidentiality, I recognize that in a school it can be hard to believe no one will talk about what happened in a class. So I want to remind you that if you have a personal story you would like to share, please come talk with me after class. This last point is an important guideline because the class can get distracted by personal sharing, which can raise issues unrelated to the curriculum.**

5. Say: **For some of you, suicide may be a very personal topic, and you may find it difficult to sit through these sessions. After today's session, which is our introduction to the topic, if any of you feel you would rather have an alternate assignment to participating in our classroom activities, please see me after class, and we'll arrange something else for you to do.**

6. Ask the class to raise their hands in response to the following three questions. Acknowledge the responses to each question before you move on to the next one.

   a. **How many of you have heard about someone in our school or community who has made a suicide attempt?**

   b. **How many of you have heard about someone from our town, neighborhood, or school who has died by suicide?** Usually about 70 to 80 percent of the class will raise their hands.

   c. **Now, how many of you know someone personally who has made a suicide attempt or died by suicide?** Comment on the percentage of the class members who respond affirmatively.

7. Explain: **As you can see from your responses, most of you have heard of or personally know someone who has been suicidal. Let me ask another question: If a teen is troubled and thinking about suicide, who do you think will be the first person who knows?** It is unusual to get an answer other than a "friend." **That's right. You are. Peers and friends are often the first to know if another teen is troubled. That's why the information we're going to be covering in the next few sessions is so important. More than anyone else, you may be able to help someone who may be thinking about suicide.**

   We will be discussing how to help a troubled friend. We'll also be talking about how you feel about asking for help for yourself and the resources for help that exist in our school and community.

   Suicide prevention is everyone's business, and you all play an important part in our school's effort to prevent suicide and other forms of violence. Learning how to prevent suicide makes our school a healthier and safer place. Everyone in the school—including teachers, administrators, school board

members, bus drivers, kitchen staff, and custodial staff—has been educated about suicide prevention. Your parents and guardians have also been provided with information. Now, these next few sessions will prepare you for your critical role in the prevention process.

<table>
<tr><td>

ALTERNATE
PART 1
5 minutes

</td></tr>
</table>

INTRODUCING THE *LIFELINES PREVENTION* PROGRAM TO STUDENTS IN A SCHOOL THAT HAS EXPERIENCED A DEATH BY SUICIDE OR OTHER TRAGIC DEATH WITHIN THE PAST SEVERAL YEARS

1. *Optional:* Give each student a copy of the pre-test and a pen or pencil. Allow a few minutes for students to fill it out, and then collect the pre-test.

2. Say: **While suicide (or other tragic death) is simply a concept for many schools, for our school it's a sad reality.** Ask students to raise their hands if they were affected by the suicide (or other tragic) death that affected your school community. Say: **We know from research that for every suicide (or other tragic) death, at least twenty people are intimately affected. I know those of you who raised your hands understand what I'm talking about.**

3. Say: **Because this may be a personal topic for some of you, or even something that's scary to talk about, we want to make sure we start by coming up with some norms for discussion that we can all follow.** Use the directions above to work with the class to create appropriate norms. *Make sure* to be clear that personal stories will *not* be shared during class discussion, but that you will be available to talk with students privately if they feel a need to share.

4. Say: **In this unit, we'll be discussing how to help a troubled friend. We'll also be talking about how you feel about asking for help for yourself and the resources for help that exist in our school and community.**

    Suicide prevention is everyone's business, and you each play an important part in our school's efforts to prevent suicide and other forms of violence. Learning how to prevent suicide makes our school a healthier and safer place. Everyone in the school—including teachers, administrators, school board members, bus drivers, kitchen staff, and custodial staff—has been educated about suicide prevention. Your parents and guardians have also been provided with information. Now, these next few sessions will prepare you for your critical role in the prevention process.

    Note: Schools that have experienced a suicide are called "survivor schools." Obviously, a wide range of reactions occur after any suicide death. Sometimes it may appear that most school members were unaffected, but you can never tell what the impact has been below the surface. That's why you want to use this alternate introduction to the curriculum. You don't need to ask who knows someone who has died by suicide, because you already know the answer. You also want to avoid asking the question about whom a troubled teen would go to if he or she were thinking about suicide. There may have been students who did know about the suicidal intent of the deceased student and did nothing. Asking that question directly may reactivate guilt. Instead, in part 2, you'll make the point of how important it is to tell someone if you find yourself in a situation like that.

<table>
<tr><td>

PART 2
20 minutes

</td><td>

WHAT WOULD YOU DO?

The purpose of part 2 is to help students recognize their personal reactions to suicide and to introduce the idea of not keeping secrets about suicidal information. The situation that students are asked to discuss involves the request from a friend to keep a suicidal confidence. It reflects a common challenge in adolescence of maintaining peer allegiances, even in matters of life and death.

</td></tr>
</table>

Be sure to thoroughly discuss student responses to each question. Sessions 2, 3, and 4 will build on what you cover in this discussion.

1. Give each student a copy of the What Would You Do? handout and a pen or pencil. Ask a student to read the situation on the handout aloud.

2. Explain: **Please answer the questions about the situation in the space provided on the handout. You won't have to hand in what you write, so feel free to be honest about your thoughts and feelings. You have two minutes to think and write. Then we'll discuss your responses.**

3. When the students have completed their answers, discuss the questions one at a time. During this discussion, write student responses to the questions on the board, and then go back and discuss each response. Leave the answers to all questions on the board, so you can refer to them later in the session. The most common (and relevant) responses are listed on the following pages. If your students miss important points, feel free to add them. Preface these remarks with something like this: **Other students have also said …**

4. a. Ask: **How did you respond to the first question: How do you feel when you hear him say this?**

    Possible answers include

    • concerned

    • scared

- angry

- worried

- upset

- nothing—he always says things like that to get attention

- it's not any of my business

- confused

- like "oh, here we go again!"

b. Explain: **So, what you're saying is that you might have a lot of different feelings, most of which don't feel very good. Some of you don't even feel anything, because sometimes we have friends we don't take too seriously, or we may have friends who threaten things like suicide so often we simply tune them out. And sometimes we may even ignore what someone is saying because we don't know what to say or do.**

5. Ask about the second question: **What do you decide to do or say?**

Possible answers include

- nothing, I decide to keep his secret

- tell another mutual friend

- tell my parent(s)/guardian(s)

- tell his teacher or my teacher

- try to talk my friend out of it

- tell him I can't keep his secret

- ask him what's upsetting him so much

- tell him it would be a dumb thing to do

- I don't know what to do

- feel proud that he trusts me

6. a. When any students who want to share have done so, continue: **Now let's look at the suggestion of trying to talk your friend out of it. Why would someone try to do that?**

Possible answers include

- You can do it right away and not have to wait to find someone to talk to.

- Since your friend trusts you, he may listen to you and take your advice.

- It keeps it between you and your friend—you don't tell the secret.

- Since you know your friend so well, your advice would probably be on target.

- You've felt that way yourself, so you understand.

b. Explain to the students: **This suggestion may let you act quickly and keep your friend's confidence. This one, in fact, may be good to try along with something else we'll talk about in a little bit. Letting your friend know you care about him and that his life is important to you, even if it isn't important to him right now, may be helpful.**

7. a. Say: **Now let's look at the option of asking your friend what is upsetting him. Why would you do this?**

Possible answers include

- You may be able to help.

- You may have experienced a similar problem.

b. When several students have offered reasons, explain: **While these things may be true, suppose your friend tells you about a serious problem: about physical or sexual abuse, or date rape, for example, or about an alcoholic parent? You would probably be surprised or shocked to hear something like that, and your reaction might convince your friend that things are hopeless. Remember, lots of problems that teens have can be very complicated. Knowing that your friend is considering suicide, without even understanding why, is enough of a problem. Your friend may really need a professional to help him figure out what to do. If you ask too many questions and get in over your head, both your friend and you may need some help.**

8. a. Continue: **Another suggestion was to do nothing. Why might someone choose this option?**

Possible answers include

- You would want someone to keep your secret if you asked them.

- Your friend is always saying things to get attention, and if you did something every time he threatened, you'd look like a fool.

- Your friend asked you to keep a secret, and it's important to be trustworthy.

b. When students have given some of these responses, continue: **I hear some of you saying that keeping a secret is important. This is true. But are all secrets the same? Keeping a secret about something that may make the difference between life and death seems to be in a special category. Not keeping a secret about suicide is not being disloyal or untrustworthy. You break this secret because you are loyal to your friend—you care about his life. Your friend may get angry with you for telling someone, but after the crisis has passed, the anger will most likely pass as well. Even if it doesn't, it's a lot easier to live with someone being angry at you than feeling guilty about a friend who is dead or seriously injured because you did nothing to help.** Write the following on the board as you say it out loud: **Losing a friendship is better than losing a friend.**

9. a. Pause for a moment before asking: **If your friend did share with you that he was feeling suicidal, and you told him that it was a really dumb idea or a stupid thing to do, how do you think that might make him feel?**

   Possible answers may include

   - more isolated and alone than ever

   - like you don't understand

   - that you aren't listening or you don't care

   - maybe he'd think that nobody cares

   b. Explain: **This points out that there are some things that are better not to do or say to someone who is feeling suicidal. While these comments won't cause a suicide, because each of us is really responsible for our own lives, they may make a person feel even worse. Think for a second: How would you feel if someone said the following things to you?**

   - **"Don't talk like that—it's a stupid idea."**

   - **"You wouldn't kill yourself over *that* would you? That's crazy!"**

   - **"Don't be so dramatic! Here's what you ought to do ..."**

10. a. Allow a moment for students to consider and respond. Then continue: **The last response we'll look at is the decision to tell some other person, such as another friend or an adult—a parent or guardian, teacher, or some-body else you trust. Why do you think someone might decide to do this?**

   Possible answers include

   - to share the responsibility

   - because you need help figuring out what to do

- because you're scared

- because you don't know what else to do

b. Ask: **How do you choose the person you decide to tell?**

Possible answers include

- The adult knows your friend and is in a good position to understand.

- You have talked to this person about other important things in the past.

- You have seen how this person responds to other students, and he or she seems okay.

- You tell this adult everything already, so this is no different.

- Your parents are helpful in situations like this.

- Your friend's parents seem okay to you, and you think they ought to know.

c. When several students have volunteered answers, continue: **No matter whom you pick, telling someone else helps both you and your friend. You get the advice and opinion of someone you trust, and you don't have to feel like your friend's life is in your hands. And your friend gets the benefit of another person's help. One of the best people to tell is an adult in your school whom you know will listen to you and take you seriously. All the adults in our school have been trained to know what to do in a situation like this. It's important to help your friend get some *adult* help!**

11. Say: **Finally, I want to return to an idea we considered earlier, because it's so important.** Write the following statement on the board as you say it: **One of the most dangerous things you can do is promise to keep suicidal thoughts or behavior a secret.**

   It is common for suicidal people to ask that you promise not to tell anyone about their thoughts or plans. They tell you that you're their most trusted friend, the only one who can help. This is a very dangerous situation. If your friend had a broken arm, you'd get help from someone who knows how to fix broken arms, like a doctor. You wouldn't try to fix it yourself, because you couldn't. The same is true for suicide. The most mature thing you can do for your friend is to get help. People who care about other people help them find help. It's a brave and courageous thing to do.

PART 3
15 minutes

INFORMATION ABOUT SUICIDE

The purpose of part 3 is to present current and accurate information about youth suicide. Because the topic of suicide is often colored by misinformation and personal attitudes that pose as facts, it's important to provide students with correct information. This section builds on the educational saying "A problem well-defined is a problem half-solved."

Students will complete a short questionnaire on basic information about suicide. (Be sure to use the word "questionnaire" so students don't get anxious about taking a "quiz" or a "test.")

Ten specific questions are included, but you may wish to emphasize different facts about suicide. You may also wish to present recent information about youth suicide as it becomes available. For these reasons, items may be substituted for current quiz items except for items 1, 2, 7, 8, 9, and 10. If you find yourself running out of time as you get to this part of the session (usually because you have had a very participatory class), you can limit class discussion to the above six questions.

1. Explain: **I'm going to hand out a questionnaire. You don't have to turn this in, and you don't have to know the right answers, because I'm going to give them to you. This is just to give you an idea of what you already know about teen suicide and provide us with some questions for discussion.**

2. Give each student a copy of the Questionnaire: True or False? handout and a pen or pencil. Allow a couple of minutes for students to complete the questionnaire.

3. When most students seem to have finished writing, explain: **I'm going to ask how many of you responded "true" and how many of you responded "false" to each question. Then I'll give you the correct answer and the facts on which it is based.**

4. Read each question aloud (or ask students to do so). Ask for an indication of who said true or false, and review the reasons for the correct answer.

   - *People who talk about suicide don't kill themselves.*
     False.

     After each question, remember to ask for a show of students' hands from those who chose each answer. Read aloud or summarize the following: **Most people who die by suicide talk with at least one other person about their suicidal feelings or plans before they finally decide to act on them. It's important to take these communications seriously, even if the person says she or he didn't really mean it.**

• *Suicide happens without recognizable warning signs.*
False.

Read aloud or summarize the following: **Most people give us clues that they're thinking about taking their lives. The warning signs include things like making direct statements about dying, losing interest in everything they used to care about before, feeling miserable and unhappy, and showing changes in attitudes or behaviors, like not taking care of themselves, quitting teams, or being tired all the time. Usually a person shows more than one sign. That's why it's going to be so important for us to learn about some of these warning signs and what to do if we spot any of them. There are, unfortunately, a small percentage of people who die by suicide without leaving clues.**

• *Suicide occurs equally as often among rich, middle class, and poor people.*
True.

Read aloud or summarize the following: **Suicidal behavior occurs in people of all income levels. In fact, people of all ages, races, faiths, cultures, and levels of society die by suicide. Both "popular" people who seem to have everything going for them and people who are "down and out" die by suicide. Suicidal teens come from all kinds of families. This is why we have to pay serious attention to all suicidal talk and behavior.**

• *Males die by suicide more often than females.*
True.

Read aloud or summarize the following: **Males do die by suicide more than females, but females make more attempts than males do. It isn't that girls and women aren't as serious about dying as boys and men are. It's just that females tend to choose methods that are less deadly and that give them time to change their minds. It's so important to understand that most people—male or female—will change their minds and want to be rescued.**

Note: If you are presenting this at a high school level, you can substitute the word "lethal" for deadly. When teaching in middle school, however, you'd be surprised to learn how many students don't know what "lethal" means. Using the word "deadly" instead generates fewer questions about what types of suicide are more lethal than others. Questions like that can lead you into an unnecessary discussion of means.

Explain: **This question does present us with another issue, and that's how we talk about suicide. The words we use are very important. When we say someone was "successful at suicide," that's a bit of a contradiction. It's like saying you're good at doing something that hurts you. And people whose lives have been touched by suicide often feel that using the term "successful" is insensitive. Even talking about "committing suicide" can seem a bit insensitive. When we talk about "committing" something in our society, we are usually talking about committing a crime. And suicide isn't a crime. It's just a very, very bad decision made by someone who isn't thinking clearly. Instead, using the words "completed suicide" or "died by suicide" is appropriate, sensitive, and correct.**

- *The only people who can really help teens are other teens.*
  False.

Read aloud or summarize the following: **This is kind of a trick question, because there may be some things that only your peers know how to do. But if we were to reword the question to say instead: "The only people to help teens who are feeling suicidal are other teens," I think the answer would be clearer. Just as we talked about in the example that started this session today, there are some things that are so complicated—like thinking about suicide— that even peers who may know you the best need to get help from a trusted adult.**

- *If a person feels better after a suicide attempt, it means he or she will probably not try to do it again.*
  False.

Read aloud or summarize the following: **If the attempt brings a lot of temporary attention and support, or even popularity, the person may feel better for a while. But unless there are changes in the person's life or the person gets help in managing problems with better coping skills, he or she may be at risk for another attempt. In addition, the person may have to deal with all the disapproving things people say about someone who has made a suicide attempt. This adds another negative issue to the problems the person had in the first place, so it can also increase his or her risk for another suicide attempt. That's why it's so important for someone who has attempted suicide or is even thinking about it to get good, professional help.**

- *Most teens who try to kill themselves don't really want to die.*
  True.

Read aloud or summarize the following: **This is true. Usually suicidal people simply want to escape the terrible way they are feeling, not end their lives. Many people who attempt suicide call on someone to help them immediately after they have made their attempt. Or they may tell someone about their plan to make an attempt and try to swear the person to secrecy. This is why suicide intervention is so important. People who attempt suicide are emotionally mixed up at the time and not thinking very calmly and clearly. Later, most are grateful that someone saved them.**

- *Talking about suicide or asking someone about suicide may put the idea in the person's head and cause suicide.*
  False.

Read aloud or summarize the following: **Actually, the opposite is often true. Asking directly about suicidal ideas or intentions can help people who feel like there's no one they can talk to about how terrible they're feeling. In fact, talking out feelings can help prevent the person from acting on them. Think about a time in your life when you were upset about something and felt like you had to keep it to yourself, that no one would understand. If you could share those worries with someone else, my guess is that you would probably feel a lot better.**

- *People who threaten to kill themselves are just seeking attention.*
  False.

Read aloud or summarize the following: **We must not dismiss a suicide threat or attempt as simply being an attention-getting device. If people are so desperate for attention that the only way they can think of getting it is to threaten to kill themselves, then they really do need attention. But they need attention from someone who can truly help them to not feel this way. All talk, threats, and attempts must be taken seriously and shared with an adult who can help.**

- *Bullying can be a suicide risk factor, not only for the person who is being bullied but also for the person doing the bullying.*
  True.

Read aloud or summarize the following: **As more research is done on the effects of bullying behavior, what we're finding is that everyone involved in the process can be at risk for bad outcomes, like thinking about suicide.**

That even includes the bystanders. Think about this example: You're out walking somewhere with a friend, and just as you get to the curb at the stop sign, two cars crash right in front of you. It's a bad accident, although both drivers are still alive. Everyone there—you and your friend who were bystanders, the person who caused the accident, and the person who was hit—will be affected by what happened, certainly in different ways, but affected nonetheless. Bullying has a similar effect on *everyone* involved.

PART 4
5 minutes

WRAP-UP

The purpose of part 4 is to remind students about the key points covered in this session and prepare them for session 2.

1. When discussion of the questionnaire draws to a close, explain: **We've learned today that youth suicide is a big problem that has touched many of our lives. We've talked about the fact that you may be one of the first people to know if a friend is having problems or thinking about suicide.**

2. Ask the students: **What did we say was one of the most important ways that you could help a friend who might be thinking about suicide?** Respond to raised hands and continue to ask for input until you get the answer **"talk to an adult."** Validate all answers, but reinforce the importance of talking with an adult.

3. Say: **And sometimes you may need to talk with someone immediately. That's why I'd like you to take out your phones right now and put the National Suicide Prevention Lifeline number in your contact list. The number is 1-800-273-TALK (8255). You can also go to the group's website to learn more about all the services they can provide: www.suicidepreventionlifeline.org.** Write the phone number and website address on the board for students to copy correctly. If students can't have phones in school, have them write this information on one of their handouts and transfer it to their phone when they get home.

4. Wait for a moment until most students have finished writing or entering the information. Then conclude: **In our next session, we're going to learn about warning signs for suicide and begin to talk about specific ways to help friends who may be in need.**

Because the National Suicide Prevention Lifeline is a 24/7 service, it can be a great resource for students after school hours. You can contact the National Suicide Prevention Lifeline on its website (www.suicidepreventionlifeline.org) to ask for relevant materials to share with students if you want to supplement this curriculum content. You may also want to write this organization's phone number on the norms poster.

Session 2:
How Do I Help a Friend?

DESCRIPTION

Through a discussion guided by a handout and video scenarios, students will begin to explore specific intervention steps to use when responding to suicidal friends. An additional handout will help them identify suicide warning signs.

LEARNER OUTCOMES

By the end of the session, students will be able to

- identify specific warning signs of suicide in themselves and others

- organize warning signs around the FACTS acronym

- explain the three basic suicide intervention steps

- describe how to ask someone about suicide

MATERIALS NEEDED

- Pens or pencils

- Handouts from the Student Curriculum Grades 7–10 packet

    - Warning Signs of Suicide (FACTS)

    - *A Teen's Guide to Suicide Prevention* Discussion Guidelines

    - Helpful Steps to Prevent Suicide

- *A Teen's Guide to Suicide Prevention* video, a video player, projector, and screen

- Norms poster from session 1
- Masking tape
- Whiteboard or flip chart and markers

PREPARATION NEEDED

- Read the session outline.
- Photocopy the handouts, one copy of each per student.
- Set up a video player, projector, and screen for showing the video.
- Preview the video *A Teen's Guide to Suicide Prevention*.
- Hang the Norms poster from session 1, if it isn't still up.
- Set up the whiteboard or flip chart and place a marker within reach.

Session 2 Outline

PART 1
10 minutes

IDENTIFYING WARNING SIGNS OF SUICIDE

The purpose of part 1 is to identify the most common warning signs of youth suicide. With this awareness, students should be better able to recognize signs of distress in a friend, a peer, or even themselves. There is a lot to cover in this session. Keep to the time limits in each part to ensure there is enough time to view the video, which is the main part of this session and reinforces the content of the other parts.

Several lists of suicide warning signs exist. Unfortunately, there is no "official" list that all experts agree on. No research to date shows that a particular set of risk factors or warning signs can accurately predict the likelihood of imminent danger of suicide for a specific individual. Even experts do not always agree when asked to assess the degree of suicide risk for given cases.

For now, it may be best to stick to the list provided in this session's Warning Signs of Suicide (FACTS) handout, which includes some of the most commonly acknowledged warning signs. Avoid including additional signs; otherwise, the list becomes useless. (To stay up to date on the most current research on risk factors and warning signs, visit the Suicide Prevention Resource Center's website at www.sprc.org.)

1. Welcome the students to the second session and begin. Explain: **Most teens give some kind of warning signs or clues that they're experiencing problems and may be considering suicide. Even though the signs don't necessarily mean that a person is suicidal, it's important to know what some of the warning signs of suicide are so you can recognize them and help appropriately.**

2. Explain: **The word "FACTS" is one way to organize different kinds of warning signs of suicidal behavior.** Write the following on the board:

    Feelings

    Actions

    Changes

    Threats

    Situations

3. Give a copy of the Warning Signs of Suicide (FACTS) handout to each student.

Don't just write the letters F-A-C-T-S and ask the class what the letters stand for. You may get some inappropriate responses.

4. Review the handout by asking students to take turns reading the introductory paragraph and each category out loud. If you feel comfortable having a discussion with the class about the handout, feel free to do so. Just remember to keep your eyes on the time.

5. Explain: **Of course, except for obvious threats or attempts, none of these signs is a definite indication that a person will die by suicide. Many people are depressed but never end their lives. Many others experience losses or show changes in behavior with no indication of suicide. However, if several of these signs occur together, they may be important clues. Since people who attempt suicide usually feel trapped and can't think of another way out of their emotional pain, it's much better to risk the possibility of overreacting rather than underreacting and to tell an adult if you're concerned about a friend.**

   It's also important to recognize that two things dramatically increase the danger of suicide:

   - **One thing that dramatically increases suicide risk is using alcohol or other drugs. These substances tend to impair a person's judgment, which means they don't make good decisions. Alcohol and other drug use also increase a person's tendency to do things without thinking, which is called "impulsivity."**

   - **The second thing that dramatically increases suicide risk is access to a gun. Guns are the number one way that teens kill themselves.**

   If you have a friend who is drinking or using other drugs, or who has a gun, leave the situation immediately, get a trusted adult involved, and call 911.

PART 2
20 minutes

VIDEO SCENARIOS: *A TEEN'S GUIDE TO SUICIDE PREVENTION*

The purpose of part 2 is to model appropriate student responses to a troubled peer. To engage students in the content, four role-played scenarios on the video are used to demonstrate the different ways teens involve adults in helping at-risk friends.

1. Explain: **The video we're going to watch next was created to demonstrate what to do and what not to do if a friend is talking about suicide or showing some of the warning signs for suicide. It reviews some of the information about suicide that we talked about in our first session and some of the warning signs we just reviewed with the word "FACTS." You'll also see four role plays that demonstrate friends helping friends. All four role plays discuss involving an adult. I'm going to pass out a handout that lists several things I'd like you to pay attention to as you watch the video.**

2. Give each student a copy of the *A Teen's Guide to Suicide Prevention* Discussion Guidelines handout and a pen or pencil.

3. Point to the first part of the handout, the table with FACTS. Say: **First, I'd like you to identify the warning signs you see in each scenario.** Point to the handout's second table, listing scenes 1 through 4, and say: **Then, I'd like you to observe who the adults are that the friends turn to for help and how they do that.**

4. Play the video *A Teen's Guide to Suicide Prevention.* Determine ahead of time how you will present the scenes. You may choose to watch all four and then hold a discussion. Or you may briefly stop the video after each of the role plays to discuss key points. Just remember this latter approach may take up more class time.

PART 3
10 minutes

A TEEN'S GUIDE TO SUICIDE PREVENTION DISCUSSION

The purpose of part 3 is twofold: to reinforce awareness of suicide warning signs, and to identify the differences and similarities in the ways that adults can be involved in the helping process.

1. Using students' answers to the *A Teen's Guide to Suicide Prevention* Discussion Guidelines handout, ask the following discussion questions. (Suggested responses are provided for your reference. If students do not make these key points, add them yourself.) Because texting is one of the main ways teens communicate, it is essential to discuss the third role play from the video. Be aware that the video was filmed in 2008, at a time when flip phones were the predominant type of cell phone. Be prepared for some students to call your attention to this detail.

    a. Ask the students: **What are some of the key warning signs or "FACTS" you saw that made the young people in the video think that their friends might be at risk for suicide?**

    Possible answers include

    *   a sudden or significant change in behavior or attitude

    *   having made a suicide attempt in the past

    *   making a suicide threat

    *   having a current suicide plan

        (***Note:*** Make the point that if the person also has the means to carry out the plan, the risk is high and immediate.)

        *   using alcohol and/or other drugs

b. Ask students: **All four role plays show the young people involving an adult. Whom did they involve and how?**

- Emphasize that if the risk is high and immediate, the nearest adult should be involved. Remind students that this was illustrated in the scene with Isaac and Blake. Say: **The minute Blake shared that he knew the location of his father's gun, Isaac suggested they talk to his older brother. If Blake had a gun with him, that's when Isaac would have left and called 911.**

- Prompt the students, if needed, to continue the discussion by saying: **In the remaining three scenes, the teens were encouraged to choose a particular adult that they would be willing to talk to, and they were given firm support by their friends for making that effort.**

- **In the role play with Teresa and Susie, Teresa suggested finding a different adult to talk to if the first person they went to wasn't helpful. This is an important point to emphasize because not everyone knows how to be the kind of trusted adult who really listens to what you have to say.**

c. Ask: **In the video, the hosts spoke about "remembering your limits." How would you know if you were in over your head when trying to help a friend?**

Possible responses include

- I'd be scared about something they said.

- I wouldn't know how to respond to them.

- They'd talk about having already tried to kill themselves.

- They would say things I wouldn't believe, like they were okay when I'd know they weren't.

- The minute they said the word "suicide," I'd know I needed to get some help.

2. When those students who want to share their responses have, summarize your discussion by saying: **In these video scenes, you saw teens interacting with friends who were showing warning signs of suicide risk. These teens demonstrated how to acknowledge concern about risk and how to suggest to their friends that they go to a trusted adult for additional help.**

PART 4
5 minutes

HELPFUL STEPS TO PREVENT SUICIDE

The purpose of part 4 is to provide students with three basic intervention steps they can use to respond to a possibly suicidal person:[1]

- Show you care.

- Ask about suicide.

- Get help.

To increase students' comfort level in their ability to intervene, encourage them to find "their own words" for carrying out these three steps.

1. Ask students to pair up with a partner. Depending on the composition of your class, this pairing may be based on either student self-selection or your assignment. If there is an odd number of students, have one group of three.

2. Give each student a copy of the Helpful Steps to Prevent Suicide handout.

3. a. Explain: **When we're trying to help a friend who might be thinking about suicide, there are three steps we need to take. You saw them demonstrated in the scenarios we just watched on the video. Now you'll get a chance to use your own words to describe how you'd intervene. The three steps are listed on your handout.**

   b. Say the highlighted words or the whole phrase describing each step. Write the highlighted words in these steps as column headings across the whiteboard as you say them, and leave them on the board for the remainder of the session:

   > Step 1: Find the words to **show you care** about your friend.

   > Step 2: **Ask about suicide.**

   > Step 3: Convince your friend to **get help.**

   c. Explain: **Your assignment with your partner is to**

   - **think about and write one or two phrases on your handout that you'd use to show caring**

   - **write two ways to ask about suicide**

   - **write two things you might say to convince a friend to get help**

d. Explain that this is going to be a brainstorming activity, so you expect the pairs of students to work quickly: **You and your partner will have a few minutes to do this assignment. Then we're going to review it together as a class.** Give students about two minutes to record their responses on the handout.

4. To reinforce and review the steps of a basic suicide intervention, when you see that most partners have finished writing, ask for responses from the class. Write their responses under each heading on the board. Keep this discussion moving very quickly. Since this is a form of brainstorming, all answers, unless mean-spirited, are acceptable.

   a. Say: **I'd like to hear the words you would use to show you care.**

      Possible answers include

      - You don't seem to be yourself. I'm worried about you.
      - I'm concerned. You have never been this "down" before.
      - What's going on? What's making you act so out of control?
      - You're my best friend and I care about you.
      - Why are you so down lately?

   b. Then ask: **How would you ask about suicide?** Ask for several examples.

      Possible answers include

      - Are you talking about suicide?
      - Are you thinking about killing yourself?
      - Do you mean you want to end your life?

   c. Reinforce that all the answers *directly* ask about suicide, just as the video demonstrated, and that it's important to be very clear with a friend about your concerns.

   d. Ask: **And finally, what words would you use to convince a friend to get help?**

      Possible answers may include

      - You're not alone. Let me help you get help.
      - This is serious. I want to help you right now. Who do you feel comfortable talking to? How about we go talk to the coach?
      - I know a crisis number we can call to talk this over.

5. Say: **These were all very thoughtful answers. You came up with them very quickly, and they really are the first steps in getting help for someone from a trusted adult.**

PART 5
1 minute

WRAP-UP

The purpose of part 5 is to reinforce the content of this session.

1. Summarize for the students: **Today, we've discussed how we move from knowledge about suicide and its warning signs to action. One of the most significant things we learned is that if you're concerned about a friend, it's important to ask this person directly about suicide.**

2. Add: **Another important thing we saw practiced in the video was how to convince a friend to go to an adult for help.**

3. Conclude the session by saying: **I'd like you to continue to think about what we learned, especially about these three intervention steps and the other things you might say to show you care, to ask about suicide, and to convince a friend to go for help. We'll learn more about these in our next class.**

4. Remind students that the National Suicide Prevention Lifeline is their 24/7 resource. Write the phone number on the board: 1-800-273-TALK (8255).

Session 3:
Where Can I Go to Get Help?

....

DESCRIPTION

Students will view the dramatization of a real-life suicide intervention undertaken by three students in Maine, using the skills they learned in the *Lifelines Prevention* curriculum. Through a classroom activity, students will identify the qualities of helpful people. A discussion will also review in-school and community resources.

LEARNER OUTCOMES

By the end of the session, students will be able to

- describe how to implement the steps of a successful peer intervention

- define traits of helpful people

- identify school resources and procedures for responding to suicidal students

MATERIALS NEEDED

- Pens or pencils

- Handouts from the Student Curriculum Grades 7–10 packet 📄

    - Warning Signs of Suicide (FACTS) (from session 2)

    - *One Life Saved* Discussion Questions

    - The Qualities of Helpful People

    - Trusted Adult Card (to print if you don't already have a sample available)

Duplicating this page is illegal. Do not copy this material without written permission from the publisher.

217

– Role-play scenarios (to hand out to selected students to study for homework)

– *Optional:* Help-Seeking Pledge (located in handouts for session 4)

- *Optional:* Handout on the school's procedure for responding to suicidal students (must be created)

- *One Life Saved: The Story of a Suicide Intervention* video, a video player, projector, and a screen ▶

- Norms poster from session 1

- Chart paper

- Masking tape

- Whiteboard or flip chart and markers

PREPARATION NEEDED

- Read the session outline.

- Select and prepare discussion questions for use in the part 2 activity, The Qualities of Helpful People. You will be dividing the class into groups of three or four and assigning each group two or three of these questions to answer.

   Choose your questions from the list that immediately follows. These questions lend themselves to small-group work. They are designed to empower students to seek help from adults and/or be helpful to others. Pick questions that will work best for your groups or write your own. It can be interesting to give each group one question that is the same. If you choose to present in this way, one question that works really well is this: **What can you do personally to make it more likely that people will turn to you for help?**

   Here are some possible discussion questions:

   – If you were on a committee to hire a new counselor at our school whose only responsibility would be to help students, what characteristics would you look for in this person?

   – In your experience, what qualities make a person trustworthy?

   – In your experience, what qualities make a person helpful?

   – If you were looking for help, how would you check out a person to find out if he or she would be a good person to approach?

   – What can you do personally to make it more likely that people will turn to you for help?

    – What makes it hard to get help from adults in our school?

    – What do you suggest should be done to improve helpful resources for students?

• Using the chart paper, write one question at the top of each sheet of paper, making sure to have two or three questions/sheets of paper per group. You will be distributing these to the groups to record their answers. Cut strips of masking tape so completed answer sheets can be posted in front of the room to facilitate discussion.

• Photocopy the *One Life Saved* Discussion Questions and The Qualities of Helpful People handouts, one copy of each per student.

• Set up a video player and screen for showing the video.

• Preview the video *One Life Saved: The Story of a Suicide Intervention.*

• Post the Norms poster from session 1, if it isn't still up.

• Make a handout describing your school's policy on handling suicide situations and make copies, one for each student. See part 3 of this session for the context in which it will be used.

• Make preparations for session 4: Read the role plays for session 4 (found in the digital files) and select two or three for class discussion. Print out three copies of each role play you selected. Feel free to adjust the dialogue of the role plays to reflect your student population. Each role play will require two actors and a moderator. Review the class roster and choose three students for each role play. These students should be reliable and outgoing and agree not to discuss the role plays with other classmates prior to class. They should also be willing to practice reading the parts out loud to get comfortable with their lines. You can enlist the participation of these students and hand out the scripts at the beginning or end of this session.

• Set up the whiteboard or flip chart and place a marker within reach.

Session 3 Outline

ONE LIFE SAVED AND DISCUSSION QUESTIONS

The purpose of part 1 is to illustrate for students how to apply the three steps of the peer intervention they learned in session 2 (show you care, ask about suicide, and get help). The real-life experience of students from Maine is dramatically described in the video and provides a concrete example of how to implement the steps. *Lifelines Prevention* author Maureen Underwood also discusses the important role of the counselor in this situation. An important reason for including this video is that it focuses on the students who performed the intervention and not on the person who was feeling suicidal.

1. Begin the session by reviewing the three steps to prevent suicide. Ask students: **In our last session, we talked about three steps we need to take when we're trying to help a friend who may be suicidal. Can anyone remember these steps?** As students respond, write these three steps on the board:

    1. Show you care.

    2. Ask about suicide.

    3. Get help.

2. Introduce the next aspect of the *Lifelines Prevention* program to the students: **We're going to start today by watching a short video that shows a real-life example of what these three steps look like in action. This video, titled *One Life Saved,* tells the true story of a suicide intervention that took place several years ago after the students in a Maine school completed these *Lifelines Prevention* lessons that we're studying now. It illustrates how three young men recognized the warning signs of suicide in a friend and what they did to help him.**

3. Ask students to get out their copy of the Warning Signs of Suicide (FACTS) handout from session 2. Give each student a copy of the *One Life Saved* Discussion Questions handout and a pen or pencil. Explain: **As you watch this video, look at the FACTS handout that we talked about in the last session. Listen carefully for the FACTS that the boys noticed in their friend: the feelings, the actions or events that led to the feelings, the changes in the way he acted, the threats that he made, and the situations you think contributed to his feelings. Use the *One Life Saved* Discussion Questions to help organize what you notice. It's okay to write on the handout. We'll talk about what you observed after we watch this short video.**

The content related to TJ's dad's death is only a small part of *One Life Saved*. Nevertheless, you need to recognize that there may be students in the class who have had personal and perhaps recent experiences with a loved one's death. If you are concerned about how a particular student might react to this video, talk to the student before class and explain that the video contains references to a parent's death. Give the student permission to leave the class if the video is upsetting, or provide the student with an alternate assignment.

4. Play the *One Life Saved* video.

5. Ask: **After hearing TJ's story, how do you think he might have been feeling— the "F" in the FACTS acronym?**

Possible answers include

- sad
- upset about his dad's death
- desperate
- confused
- hating his life
- like no one liked him

6. a. Acknowledge the students' responses. Then ask: **What "A" actions or events was TJ experiencing that were very stressful for him?**

Possible answers include

- teasing from others about his athletic ability and girls
- his mother's sadness about his dad's death

b. Explain: **When a parent dies, like TJ's dad did, everyone in the family is affected. And although everyone in the family experiences the same loss, each family member will react to it in a very personal way. Because of these different reactions, family members can often feel very alone and isolated, even from each other. His dad's death sounds like it's the "S" situation that pushed TJ over the edge, doesn't it?**

The support of peers and friends can help someone like TJ in a difficult situation like this. And it's important to recognize that even though these three boys used to tease TJ, they could still be helpful, caring friends.

7. a. Ask: **What changes, the "C" in FACTS, did his friends observe?**

Possible answers include

- no longer "happy-go-lucky"
- saying things like "Nobody would care if …"

b. Acknowledge the students' responses. Then explain: **If the boys—Gabe, Sean, and Sam—had not learned these warning signs, they may not have realized that the behavior changes and comments they noticed in TJ were actually warning signs of suicide. Research shows that many people who are thinking about suicide often give some warning signs, especially in the week or two before an attempt.**

8. a. Next ask students: **What "T" threats did the boys hear TJ mention?**

    Possible answers include

    - "Everybody would be better off without me."
    - "I'm gonna kill you or kill myself."
    - The plan of using his "very high roof" to kill himself.

    b. If students don't mention TJ's plan, remind them of that. Explain: **What the boys heard was not just a threat from TJ but an actual plan. The threat itself was serious, but the fact that TJ had a plan made the situation even more dangerous. And what the boys did was the absolutely correct thing to do: they went to talk to a trusted adult.**

9. Ask: **What "S" situations contributed to TJ's feelings? We already mentioned one earlier. Do you remember?**

    Possible answers include

    - his dad's death
    - being worried about making his mom even sadder

10. a. Say: **Now let's talk about some of the positive things TJ had going for him. What were they?**

    Possible answers include

    - friends and adults who knew what to do
    - the ability to communicate his feelings
    - a caring parent who was very willing to help
    - a good school counselor

    b. Acknowledge students' responses. Explain: **These positive things are called "protective factors," because they help protect us in difficult situations. They're kind of like the bumper that protects the people inside the car when it gets bumped in an accident, or those bumper cars you ride where you purposely run into someone else's car and the bumpers absorb the shock. Protective factors can be your friends, your involvement in school activities or after-school activities, your faith organization, or having a caring adult in your life that you trust.**

11. a. Say: **So Gabe, Sean, and Sam were "protective factors" for TJ. What did they do to try to help him?**

Possible answers include

- showed they cared (listened, noticed different behaviors)
- asked about suicide (twice!)
- got help from an adult they trusted
- stayed with TJ until the school counselor got there

b. Explain: **These three steps—show you care, ask about suicide, and go to an adult you trust for help—are simple and easy to remember.**

12. a. Ask: **What was TJ's immediate response to his friends' trying to help him?**

Possible answers include

- He accused the boys of overreacting.
- He told them that they weren't his friends anymore.

b. Explain: **TJ's reaction isn't so unusual. Even if friends have told you upsetting or scary things, they might initially get angry when you suggest they need some help from an adult. Usually their anger passes once the crisis is over and they've gotten help. Even if the anger doesn't go away, it is easier to live with a friend's anger than with your own guilt over a friend who is dead or seriously injured. We must not keep suicide a secret.**

And to give you the inside story on this real-life situation, TJ's anger lasted less than a week, and all the boys remained friends; if students ask directly, feel free to share this information with them.

13. a. Ask: **How did Gabe, Sean, and Sam feel about what they did?**

Possible answers include

- really proud
- happy they could help a friend

b. Explain: **This story shows us that friends who pay attention and know what to do can really make a lifesaving difference. These boys are teaching us that suicide can be prevented and that any one of us can make a difference.**

Caution: Questions may surface about TJ and the outcome of the intervention; feel free to share this information with them. Remind the class that the purpose of the video is to highlight the three boys and the steps they took to intervene with a friend. They were in no way responsible for the outcome. If TJ had ultimately decided to take his life, the boys would not be responsible for his decision. However, TJ did receive both immediate crisis intervention and ongoing help. He and his family worked through their grief over the death of his father. TJ graduated from high school in June 2007.

PART 2
15 minutes

THE QUALITIES OF HELPFUL PEOPLE

The purpose of part 2 is to help students define the qualities in people that they find helpful. Because the perception of helpfulness is so individual, this topic creates the opportunity for an interesting classroom discussion.

1. Ask students for a show of hands in response to these two questions:

    • **How many of you have ever helped someone else at some point in your life?**

    • **How many of you have ever needed help from somebody else?**

2. Make the point that everyone needs help at some time in his or her life. Also, explain that your school system has planned how adults can and will be helpful in the event of suicide-related concerns.

3. Explain: **In the story about TJ, we saw that when his friends realized they couldn't handle the situation, they went to their school counselor for help. I'd like to think that all young people have an adult like that school counselor to talk to. But I know that sometimes young people are reluctant to turn to adults for help.**

4. Ask: **What are some reasons teens might be reluctant to go to adults for help?**

    Possible answers include

    • We don't know what the adult will do or what will happen if we tell an adult.

    • The adult may not know what to do.

    • Adults don't understand us the way friends do.

    • The adult won't take us seriously or will overreact.

    • The adult will cause even more trouble: Our parents will be angry if we call them.

    • Our friends will be mad at us if we tell an adult.

    • We don't want to "rock the boat" or disappoint parents or admit to needing help.

5. Acknowledge students' answers. Then summarize: **There may be a lot of reasons why adults may not seem approachable when you need help. But I'm sure there are also many reasons to talk to an adult when you have a problem. That's what we're going to explore next.**

6. Divide the class into groups of three or four. Use your knowledge of the students to create functional work groups.

7. Give each student a copy of The Qualities of Helpful People handout. Then, distribute the chart paper with the questions you prepared, giving each group two or three sheets and a marker.

8. Explain: **Each small group will have two (or three) questions to answer about the qualities of helpful people. Your questions are written on these large sheets of paper. I'll give each group a marker so you can write your answers on the paper to share with the rest of the class. You will have about five minutes to complete the assignment. Use the handout to help answer the questions.**

9. When the groups have finished answering their questions, tell them to use the pieces of masking tape to post their responses in the front of the room to facilitate discussion. Briefly review and discuss what they wrote.

10. Review The Qualities of Helpful People handout briefly and ask students if they would add anything based on their group discussions or their own experiences with people they found helpful.

PART 3
8 minutes

INFORM STUDENTS OF YOUR SCHOOL'S PREPAREDNESS TO HELP

The purpose of part 3 is to assure students that the adults in your school have received training so they know how to respond to situations involving suicidal behavior. Students are reminded that not every member of the staff may demonstrate the qualities they personally find helpful and that if students are not satisfied with the response from the first adult they approach, they should immediately find another trusted adult. They can also check for the Trusted Adult Card that many of the faculty and staff have placed in their classrooms or offices to indicate they're prepared to assume that role. The school's response when a potentially suicidal student is identified is explained briefly.

1. Explain: **The question of whom you can go to in order to get help is so crucial that everyone who works in our school has been trained to know what to do if you or other students approach them with a concern about suicide. It's also important to remember what we just learned in our activity today about the different qualities of helpful people—that what one person finds helpful may be very unhelpful to someone else. So, if you go to a teacher to ask for help and that person responds in a way that isn't helpful to you, go find another teacher or staff member to talk to.**

2. Say: **You may have already noticed that some of the faculty and staff have placed cards in their rooms that say, "I am a trusted adult."** Show a sample of the card. **Adults who display these cards agree about the qualities that make an adult helpful and are willing to be approached by anyone who needs someone to listen to them in a nonjudgmental, trustworthy way.**

3. Next, students should be told *exactly* what the school's procedure is when a potentially suicidal student is identified. This can be summarized in a handout that you can create, distribute, and then paraphrase or read aloud, emphasizing that this is the school's commitment to the students. The handout's language, for example, might be similar to this:

> When a potentially suicidal student has been called to the attention of any adult in the school, that adult will contact one of the school personnel who has been trained and designated to respond to this kind of situation. In our school, those people are (*name the individuals*). One of these individuals will talk privately with the student to find out what is bothering him or her. If the adult is concerned about this young person being at risk for suicide, his or her parents/guardians will be contacted, and the student will be referred for help. You may contact any adult in the school on your own if you're worried about someone else, and if you wish, your name won't be revealed.

4. Explain: **Sometimes students worry that their parents or guardians will be angry or upset with them if the school contacts them. And while there's no guarantee that this won't happen, remember that the resource person is there to explain to parents and guardians the reasons for the school's concerns and how important it is for the student to get help.**

    Students may also worry about the reactions of a friend, but the video we saw today reminds us that it's a lot better to have an angry friend than a dead friend.

<table>
<tr><td>

PART 4
2 minutes

</td><td>

WRAP-UP

Part 4 reinforces the three steps of an intervention.

</td></tr>
</table>

PART 4
2 minutes

WRAP-UP

Part 4 reinforces the three steps of an intervention.

1. When all questions about the school policy handout have been answered, move to conclude this session. Explain: **This class gave us a dramatic picture of how helpful friends can be to each other when one of them is thinking about suicide. We saw a real-life example of how three students took these steps:**

    1. **Showed they cared**

    2. **Asked about suicide**

    3. **Got help for their friend**

    Their story also demonstrated how to use some of the suggestions for helping that we've been learning about in this *Lifelines Prevention* program.

2. Ask: **What were some of the qualities you identified as important in helpful people?** Respond to raised hands to get a sampling of responses.

3. When students have responded with a range of helpful qualities, conclude: **In our next session, you'll see how you can put into practice what you've learned about helping a friend who may be thinking about suicide.**

Note: At the end of this session, hand out the role plays to the students you have selected.

The next section involves a help-seeking pledge. If you prefer, you may introduce that exercise here, after discussing the qualities of helpful people, or as part of the closing activities in session 4. See session 4, part 2 for instructions.

Session 4:
How Can I Use What I've Learned?

....

DESCRIPTION

Session 4 uses scripted role plays to practice intervening in suicidal behavior. A help-seeking pledge further commits students to taking action for themselves and others and also clarifies the limits of their responsibility. A Lifelines Card serves as a review and a resource.

LEARNER OUTCOMES

By the end of the session, students will be able to

- demonstrate the ability to help a troubled friend through scripted role plays

- demonstrate a willingness to help themselves or a troubled friend by signing a help-seeking pledge

- explain the purpose of the Lifelines Card

MATERIALS NEEDED

- Pens or pencils

- Scissors

- Handouts from the Student Curriculum Grades 7–10 packet

   – Role-play scenarios (for actors and moderators, from session 3)

   – Role-Play Discussion handouts for the role plays you selected

    – Warning Signs of Suicide (FACTS) (from session 2)

    – Help-Seeking Pledge

    – Lifelines Card

    – *Optional: Lifelines Prevention Post-test: Students*

- Norms poster (from session 1)
- Masking tape
- Whiteboard or flip chart and markers

PREPARATION NEEDED

- Prior to class, check in with the students you selected to participate in the role plays to make sure they are prepared. Make extra copies of the role plays in case they've forgotten to bring the copies you gave them during the last session. If one of the actors is absent, the teacher should be prepared to step into that role.

- Review the instructions for the role plays.

- Photocopy the Role-Play Discussion and Help-Seeking Pledge handouts, one copy of each per student.

- Print the Lifelines Card handout and cut the cards apart. You should have one card for each student. These cards are designed to be carried by the students at all times. They should, therefore, be printed on sufficiently strong stock to stand up to use; 8-point white-coated cover stock is recommended. Students won't want to advertise the fact that they are carrying a card with help-seeking information, so use an unobtrusive color. Alternatively, you can create your own Lifelines Cards. Use an easy-to-read font and print them on heavy paper stock.

- Hang the Norms poster from session 1, if it isn't still up.

- Set up the whiteboard or flip chart and place a marker within reach.

Session 4 Outline

GUIDED PRACTICE THROUGH SCRIPTED ROLE PLAYS

The purpose of this part of the session is to use role plays to involve all students as "helpers." Class members have been preselected to present the role plays while the rest of the class is instructed to concentrate on the student in the "helper's role."

Each role play has two scenes. The first scene presents the warning signs of suicide and the suicidal person's resistance to help. There is a "break" between scenes with discussion questions provided to give the class time to make comments and suggestions. The second scene demonstrates the "helper" completing a suicide intervention, followed by more questions to discuss. The questions can be facilitated by the student moderator and/or the teacher. Depending on the level of student engagement in these discussions, you will probably have time for two or three role plays.

The role plays are purposely scripted to ensure that participating students have emotional distance from the content and that the role plays specifically reinforce material that's been covered in the previous three sessions.

One of the role plays (number 3, with Maria and Olivia) involves an intervention that is made via cell phone. It can be useful to include this for discussion, because it brings up the issue of how to make an intervention when it's not in person. You can expand this conversation to include the example used in the video from session 2 of the two girls texting each other. Because this form of remote communication is very popular, it can be helpful to identify the differences between these communication techniques and whether one form—in person or remote—has an advantage over the other.

When responding to the discussion questions, many students will initially answer in the way they feel is expected of them. For example, they will indicate that they would break their friend's (or relative's) confidence and "tell an adult" even if they honestly remain unconvinced that they would or should, especially if the situation is ambiguous. The break between the two role-play scenes gives students the opportunity to explore the reasons for and the consequences of different responses.

This session provides the opportunity to emphasize the following:

- Keeping suicidal behavior a secret is a form of assuming responsibility.

- One should never promise to keep suicidal thoughts, plans, or actions a secret.

- One of the best things a friend can do is to recognize his or her limits and get the help needed from trusted adults.

1. Explain: **Today, we'll be participating in role plays of some situations where an intervention is needed for suicidal behavior. We'll do this by using the suicide prevention steps we learned in sessions 2 and 3.**

2. Ask: **What were those steps?**

    1. Show you care.

    2. Ask about suicide.

    3. Get help.

3. Give each student copies of the Role-Play Discussion handouts and ask them to take out their copy of the Warning Signs of Suicide (FACTS) handout first discussed in session 2. Give each student a pen or pencil.

4. Explain: **Today, some of your classmates have agreed to present some role plays that were actually written by other students who have participated in the *Lifelines Prevention* program in the past. Each role play has two scenes. In the middle of each role play, there will be an opportunity to talk about what might be going on. As you watch and listen, use your Role-Play Discussion handout to record the FACTS—the feelings, actions, changes, threats, and situations—that may signal suicide risk. Also think about what you would do and say if you were trying to help this friend or relative.**

5. Taking time to set up the role plays will make it easier to debrief the actors after the role plays are over. Select a location in front of the class for the stage. Invite the actors in the first role play to take their places and explain to the class: **As you know, role plays are like acting. So, we're going to help our actors take their cues by using the technique that's used in filming: starting the role play by calling out as a group "One—Two—Three—Action!" At the end of the scene, the moderator for that scene will call "Cut" to bring our actors out of their roles.**

    These simple techniques help define boundaries on the role playing and make it easier for the involved students to step out of the action and back into the regular structure of the class. You will want to encourage that transition as quickly and effectively as possible, especially for the actor playing the suicidal student.

6. After the student actors have acted the first part of a role play, stop and discuss the warning signs that students see in the scenario. Then have the actors act out the rest of the role play. Have the group discuss the intervention steps that were taken.

7. At the end of each role play, be sure to recognize and reinforce that all three steps were taken:

    1. Caring words were expressed.

    2. A direct suicide-related question was asked.

    3. The need for help was identified and sought after.

8. Emphasize that caring alone is not enough when suicidal behavior is being expressed. The second and third steps are essential.

9. In between scenes and after the role play, the moderator poses questions from the Role-Play Discussion handouts to the class. Between scenes in the first role play, for example, the moderator would ask the following:

    • In scene 1, what warning signs and clues did you notice about Owen?

    • Which intervention steps, if any, did Alexa use?

    • And as role play 1 ends, the moderator can ask questions like these:

        – Alexa continues her suicide intervention in scene 2. What specifically does she do? How does she handle it when Owen asks her to promise not to tell anyone?

        – Where could Alexa turn for additional support for herself and Owen?

    Be prepared to step in and help the moderator manage the discussion, if needed.

If you would like to learn more about maximizing the effectiveness of this role-playing technique, a helpful resource is *Clinical Applications of Drama Therapy in Child and Adolescent Treatment,* edited by A. M. Weber and C. Haen (New York: Brunner-Routledge, 2005).

10. As soon as the role play is over, ask the actors to take a deep breath, shake off the characters they were playing, and return to their seats for the debriefing. By giving these directions, you begin to help the students disengage from their roles. Use the real names of the students involved and thank them for their participation. Ask the actors if they would like to share anything about what it was like to play their roles.

11. Repeat this process for the next role play. Conduct as many role plays as you can in the time you have.

PART 2

5 minutes

The pledge can be used at the close of session 3 after discussing the qualities of helpful people or as part of the closing activities in session 4. The pledge can be kept by the students, collected by the teacher, or even signed in duplicate so that one copy can be kept and one copy can be collected.

You'll rarely have a student who cannot name even one trusted adult; however, it does happen sometimes. If the student is open enough to share this information with you, set up a brief meeting to get a little more information and suggest some trusted adults.

THE HELP-SEEKING PLEDGE

The purpose of part 2 is to invite students to formally commit to the idea of seeking help for themselves or a friend. Created by real students in Maine, this simple pledge is designed to encourage students to identify and seek out helpful adults.

1. Say: **In the last part of our session today, we're going to talk about making a help-seeking pledge.**

2. Ask: **Can anyone tell me the meaning of a pledge?** Solicit responses from the students until you get the answer that a pledge is a promise.

3. Explain: **The promise I'm going to ask you to make today is a promise to yourself. In these** *Lifelines Prevention* **classes, you've learned to recognize the signs of suicidal behavior and how to get help. The promise you're making to yourself is if you see signs of suicidal behavior in yourself or someone else, you'll get help from a trusted adult. This help-seeking pledge was created by students in Maine as a way to formally commit to the idea of seeking help for yourself or for a friend.**

4. Give each student a copy of the Help-Seeking Pledge handout and a pen or pencil.

5. Explain: **On this pledge, you'll see that you're asked to identify three trusted adults to whom you would turn if you needed help for yourself or someone else. I'd like you to write in the names of three adults you trust, and if you have their contact information, add that, too. You can also put this information into your cell phones. If there is anybody who can't think of even one name to put on the list, come talk with me at the end of class.**

PART 3

5 minutes

WRAP-UP

1. Explain: **We've learned a lot about suicide prevention in these four sessions, and it's the kind of information that you'll be able to use for the rest of your lives. What are some of the things you remember from the last four sessions?**

    Possible responses include

    - Tell a trusted adult.

    - It's okay to ask about suicide.

    - If those students from Maine in the video could ask about suicide, I can, too.

- Our school has trained all the staff to be trusted adults.

- Don't keep a secret about suicide.

- FACTS: feelings, actions, changes, threats, situations.

2. Validate the responses you receive and continue: **Although we've had a lot of thoughtful and interesting classroom discussions, there are some key points that are important for you to remember.**

    This information has been printed for you on a small card that you can keep in your wallet or another safe, easily accessible place.

3. Hand out a Lifelines Card to each student.

4. Explain: **This small card summarizes all the information we've covered in this *Lifelines Prevention* unit on suicide prevention. It reminds us about the warning signs we've talked about. And, more importantly, it reinforces the fact that the first thing to do if you're worried about yourself or a friend being suicidal is to tell a trusted adult. It lists the number for the National Suicide Prevention Lifeline. It even gives you room to write down the names and phone numbers of the adults you know you can go to if you need help. Program these phone numbers into your cell phone so you have them with you at all times.**

    a. Give students a few minutes to fill in their Lifelines Cards.

    b. Remind students of these three key points:

    - Show a friend you care.

    - Ask about suicide.

    - Get help from a trusted adult!

5. Conclude: **We don't have a lot of time left, but I'd like to ask you all one last important question. We've been talking a lot about what our school is doing to take youth suicide prevention more seriously. Yet as we've talked over the last four sessions, you've made it very clear that you feel you're also in a great position to help each other. So, I want you to think about this: What can *you* do to be part of our school's suicide prevention plan? And don't just think about it—be like the students we saw in the videos and do something yourself about youth suicide prevention!**

6. *Optional:* Plan to have students take the post-test about a month after this last session.

GRADES 7–10 CURRICULUM HANDOUTS

These handouts can be found in the Student Curriculum Grades 7–10 packet of digital files.

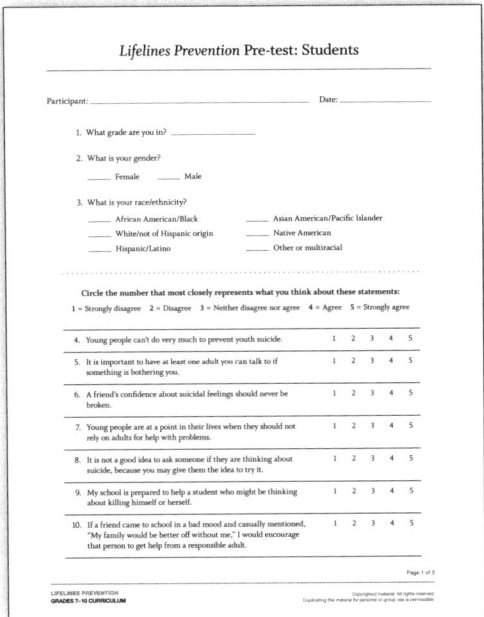

Lifelines Prevention Pre-test:
Students

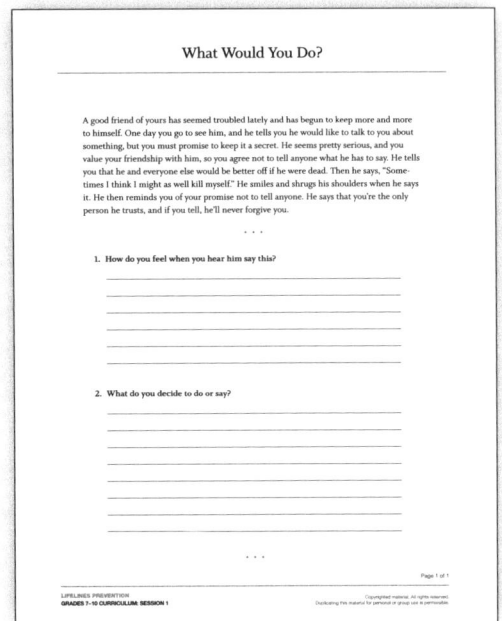

Session 1:
What Would You Do?

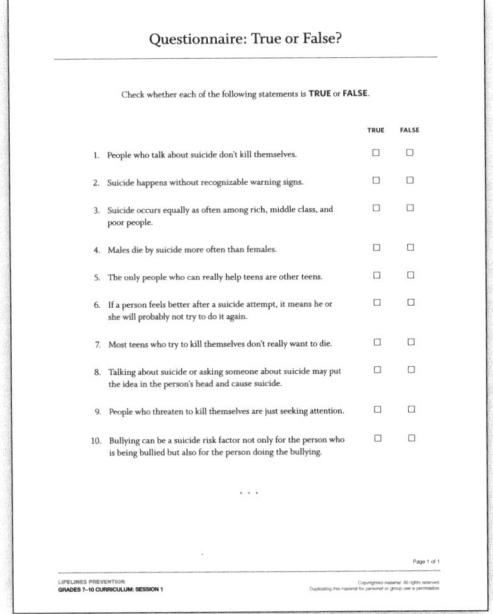

Session 1:
Questionnaire: True or False?

Session 2:
Warning Signs of Suicide (FACTS)

GRADES 7-10 CURRICULUM HANDOUTS

These handouts can be found in the Student Curriculum Grades 7–10 packet of digital files.

Session 2:
A Teen's Guide to Suicide Prevention
Discussion Guidelines

Session 2:
Helpful Steps to Prevent Suicide

Session 3:
One Life Saved **Discussion Questions**

Session 3:
The Qualities of Helpful People

GRADES 7–10 CURRICULUM HANDOUTS

These handouts can be found in the Student Curriculum Grades 7–10 packet of digital files.

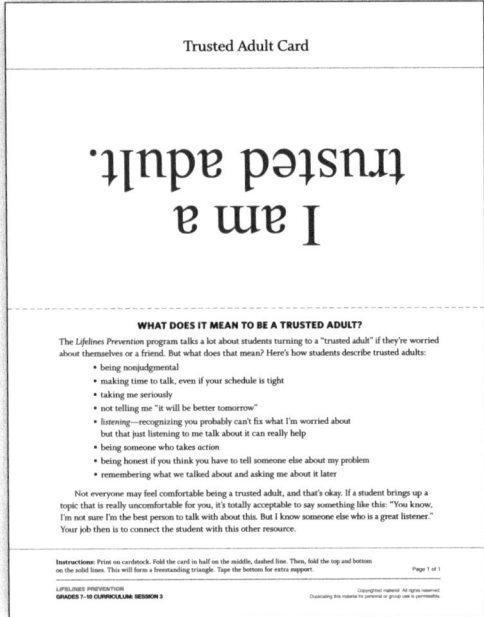

Session 3:
Trusted Adult Card

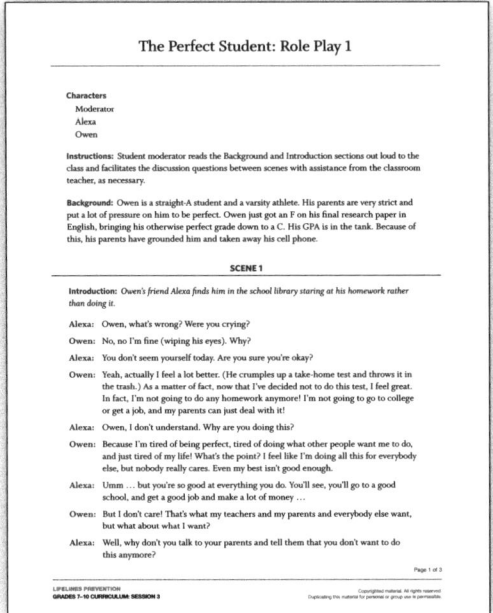

Session 3:
The Perfect Student: Role Play 1

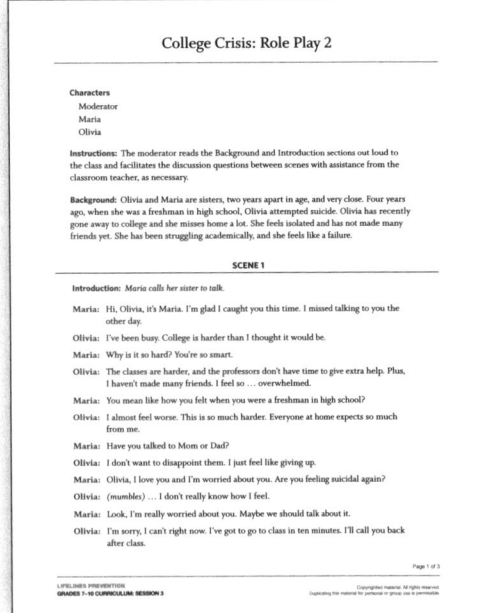

Session 3:
College Crisis: Role Play 2

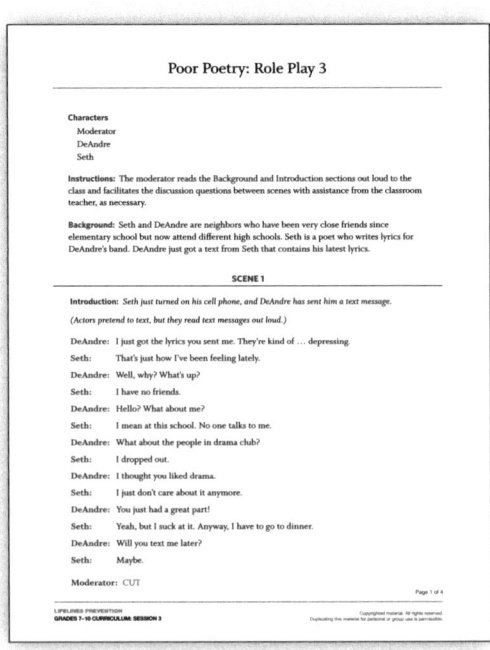

Session 3:
Poor Poetry: Role Play 3

GRADES 7–10 CURRICULUM HANDOUTS

These handouts can be found in the Student Curriculum Grades 7–10 packet of digital files.

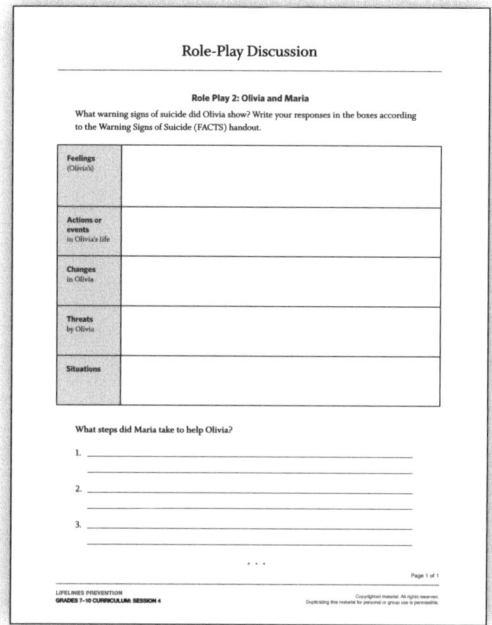

Session 4:
Role-Play Discussion:
Role Play 1: Owen and Alexa

Session 4:
Role-Play Discussion:
Role Play 2: Olivia and Maria

Session 4:
Role-Play Discussion:
Role Play 3: Seth and DeAndre

Session 4:
Help-Seeking Pledge

GRADES 7-10 CURRICULUM HANDOUTS

These handouts can be found in the Student Curriculum Grades 7–10 packet of digital files.

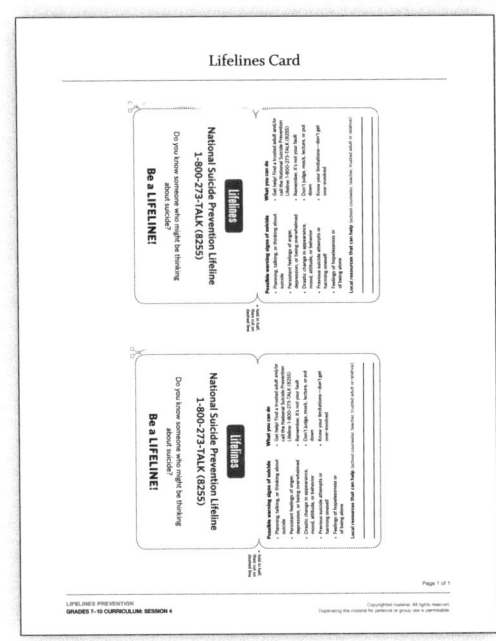

**Session 4:
Lifelines Card**

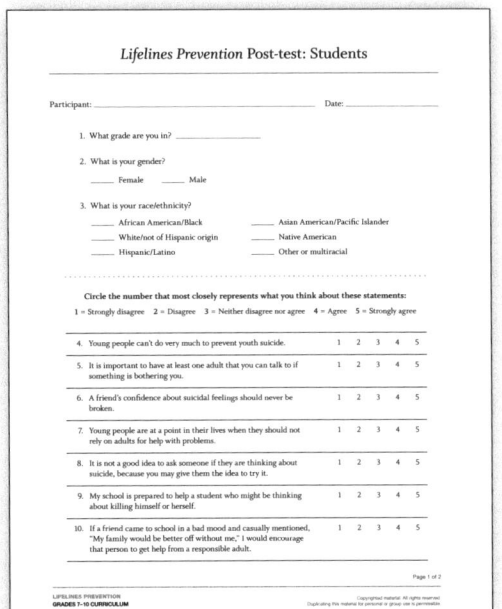

***Lifelines Prevention* Post-test:
Students**

Grades 11–12 Curriculum

....

DESCRIPTION

Myriad challenges face students after graduation from high school. Dozens of programs already exist that address practical realities like time-management skills, workload organization, and goal setting. Many high school curricula also include stress-management tools, such as classes in relaxation and breathing techniques, and some schools have even incorporated wellness into either curricula or extra-curricular activities. What are harder to find, however, are guides to help students address the emotional challenges that come from dealing with the massive life changes that accompany graduation.

Obviously, a unit that addresses all those challenges would need to be extremely comprehensive and cover several class periods. But with already extensive academic graduation requirements, it might seem unrealistic in many schools to embark on such an undertaking. There are, however, some core elements of mental wellness that are essential components to personal adjustment, whether a student is entering college, the military, or the workforce. These elements were introduced to students in the *Lifelines Prevention* grades 7–10 curriculum, so the foundation has been set to reintroduce them in the sessions for grades 11–12.

This two-session unit begins with a brief recap of the grades 7–10 *Lifelines Prevention* curriculum. The difference in this unit is that it focuses on caring for yourself rather than for others and emphasizes knowing how to identify trusted sources for help outside the high school community. The concepts of self-care and social connection have been recognized as increasingly important variables in emotional health and can be covered easily in a two-class unit. Self-care and social connection are called "protective factors" because they buffer youth from stress. The self-care element of the curriculum will help students identify their personal expectations for the future and how they will handle the stress they may experience when high expectations for life after high school are challenged or unmet. Students will be provided with both hard copy and online resources to identify and address these stressors.

The teaching methods used in this curriculum include whole class activities, individual questionnaires, and guided discussion about videos. Although there is some didactic material, it is presented in discussion with students rather than in lecture format to help them translate the content to their own life situations.

Some schools may choose to do an evaluation of the program. A pre-test and post-test are included for that purpose. The pre-test may be completed in the class before this unit begins rather than in the unit itself, or it can be done quickly at the beginning of the first session. For best measurement of program retention, it is advised that the post-test be completed at least one month after the unit has been completed. Both the pre-test and post-test can be found in the accompanying digital files.

Scope and Sequence

By the end of each session, students will be able to do the following:

Session 1: Do You Need a Crystal Ball to See the Future?	Session 2: How to Get from Here to There
• Explain the reasons for a unit on the transition after high school • Identify the key intervention steps from the grades 7–10 *Lifelines Prevention* curriculum • Identify their assumptions about the transition after high school	• Explain how their expectations about life after high school may be unrealistic • Assess the extent of their current support system • Identify where to find resources for help after high school

Related National Academic Standards[*]

Grades 11–12

Students will

- Predict how healthy behaviors can affect health status

- Describe the interrelationships of emotional, intellectual, physical, and social health

- Propose ways to reduce or prevent injuries and health problems

- Analyze personal susceptibility to injury, illness, or death if engaging in unhealthy behaviors

- Analyze the potential severity of injury or illness if engaging in unhealthy behaviors

- Analyze how peers influence healthy and unhealthy behaviors

- Evaluate how the school and community can affect personal health practice and behaviors

- Use resources from home, school, and community that provide valid health information

- Determine when professional health services may be required

- Access valid and reliable health products and services

- Use skills for communicating effectively with family, peers, and others to enhance health

- Demonstrate refusal, negotiation, and collaboration skills to enhance health and avoid or reduce health risks

- Demonstrate strategies to prevent, manage, or resolve interpersonal conflicts without harming self or others

- Demonstrate how to ask for and offer assistance to enhance the health of self and others

- Examine barriers that can hinder healthy decision-making

- Determine the value of applying a thoughtful decision-making process in health-related situations

- Justify when individual or collaborative decision-making is appropriate

- Generate alternatives to health-related issues or problems

- Predict the potential short-term and long-term impact of each alternative on self and others

- Defend the healthy choice when making decisions

---

[*] Source: *National Health Education Standards—Achieving Excellence,* Joint Commission on National Health Education Standards, 2004, www.cdc.gov/healthyschools/sher/standards/index.htm.

- Evaluate the effectiveness of health-related decisions
- Demonstrate a variety of healthy practices and behaviors that will maintain or improve the health of self and others
- Demonstrate a variety of behaviors to avoid or reduce health risks to self and others
- Demonstrate how to influence and support others to make positive health choices

Session Descriptions and Preparation

Session Title	Session Description	Materials Needed	Preparation Needed
Lifelines Prevention Pre-test: Students	Taking a pre-test before beginning the sessions helps students assess their views and knowledge of suicide and suicide prevention, alerting them to aspects they may want to listen carefully for or ask questions about.	• *Lifelines Prevention* Pre-test: Students 📄 • Pens or pencils	• Photocopy the pre-test, one for each student.

Session 1: Do You Need a Crystal Ball to See the Future?	After review of the grades 7–10 *Lifelines Prevention* sessions, the class engages in a discussion about how we make assumptions about future events and how we respond if these assumptions fall short. What they assumed in middle school about high school sets the stage for discussion about how lessons from our past can inform our future.	• Pens or pencils
		
		• Handouts from the Student Curriculum Grades 11–12 packet 📄
		  – Middle School Assumptions
		  – My Crystal Ball Predictions: Life After High School
		
		• Envelopes, one for each student
		
		• Whiteboard or flip chart and markers
			• Read the session outline.
			
			• Photocopy the handouts, one copy of each per student.

Session Title	Session Description	Materials Needed	Preparation Needed

Session 2: How to Get from Here to There	The assumptions students have made about life after high school are demonstrated in short videos. Personal strategies for coping with disappointment are reviewed. The importance of being socially connected or having a support system as a coping tool is highlighted.	• Pens or pencils
		
		• Student envelopes with My Crystal Ball Predictions handout from session 1
		
		• Handouts from the Student Curriculum Grades 11–12 packet 📄
		  – When Things Don't Go According to Plan
		  – When You Need to Take a Detour
		  – When You Need a Friend
		  – Local resource list, created from the Resources for Suicide Prevention and Support handout
		  – Lifelines Card
		  – *Optional: Lifelines Prevention* Post-test: Students
		
		• *What I Know Now* video, a video player, projector, and screen ▶
			• Read the session outline.
			
			• Fill out the Resources for Suicide Prevention and Support handout with local resources, and then make a copy for each student.
			
			• Print the Lifelines Card handout and cut the cards apart. Make enough cards for all students. It is recommended that you print these cards on a heavier paper stock.
			
			• Photocopy the rest of the handouts, one copy of each per student.
			
			• Set up a video player, projector, and screen for showing the video.
			
			• Preview the video.

***Lifelines Prevention* Post-test: Students**	*Lifelines Prevention* Post-test: Students	• *Lifelines Prevention* Post-test: Students 📄 • Pens or pencils	• Photocopy the post-test, one copy per student.

Session 1:
Do You Need a Crystal Ball to See the Future?

···

DESCRIPTION

Even in eleventh grade, high school students understand that their future lies ahead, after high school. For twelfth-grade students, the clock of the future is ticking. Understanding, however, that there may be ways to think about life after high school that might make this challenging transition easier does not usually register in conscious thinking. This session begins by reminding students that the lessons from the earlier grades 7–10 *Lifelines Prevention* curriculum still apply as they become older. In fact, the lessons can be expanded to include strategies to help them after graduation. It briefly reviews the grades 7–10 *Lifelines Prevention* curriculum, including summarizing the three action steps in a helpful intervention, which aids any students who may not have received the earlier curriculum. The idea that we carry learning from the past into the future sets the stage for a discussion about the transition of students from middle school to high school, what students recall about it, how they coped, and what they learned about themselves in the process. Discussion and an activity about the transition after high school follow, with an emphasis on how assumptions about the future can create personal stress.

LEARNER OUTCOMES

By the end of the session, students will be able to

- explain the reasons for a unit on the transition after high school

- identify the key intervention steps from the grades 7–10 *Lifelines Prevention* curriculum

- identify their assumptions about the transition after high school

MATERIALS NEEDED

- Pens or pencils
- Handouts from the Student Curriculum Grades 11–12 packet
    - Middle School Assumptions
    - My Crystal Ball Predictions: Life After High School
- Envelopes, one for each student
- Whiteboard or flip chart and markers

PREPARATION NEEDED

- Read the session outline.
- Photocopy the handouts, one copy of each per student.

Session 1 Outline

OUTLINE REASONS FOR THE UNIT ON TRANSITIONS

The purpose of part 1 is to explain some of the challenges students may face during the transition to life after high school and review how the *Lifelines Prevention* curriculum can provide a foundation for problem-solving strategies to address them.

1. a. Say to twelfth-grade students: **In our next two classes, we're going to be talking about life after high school. After all, that life will be coming shortly.**

    b. Say to eleventh-grade students: **Although it may not seem like it, life after high school is just around the corner.**

2. Continue with students of either grade: **Despite the differences in the paths you choose to take after high school, one thing will be the same for all of you: changes or transitions will happen, and they can be challenging. Our school thinks it's really important to help you anticipate and understand what some of these challenges may be and what skills you need to deal with them.**

3. Explain: **The foundation we'll use for our discussion is the *Lifelines Prevention* course that many of you took in middle school or earlier in high school.**

4. Say: **By a show of hands, how many of you participated in the *Lifelines Prevention* lessons on suicide prevention? For those of you who did, what are some of the things you remember?**

    Possible responses include

    *   learning to identify the FACTS about suicide: Feelings, Actions, Changes, Threats, and Situations

    *   recognizing the warning signs of suicide in themselves or others

    *   knowing the three basic suicide intervention steps: show you care, ask about suicide, and get help

    *   identifying a trusted adult

    *   I don't remember anything

5. Ask: **For those of you who do remember these lessons, how many of you have used anything you learned in those past sessions of the *Lifelines Prevention* program? You don't have to tell us what or how you used these tools; just raise your hand if you did.** Comment on responses. If no one remembers using any tools from the program, acknowledge that this is one of the reasons the school is presenting this booster course: to reinforce important messages that can help them as they make the transition to life after high school. Review the following key concepts from the grades 7–10 curriculum: caring for others and seeking help from trusted adults.

> Don't be concerned if students did not participate in the grades 5–6 or grades 7–10 *Lifelines Prevention* curriculum. The concepts you are reviewing can be understood quickly, especially by students in these later grades. In fact, this unit could stand alone without any reference to the previous lessons.

6. Say: **In this unit, we'll talk about those basic *Lifelines Prevention* concepts in a slightly different way. Instead of showing you how to care for others, we'll talk about "self-care," especially as it relates to our expectations about our future after high school. And we'll be expanding our definition of "trusted adult" to consider something called "social connections."** Write these two phrases in quotation marks on the board.

7. Explain: **We're going to start, however, by going back to another time in your life when many of you faced another big change: when you left middle school to come to high school.**

PART 2
20 minutes

EXPECTATIONS VERSUS REALITY

The purpose of this section is to help students begin to understand that there are times in life when our expectations about transitions do not match reality. A class activity is used to help students identify their middle school expectations about high school and whether those came true.

1. Say: **Now that you're in your last year(s) of high school, I want you to think back to middle school and try to remember what you thought life would be like in high school. I know it may seem like middle school was a lifetime ago, so I'm going to ask you to get in groups of three or four to make this discussion a little easier. Something one of your classmates says may remind you of something you forgot.**

2. Give each student a copy of the Middle School Assumptions handout and a pen or pencil. Divide the class into groups of three to four students.

3. Explain: **Groups on one side of the room** (identify which groups) **are going to come up with a list of all the things you expected about how high school would be different from middle school that turned out to be true.**

4. **Groups on the other side of the room are going to list the things you didn't expect: the things you weren't prepared for. I'd like you to appoint a recorder in each group, and after you make your list on your handouts, your recorder will come up and write your group's responses on the board. You will have about five minutes to do this.**

    Note: Create two columns on the board: "Expected and True" and "Unexpected." Monitor the groups to ensure they stay on task. This activity can take less than five minutes, but many student groups seem to enjoy reminiscing about their middle school naïveté, so you may have to cut it short.

    Possible student responses include these:

Expected and True	Unexpected
• More freedom.	• I'd like school better.
• More homework.	• I'd have more friends.
• I'd meet more people.	• I expected schoolwork would be hard, but not THIS hard.
• I could get involved in sports.	• Teachers are nice—unexpected!
• There'd be a lot to do on weekends.	• There's just as much drama at lunch.
• I'd have more free time.	• People wouldn't be so mean.
• Changing classes would be fun.	• My parents would ease up on me.
	• I have less free time.
	• I didn't know I'd have to get a job.
	• I thought I was more prepared than I was.

5. After the recorders have written their answers on the board, comment on these responses and ask for student input. (Ignore responses like "drink and party more.") The usual response to this activity is that students are surprised that there are more things that they didn't expect or that didn't turn out to be true.

6. Say: **It's interesting, isn't it, that there seem to be more things that *didn't* turn out the way you expected than *did* turn out the way you expected. How do you feel when life doesn't turn out the way you hoped it would?**

Possible responses include

- disappointed

- angry

- depressed

- frustrated

- cheated

- like I didn't know how good I had it before!

7. Say: **So, it seems pretty clear that we don't feel really good when our expectations aren't met. Yet you're juniors/seniors now, so you somehow managed to get through your disappointments about what high school would be like. How did you do that?** Write student responses on the board.

   Possible responses include

   - stopped expecting so much

   - I'm still disappointed

   - I had to get a tutor

   - sat with different students at lunch

   - talked to the counselor

   - talked about it with an older sibling

   - it is what it is, so deal!

8. Say: **What I hear you saying is that in order to not stay disappointed, most of you did something. And several times, that involved talking to someone else about what was going on. If you remember the *Lifelines Prevention* curriculum you took in past grades, we talked about the importance of having a trusted adult in your life to talk to if you are worried about yourself or if a friend may be at risk for suicide. What this list demonstrates is that as you get older, you still can turn to people for help for different reasons. We're going to talk about the people you turn to in our next class, but for now, we're going to stay on the theme of assumptions about the future a little longer.**

PART 3
7-10 minutes

WHAT DO YOU SEE IN YOUR CRYSTAL BALL?

The purpose of part 3 is to help students identify the assumptions they've made about their lives after high school. Because you want to encourage your students to be honest with themselves, a degree of privacy is ensured by placing the personal lists that the students generate in the class activity into sealed envelopes, which you will keep and redistribute at the start of the next class.

1. Say: **The assumptions we make about what our lives will be like after a transition like graduation are like gazing into a crystal ball, looking through the crystal for a glimpse of the future. Even though we know that's impossible, we still hold on to the illusion that we can predict what's going to happen to us. Now I'm going to give each of you your own crystal ball. Inside the ball, I want you to write down some of your personal assumptions about what your life will be like after high school. These are your private thoughts, not to be shared with the rest of the class or with me, which is why I'm also handing out envelopes.**

2. Give each student a copy of the My Crystal Ball Predictions: Life After High School handout. Continue: **After you've finished writing down your assumptions, fold the handout, put it into the envelope, and seal it. Write your name on the front of the envelope and drop it off at my desk at the end of class. I'll return them to you in our next class.**

3. Explain: **My only instruction to you is that you really think about what you're imagining your life will be like after high school. Give yourself permission to be honest with yourself—no one will see what you've written but you—and writing things down can help them become clearer in your mind. You'll have five minutes to do this.**

4. Hand out an envelope to each student. Instruct students to fold their handout, place it in the envelope, and seal it. Have them write their first and last names on the front of the envelope and collect them for use in session 2. Tell students that they will open the envelopes to refer to their answers on the handout in the next session, but no one will open them in the meantime.

   Note: You will find that the simple inclusion of the envelopes seems to result in students taking this activity more seriously.

<table>
<tr><td>

PART 4
5 minutes

</td><td>

WRAP-UP

</td></tr>
</table>

1. Explain: **What we've reviewed today reminds us that we make assumptions or have expectations about how things in our lives are going to turn out. We can be disappointed if those assumptions don't turn out to be true.**

2. Ask: **As you look back to middle school and at what you expected high school would be like, what are your reactions?**

   Possible responses include

   • silly

   • very idealistic

   • hopeful

3. Ask: **And if you could talk to middle school students right now, what advice would you give them about high school?**

   Possible answers include

   • It's not as different as you think.

   • You're still the same person as you were in middle school—for good or bad. Like, if you weren't athletic in middle school, that's not going to change.

   • You can make new friends.

   • Don't get behind in your classes.

   • Find a teacher who's got your back.

4. Conclude: **What I hear you telling me is that from your perspective as juniors or seniors, you're able to give middle school students a more realistic picture of what high school will be like. In our next class, we'll take a look at your assumptions about your future after high school and see how realistic they may be.**

Session 2:
How to Get from Here to There

....

DESCRIPTION

What students learned in session 1 about the differences between their middle school predictions about high school and its reality form the foundation for this session. This session is bookended by a series of short video interviews of graduates who share what their expectations were for life after graduation and what they did when reality didn't measure up. Although these same messages could be delivered in lecture format, students seem to listen more attentively to advice from peers rather than from adults. The critical message highlighted in session 1—that life doesn't always go according to plan—will now include some examples of what to do when that happens. The key resource of identifying who in your social network to go to for help parallels the message from the grades 5–6 and 7–10 *Lifelines Prevention* curriculum of identifying and using trusted adults when you need help for yourself or a friend.

LEARNER OUTCOMES

By the end of the session, students will be able to

- explain how their expectations about life after high school may be unrealistic
- assess the extent of their current support system
- identify where to find resources for help after high school

MATERIALS NEEDED

- Pens or pencils

- Student envelopes with My Crystal Ball Predictions handout from session 1

- Handouts from the Student Curriculum Grades 11–12 packet

  – When Things Don't Go According to Plan

  – When You Need to Take a Detour

  – When You Need a Friend

  – Local resource list, created from the Resources for Suicide Prevention and Support handout

  – Lifelines Cards

  – *Optional: Lifelines Prevention* Post-test: Students

- *What I Know Now* video interviews, a video player, projector, and screen ▶

PREPARATION NEEDED

- Read the session outline.

- Fill out the Resources for Suicide Prevention and Support handout with local resources, and then make a copy for each student.

- Photocopy the Lifelines Cards handout and cut the cards apart. You should have one card for each student. These cards are designed to be carried by the students at all times. They should, therefore, be printed on sufficiently strong stock to stand up to use; 8-point white-coated cover stock is recommended. Students won't want to advertise the fact that they are carrying a card with help-seeking information, so use an unobtrusive color. Alternatively, you can create your own Lifelines Cards. Use an easy-to-read font and print them on heavy paper stock.

- Photocopy the rest of the handouts, one copy of each per student.

- Set up the video player, projector, and screen for showing the video.

- Preview the video interviews, so you are familiar with the content.

Session 2 Outline

PART 1
15 minutes

THE WISDOM OF OTHERS

The purpose of part 1 is to help students better articulate their personal assumptions about life after high school by listening to the experiences of matriculated students with whom they might identify. The clearer students can be about their personal assumptions for the future, the easier it might be for them to adjust course when things start to get off track.

1. Begin by handing back the envelopes that contain the completed My Crystal Ball Predictions handouts. Also give each person a pen or pencil. Tell students to take a minute or so to review what they wrote. They can add to what they have written if they want.

2. Say: **We ended our last session with you sharing your hard-earned wisdom with middle school students about the realities of the transition to high school. We're going to begin this session by listening to some high school graduates briefly tell us about some of their assumptions about life after high school. I'd like you to listen to what they have to say and see if any of their crystal ball predictions are similar to yours.**

3. Play *What I Know Now* video, part 1.

   Synopsis: Three students who took different paths after high school—work, college, and the military—provide short descriptions of what they hoped their lives would be like after graduation.

   Common themes for post-graduates include

   • having more freedom and independence

   • life being easier

   • having lots of free time

   • nobody will tell me what to do

   • I would find other people who finally understand me

   • I was going to do well

   • making my own money

4. Ask the following questions to stimulate discussion:

- **What are some of the expectations these young people talked about?**

- **Are they similar to the ones you identified? Different?**

- **Are there things you expected them to say that they didn't? What were these things?**

- **Do some of their predictions seem more likely to happen than others? Which ones?**

- **Does listening to them make you think of other things to put into your crystal ball? If so, add them now.**

5. Leave a minute at the end of the activity for students to add things to their crystal balls if they'd like.

PART 2
10 minutes

WHEN THINGS DON'T GO ACCORDING TO PLAN

The purpose of part 2 is to provide real-life examples of the ways in which expectations can get derailed and to identify some of the most common personal reactions to these experiences.

1. Say: **We just heard these young people talk about what was in their crystal balls. Now let's listen to them tell us if their predictions turned out to be true.**

2. Play the *What I Know Now* video, part 2.

    Synopsis: While some of the expectations or assumptions these graduates had about life after high school did turn out as they had hoped, there were others that didn't go according to plan.

3. Distribute the When Things Don't Go According to Plan handout. Take turns having students read the assumptions at the top of the handout out loud. Then spend some time discussing the questions at the bottom of the handout.

PART 3 15 minutes	**WHEN YOU NEED TO TAKE A DETOUR**

The purpose of part 3 is to reinforce the fact that, even when we apply our best efforts, life doesn't always follow our plans—but we can think ahead about how we're going to respond when that happens. The invaluable importance of a support system will be reinforced, and students will complete a personal assessment of their current sources of support. This activity will also help them identify the sources of support that are helpful to them in a personal crisis and other sources that might change after high school and need to be replaced.

1. Say: **Let's look at these young people one last time as they tell us what they did to handle their situations.**

2. Play the *What I Know Now* video, part 3.

    Synopsis: The graduates explain how they responded when they realized life was not going as expected.

3. Distribute the When You Need to Take a Detour handout. Ask the following questions to stimulate discussion:

    - **Did how these students react seem reasonable to you? Why or why not?**

    - **Could you imagine yourself handling these kinds of disappointments in similar ways?**

    Expect that responses may include those from students who tell you they wouldn't ask advice from anyone else, would never tell parents/guardians, or would never go to a counseling center for help. Try not to get defensive if these responses are presented; you're not going to change long-held opinions in a class that lasts forty-five minutes. A helpful response would be to first validate feelings, for example, **I know some people keep things very private** or **For some people, their family is the last place they would go for support.** The next step is to simply ask them how they would have handled the situation in a different way. Remember, your objective here is not to make everyone agree on the same choices, but to get students thinking about which alternatives would work best for them.

4. Say: **Whether you would have done the same thing if you were in the shoes of these graduates isn't really the point. We all learn to cope with disappointment in different ways. And whether we agree or disagree with what these young people did, there are several coping techniques we can use when life takes a detour.**

5. Ask three students to take turns reading the three techniques on the handout. Stop after each technique and ask students what that technique means to them.

   Here are the three techniques:

   - Own it: Recognize there is a problem and don't deny it.

   - Change it: Don't give up on having expectations; just change your expectations.

   - Share it: Involve someone else as part of your decision-making process.

6. Write these three key points on the board as a reference point: Own it! Change it! Share it!

7. Say: **What we see in these examples reflects what we've been talking about over these two classes. The first point is recognizing you have a problem—*own it*—when reality isn't matching up to that vision you created in your crystal ball. That's why we spent so much time on that activity, and you get to take what you wrote home with you. Putting our expectations or dreams down on paper can help us recognize when a detour is needed. The second point of this is taking responsibility for your part of the problem or for fixing it.**

8. Continue: **That second point you mentioned—*change it*—is equally important. None of those young people gave up on their dreams—they just adjusted them to match reality. What you've written in those crystal balls is really important. Your life belongs to you, and as corny as it sounds, it's the only one you've got. Give yourself permission to believe in possibilities. And be brave enough to realize when you need to correct your course and adjust the direction of your dreams.**

9. Explain: **The third point has to do with what these people did when they realized they needed that course adjustment—*share it*. Even if they didn't exactly tell someone else what their problem was, they engaged someone else so they weren't so alone. Those other people are what is called "a support system." We all have one and it provides the kinds of connections that help us get through life. And just as you may have never before thought about all the future expectations you wrote in your crystal ball, many of you have probably never thought much about who's in your support system and why they're important to you.**

10. Say: **Speaking of support systems, I'm going to pass around a handout called When You Need a Friend. It asks you to identify the people you would turn to in a variety of common life situations. I'd like you to read each question and write the name or initials of the person you'd turn to in that situation. And just like the crystal ball activity, you will not be asked to share your answers in class. You'll have a few minutes to do this.**

11. Give each student a copy of the handout. Watch the class, and when most students have finished writing (usually about three minutes), ask the following questions to stimulate discussion:

    • **Did any of you have trouble filling in any of the categories? Which ones?**

    • **How many of you listed five or more names? Four? Three? Two? Just one?**

    • **I only asked you to fill in one name for each category. Now take a minute or so and see if you can come up with a backup name for each question.** Allow a couple of minutes for students to write. **How many of you had trouble doing that?** Pause for a few responses. **Any idea why?** Pause for a few responses. **It's important to recognize that, while it is totally okay to have one person we count on for everything, we'll be in *big* trouble if something happens to that person. That's why those backup people are so important.**

12. Say: **Now look at your list and see if you can identify any of the names that might change after graduation. Be honest with yourself. Sometimes, for example, we may think we've found the love of our life, but after graduation our paths start to go in different directions. Or you may feel you can turn to your parents for everything right now, but that may change as you get older. You don't have to replace those names right now—just be aware of the roles you may need other people to fill after graduation.**

13. Ask: **How many of you could identify names that you think will be different after high school? You don't have to share the names, but what were some of the categories where you think your support system might need to be different?**

14. Explain: **There are two roles, though, that are really important to always have filled: who would you turn to if you were worried about a friend and who would you turn to if you were worried about yourself? Did all of you have a name in each of those places?**

15. Ask: **Don't tell us the name of that person, but what were the reasons you chose them?**

    Possible answers include

    • I've known him since grade school.

    • She never judges me.

    • I can trust her to respect a confidence.

    • He's always there.

16. Continue: **And although most of you will never have thoughts about life being so bad you want to end it, some of you will have thoughts about suicide somewhere along the course of your lives. Listen to me carefully: when your life is at a point that you think about suicide, you MUST reach out to someone you trust and tell them about it. You may feel alone, but you're not, and support IS there to help you get out of that dark place.**

17. Say: **Sometimes the people who fill those roles are going to be people you know, but after you leave high school, that may change. What's good to know is that, wherever you are, you can usually find local mental health resources by simply doing a Google search.**

18. Give each student a copy of the Resources for Suicide Prevention and Support that include local resources that you've added.

19. Also pass out Lifelines Cards and say: **I'm going to hand out a small card where some of those resources are listed, and I suggest you take a picture of it with your phone so it will be handy at all times. One really important resource I want to highlight is the National Suicide Prevention Lifeline: 1-800-273-TALK (8255).** Write the phone number on the board.

    You don't have to be thinking about suicide to call them. The phones are answered by trained volunteers who will listen to all types of problems or concerns. And your call will be anonymous.

PART 4
5 minutes

WRAP-UP

The purpose of part 4 is to summarize the key points of the unit and to leave students with a thought-provoking exercise that reminds them of another element of self-care: focusing on the positive.

1. Explain: **In a very short time, we've covered what may be some of the most important life lessons you can take with you after high school.**

2. Ask: **What are the lessons you'll be taking away?**

    Possible answers include

    - It's helpful to identify your expectations about your life after graduation.

    - Even if your plans or dreams get derailed, you can take control by adjusting them to reality.

    - They *will* get derailed—that's normal!

    - Having support is important.

    - You need different people to do different things to support you.

    - It's important to have backup plans if your first plan falls through.

    - Resources to address suicidal thoughts and actions are available.

    - You can find many resources online.

3. Say: **Now there's one last lesson I'd like to leave with you. I know all of you have heard about the ship the *Titanic*, but how many of you have heard about the ship named the *Olympic*? Raise your hands.**

    Usually no one has heard about this ship. Pause for a moment, and then continue: **The *Olympic* was a transatlantic ocean liner, the sister ship to the *Titanic*. And the reason most of us have never heard about the *Olympic* was that it never sank. The *Olympic* started sailing in 1911 and went back and forth across the ocean until the 1930s. Obviously, a ship that simply did its job, day by day, isn't half as interesting as one that hits an iceberg on its maiden voyage and sinks.**

And I think, perhaps, that is the way most of us live our lives. We can identity those "*Titanic*" moments. We may even catalog them—our list of personal disasters—and forget to pay attention to all the *Olympic* moments that make up each and every day. The *Olympic* moments can be as simple as getting up before the alarm clock, having a "good hair day," or not getting called on in class when we don't know the answer. But these *Olympic* moments really are the essential stuff of our lives.

I'd like to suggest to you that by paying attention to your *Olympic* moments, your days may seem just a little bit brighter. They won't change the *Titanic* moments when they happen, but the *Olympic* moments will be a whole lot more frequent, and they may remind us that even when things get dark, the ship doesn't always sink.

4. Conclude: **So as we leave today, I'd like you to think of one *Olympic* moment. Keep that thought in your head. Try to think of *Olympic* moments as often as you can—and see if doing that makes a difference. It's just another way you can take better care of yourself. Smooth sailing!**

5. *Optional:* About a month after this last session, give each student a copy of the post-test and have the students fill it out.

GRADES 11–12 CURRICULUM HANDOUTS

These handouts can be found in the Student Curriculum Grades 11–12 packet of digital files.

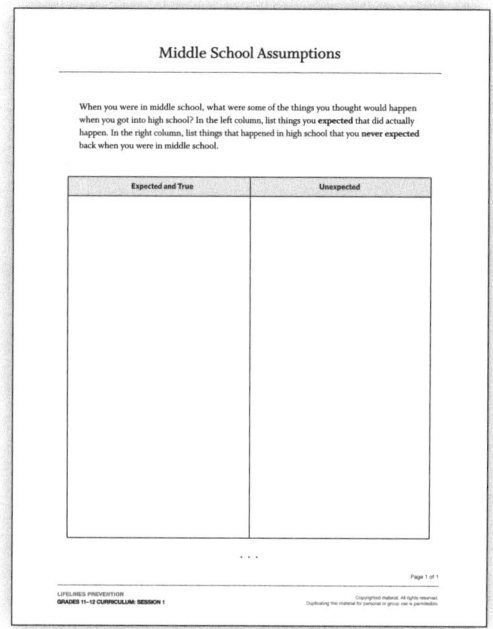

Lifelines Prevention Pre-test:
Students

Session 1:
Middle School Assumptions

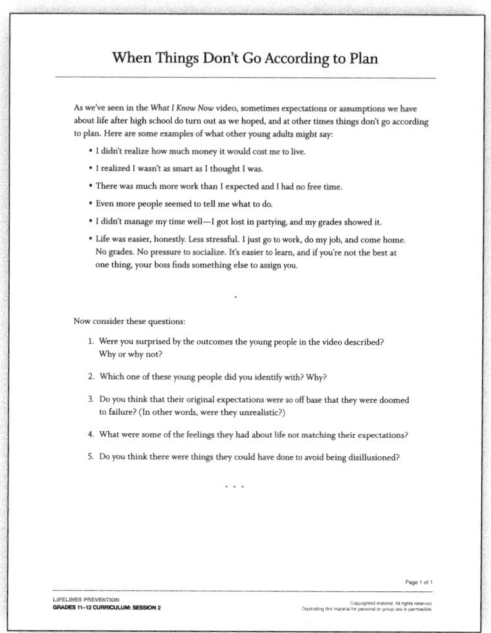

Session 1:
My Crystal Ball Predictions:
Life After High School

Session 2:
When Things Don't Go According to Plan

GRADES 11-12 CURRICULUM HANDOUTS

These handouts can be found in the Student Curriculum Grades 11–12 packet of digital files.

When You Need to Take a Detour

In the *What I Know Now* video, we saw the graduates explain how they responded when they realized life was not going as expected.

Now consider these questions:

1. Did the way these people reacted seem reasonable to you? Why or why not?

2. Could you imagine yourself handling these kinds of disappointments in similar ways?

Remember, whether you would have done the same thing if you were in the shoes of these graduates isn't really the point. We all learn to cope with disappointment in different ways. And whether we agree with what these graduates did or not, there are several coping techniques we can use when life takes a detour:

- Own it: Recognize there is a problem and don't deny it.
- Change it: Don't give up on having expectations; just change your expectations.
- Share it: Involve someone else as part of your decision-making process.

. . .

Session 2:
When You Need to Take a Detour

When You Need a Friend

Take a quick inventory of the people in your life, and then write someone's name or initials next to the following questions.

Who would you turn to . . .

1. If you want to have fun? _____

2. If you want to complain about school or a teacher? _____

3. When you need help with homework? _____

4. When you are worried about a friend? _____

5. If you were worried about yourself? _____

6. When you just want to hang out? _____

7. If you need to talk about something serious? _____

8. If you want to blow off steam? _____

9. If you want to talk about a personal relationship? _____

10. When you want to talk about your future? _____

. . .

Session 2:
When You Need a Friend

Resources for Suicide Prevention and Support
Instructions

Use these instructions to complete the Resources for Suicide Prevention and Support handout that appears on the following pages. The handout includes writing lines for you to add information for local resources, online resources, and survivor of suicide loss groups. This allows you to tailor the handout to your specific community's available services before you distribute it to *Lifelines Prevention* program participants.

Local Resources

In the first section of your Resources handout (on the following pages), list local mental health resources and local hospital mental health resources if your community has them. Also list faith community leaders with whom you have spoken about the goals and objectives of the *Lifelines Prevention* program. If your school has a cadre of local therapists to whom you refer youth who may be at risk for suicide, list them as well.

Online Resources

There is an ever-increasing number of web-based resources for information and support related to mental health problems. The list included in the handout's second section is not all-inclusive and allows space for you to add other sites. Make sure, though, if you add websites, that you check them out first to make sure the content is safe.

Resources for Survivors of Suicide Loss

Sometimes you may be asked to provide resources for people who have lost someone they knew from suicide. They are often referred to as "survivors of suicide loss." In addition to the national American Foundation for Suicide Prevention, whose information is provided in this section, your community may have specialized services for survivors that you can also list in the space provided.

Session 2:
Resources for Suicide Prevention
and Support

Lifelines Card

Session 2:
Lifelines Card

GRADES 11-12 CURRICULUM HANDOUTS

These handouts can be found in the Student Curriculum Grades 11–12 packet of digital files.

Lifelines Prevention Post-test:
Students

Introduction to Hazelden Lifelines

1. J. Kalafat and M. Elias, "Adolescents' Experience with and Response to Suicidal Peers," *Suicide and Life-Threatening Behavior* 22 (1992): 315–21; J. Kalafat, M. Elias, and M. A. Gara, "The Relationship of Bystander Intervention Variables to Adolescents' Response to Suicidal Peers," *Journal of Primary Prevention* 13 (1993): 213, 231–44; J. Kalafat and M. Elias, "An Evaluation of Adolescent Suicide Intervention Classes," *Suicide and Life-Threatening Behavior* 24 (1994): 224–33; J. Kalafat, "The Prevention of Youth Suicide," in *Healthy Children 2010: Enhancing Children's Wellness,* eds. R. P. Weissberg, T. P. Gullota, B. A. Ryan, and G. R. Adams (Thousand Oaks, CA: Sage, 1997), 175–213; C. R. Lindsay and J. Kalafat, "Adolescents' Views of Preferred Helper Characteristics and Barriers to Seeking Help from School-Based Adults," *Journal of Educational and Psychological Consultation* 9 (1998): 171–93; and J. Kalafat, "A Systems Approach to Suicide Prevention," in *Suicide Prevention and Intervention: Summary of an Institute of Medicine Workshop,* ed. S. K. Goldsmith (Washington, DC: National Academy Press, 2001), 4–7.

2. Erin M. Sullivan, Joseph L. Annest, Thomas R. Simon, Feijun Luo, and Linda L. Dahlberg, "Suicide Trends Among Persons Aged 10–24 Years—United States, 1994–2012," *Morbidity and Mortality Weekly Report (MMWR)* 64, no. 8 (March 6, 2015): 201–205, www.cdc.gov/mmwr/preview/mmwrhtml/mm6408a1.htm.

3. John Kalafat and Maurice Elias, "Adolescents' experience with and response to suicidal peers," *Suicide and Life-Threatening Behavior* 22 (1992): 315–21.

4. J. Kalafat, M. Madden, D. Haley, S. O'Halloran, and C. DiCara, "Evaluation of Lifeline Classes: A Component of the School-Community Based Maine Youth Suicide Prevention Project U17/Ccu122311-02," unpublished report submitted to National Registry of Evidence-Based Prevention Programs (2007).

5. Conversation with Harvey Doppelt, PhD, Director, Specialized Services, Division of Prevention and Behavioral Health Services, Wilmington, Delaware.

Introduction to Youth Suicide

1. American Association of Suicidology, 2017. Data gathered in 2015. Check www.suicidology.org for updated statistics.

2. L. Kann, T. McManus, W. A. Harris, S. L. Shanklin, K. H. Flint, J. Hawkins, and B. Queens. "Youth Risk Behavior Surveillance—United States, 2015," *Morbidity and Mortality Weekly Report (MMWR)* 65, no. 6 (June 10, 2016), www.cdc.gov/healthyyouth/data/yrbs /pdf/2015/ss6506_updated.pdf.

3. Kann et al., "YRBS."

4. A. H. Sheftall, L. Asti, L. M. Horowitz, A. Felts, C. A. Fontanella, J. V. Campo, J. A. Bridge, "Suicide in Elementary School-Aged Children and Early Adolescents," *Pediatrics* 138, no. 4 (October 2016).

5. Ernest L. Boyer, *The Basic School: A Community for Learning* (Princeton, NJ: Carnegie Foundation for the Advancement of Teaching, 1995).

6. P. Hazell and P. Lewin, "An Evaluation of Postvention Following Adolescent Suicide," *Suicide and Life-Threatening Behavior* 23 (1993): 101–9; M. M. Underwood and K. Dunne-Maxim, *Managing Sudden Traumatic Loss in the Schools: New Jersey Adolescent Suicide Prevention Project* (Piscataway, NJ: University Behavioral HealthCare, 1997); S. Poland, "Suicide Intervention," in *Best Practices in School Psychology-II*, eds. A. Thomas and J. Grimes (Washington, DC: National Association of School Psychologists, 1995), 259–74; J. Kalafat and M. Elias, "An Evaluation of Adolescent Suicide Intervention Classes," *Suicide and Life-Threatening Behavior* 24 (1994): 224–33; V. Vieland, B. Whittle, A. Garland, R. Hicks, and D. Shaffer, "The Impact of Curriculum-Based Suicide Prevention Programs for Teenagers: An 18-Month Follow-Up," *Journal of the American Academy of Child and Adolescent Psychiatry* 30 (1991): 811–15; J. Cliffone, "Suicide Prevention: A Classroom Presentation to Adolescents," *Social Work* 38 (1993): 197–203; and Anthony R. Pisani, Daniel C. Murrie, and Morton M. Silverman, "Reformulating Suicide Risk Formulation: From Prediction to Prevention," *Academic Psychiatry* 40, no. 4 (2016): 623–29.

7. J. Kalafat and M. Elias, "Adolescents' Experience with and Response to Suicidal Peers," *Suicide and Life-Threatening Behavior* 22 (1992): 315–21.

8. *Youth Suicide Prevention Programs: A Resource Guide* (Atlanta: Centers for Disease Control and Prevention, 1992), 66.

9. L. Potter, K. E. Powell, and S. P. Kacher, "Suicide Prevention from a Mental Health Perspective," *Suicide and Life-Threatening Behavior* 25 (1995): 87.

10. J. Cliffone, "Suicide Prevention: A Classroom Presentation to Adolescents," *Social Work* 38 (1993): 197–203; L. L. Eggert, E. A. Thompson, J. R. Herting, and L. J. Nicholas, "Reducing Suicide Potential among High-Risk Youth: Tests of a School-Based Prevention Program," *Suicide and Life-Threatening Behavior* 25 (1995): 276–96; J. Kalafat and M. Elias, "An Evaluation of Adolescent Suicide Intervention Classes," *Suicide and Life-Threatening Behavior* 24 (1994): 224–33; J. Kalafat and C. Gagliano, "The Use of Simulations to Assess the Impact of an Adolescent Suicide Response Curriculum," *Suicide and Life-Threatening Behavior* 26 (1996): 359–64; I. Orbach and H. Bar-Joseph, "The Impact of a Suicide Prevention Program for Adolescents on Suicidal Tendencies, Hopelessness, Ego Identity, and Coping," *Suicide and Life-Threatening Behavior* 23 (1993): 120–29; and A. M. Weber and C. Haen, eds., *Clinical Applications of Drama Therapy in Child and Adolescent Treatment* (New York: Brunner-Routledge, 2005).

11. J. Kalafat and D. M. Ryerson, "The Implementation and Institutionalization of a School-Based Youth Suicide Prevention Program," *Journal of Primary Prevention* 19 (1999):

157–75; and F. J. Zenere III and P. J. Lazarus, "The Decline of Youth Suicidal Behavior in an Urban, Multicultural Public School System Following the Introduction of a Suicide Prevention and Intervention Program," *Suicide and Life-Threatening Behavior* 27 (1997): 387–403.

12. D. Shaffer, P. Fisher, R. H. Hicks, M. Parides, and M. Gould, "Psychiatric Diagnosis in Child and Adolescent Suicide," *Archives of General Psychiatry* 53 (1996): 339–48.

13. D. Brent, "Risk Factors for Adolescent Suicide and Suicidal Behavior: Mental and Substance Abuse Disorders, Family Environmental Factors, and Life-Stress," *Suicide and Life-Threatening Behavior* 25 (1995): 52–63.

14. M. Gould, P. Fisher, M. Parides, M. Flory, and D. Shaffer, "Psychosocial Risk Factors of Adolescent Completed Suicide," *Archives of General Psychiatry* 53 (1996): 1155–62.

15. P. Lewinson, P. Rohde, and J. Seely, "Adolescent Suicide Ideation and Attempts: Prevalence, Risk Factors and Clinical Implications," *Clinical Psychology Journal and Practice* 3, no. 1 (1996): 25–26.

16. J. Kalafat and C. Gagliano, "The Use of Simulations to Assess the Impact of an Adolescent Suicide Response Curriculum," *Suicide and Life-Threatening Behavior* 26 (1996): 359–64.

17. C. J. Wilson and F. P. Deane, "Adolescent Opinions about Reducing Help-Seeking Barriers and Increasing Appropriate Help Engagement," *Journal of Educational and Psychological Consultation* 12, no. 4 (2001): 345–64.

Section 1: Administrative Perspective

1. L. Kann, T. McManus, W. A. Harris, S. L. Shanklin, K. H. Flint, J. Hawkins, and B. Queens. "Youth Risk Behavior Surveillance—United States, 2015," *Morbidity and Mortality Weekly Report (MMWR)* 65, no. 6 (June 10, 2016), www.cdc.gov/healthyyouth /data/yrbs/pdf/2015/ss6506_updated.pdf.

Section 2: Faculty and Staff Training

1. A. VanOrman and B. Jarosz, "Suicide Replaces Homicide as Second-Leading Cause of Death Among U.S. Teenagers," Population Reference Bureau, www.prb.org/Publications /Articles/2016/suicide-replaces-homicide-second-leading-cause-death-among-us-teens.aspx.

2. Centers for Disease Control and Prevention, "YRBSS Data & Documentation," last updated August 9, 2017, www.cdc.gov/healthyyouth/data/yrbs/data.htm?.

3. J. Kalafat and M. Underwood, *Lifelines: A School-Based Adolescent Suicide Response Program* (Dubuque, IA: Kendall, 1989).

4. American Association of Suicidology, "Guidelines for School-Based Suicide Prevention Programs," Prevention Division of the American Association of Suicidology (1999).

5. S. Curtin, H. Hedegaard, A. Minino, M. Warner, and T. Simon, "Quickstats: Suicide Rates for Teens Aged 15–19 Years, by Sex—United States, 1975–2015," *Morbidity and Mortality Weekly Report (MMWR)* 66, no. 30 (August 4, 2017): 816, www.cdc.gov/mmwr /volumes/66/wr/mm6630a6.htm.

Section 3: Parent/Guardian Workshop

1. L. Greenspan and J. Deardorff, *The New Puberty: How to Navigate Early Development in Today's Girls* (New York: Rodale Inc., 2014).

2. Greenspan and Deardorff, *The New Puberty.*

3. L. Kann, T. McManus, W. A. Harris, S. L. Shanklin, K. H. Flint, J. Hawkins, and B. Queens. "Youth Risk Behavior Surveillance—United States, 2015," *Morbidity and Mortality Weekly Report (MMWR)* 65, no. 6 (June 10, 2016), www.cdc.gov/healthyyouth /data/yrbs/pdf/2015/ss6506_updated.pdf.

4. Kann et al., "YRBS."

5. American Association of Suicidology, "Facts & Statistics: National Suicide Statistics," last updated January 2017, www.suicidology.org/resources/facts-statistics.

6. AAS, "Facts & Statistics."

7. L. Kann, T. McManus, W. A. Harris, S. L. Shanklin, K. H. Flint, J. Hawkins, and B. Queens. "Youth Risk Behavior Surveillance—United States, 2015," *Morbidity and Mortality Weekly Report (MMWR)* 65, no. 6 (June 10, 2016), www.cdc.gov/healthyyouth /data/yrbs/pdf/2015/ss6506_updated.pdf.

Section 4: Student Curriculum

Grades 5–6

1. Q. S. Curtin, H. Hedegaard, A. Minino, M. Warner, and T. Simon, "Quickstats: Suicide Rates for Teens Aged 15–19 Years, by Sex—United States, 1975–2015," *Morbidity and Mortality Weekly Report (MMWR)* 66, no. 30 (August 4, 2017): 816, www.cdc.gov /mmwr/volumes/66/wr/mm6630a6.htm.

Grades 7–10

1. Q. S. Curtin, H. Hedegaard, A. Minino, M. Warner, and T. Simon, "Quickstats: Suicide Rates for Teens Aged 15–19 Years, by Sex—United States, 1975–2015," *Morbidity and Mortality Weekly Report (MMWR)* 66, no. 30 (August 4, 2017): 816, www.cdc.gov /mmwr/volumes/66/wr/mm6630a6.htm.

Grades 11–12

1. This three-step intervention model is used with permission of the Youth Suicide Prevention Program, Seattle, WA.

References

American Association of Suicidology. "Guidelines for School-Based Suicide Prevention Programs." Prevention Division of the American Association of Suicidology, 1999.

Berman, A. L. "School-Based Suicide Prevention: Research Advances and Practice Implications." *School Psychology Review* 38, no. 2 (2009): 233–38. http://knoxvillepsychs .pbworks.com/f/School-Based+Suicide+Prevention-2009.pdf.

Berman, A. L., and D. A. Jobes. *Adolescent Suicide: Assessment and Intervention.* Washington, DC: American Psychological Association, 2007.

Campo, J. V. "Suicide Prevention: Time for 'Zero Tolerance.'" *Current Opinion in Pediatrics* 21, no. 5 (2009): 611.

Cantrell, S. G. "FERPA: To Release or Not to Release—That Is the Question." *Journal of Research Initiatives* 1, no. 1 (2013).

Cash, S. J., M. Thelwall, S. N. Peck, J. Z. Ferrell, and J. A. Bridge. "Adolescent Suicide Statements on MySpace." *Cyberpsychology Behavior and Social Networking* 16, no. 3 (2013): 166–74. https://doi.org/10.1089/cyber.2012.0098.

Centers for Disease Control and Prevention. "Sexual Identity, Sex of Sexual Contacts, and Health-Related Behaviors among Students in Grades 9–12: United States and Selected Sites, 2015." *Morbidity and Mortality Weekly Report* 65, no. 9 (2016): 1–202.

Centers for Disease Control and Prevention. "Suicide Contagion and the Reporting of Suicide: Recommendations from a National Workshop." *Morbidity and Mortality Weekly Report* 43, no. RR-6 (1994): 13–18.

Cobain, B. *When Nothing Matters Anymore: A Survival Guide for Depressed Teens.* Minneapolis: Free Spirit Publishing, 1998.

Curtin, S. C., M. Warner, and H. Hedegaard. "Increase in Suicide in the United States, 1999–2014." NCHS data brief no. 241. Hyattsville, MD: National Center for Health Statistics, 2016.

Eastgard, S. "Comprehensive Packaged School Community Suicide Prevention Programs." *Youth Suicide Prevention Program Toolkit.* Seattle: Youth Suicide Prevention Program, 2000, www.yspp.org.

Erbacher, T., J. Singer, and S. Poland. *Suicide in Schools: A Practitioner's Guide.* New York: Routledge, 2015.

Freedenthal, S., and A. R. Stiffman. "Suicidal Behavior in Urban American Indian Adolescents: A Comparison with Reservation Youth in a Southwestern State." *Suicide and Life-Threatening Behavior.* Wiley Online Library, 2004.

Gibbons, M, and J. Studer. "Suicide Awareness Training for Faculty and Staff: A Training Model for School Counselors." *Professional School Counseling* 11, no. 4 (2008): 272–76.

Greenspan, L., and J. Deardorff. *The New Puberty.* New York: Rodale, 2014.

Jensen, F. *The Teenage Brain.* New York: Harper Collins, 2015.

Kalafat, J. "The Prevention of Youth Suicide." In *Healthy Children 2010: Enhancing Children's Wellness,* edited by R. P. Weissberg, T. P. Gullotta, B. A. Ryan, and G. R. Adams. Thousand Oaks, CA: Sage, 1997, 175–213.

Kalafat, J. "School Approaches to Youth Suicide." *American Behavioral Scientist* 46, no. 9 (2003): 1211–23.

Kalafat, J., and M. Elias. "An Evaluation of Adolescent Suicide Intervention Classes." *Suicide and Life-Threatening Behavior* 24 (1994): 224–33.

Kalafat, J., and C. Gagliano. "The Use of Simulations to Assess the Impact of an Adolescent Suicide Response Curriculum." *Suicide and Life-Threatening Behavior* 26 (1996): 359–64.

Kalafat, J., and D. M. Ryerson. "The Implementation and Institutionalization of a School-Based Youth Suicide Prevention Program." *Journal of Primary Prevention* 19 (1999): 157–75.

Kieland, J. M., and L. M. Knoblauch. "HIPAA and FERPA: Competing or Collaborating?" *Journal of Allied Health* 39, no. 4 (2010): 161E-165E.

Lamis, D. A., M. Underwood, N. D'Amore. "Outcomes of a Suicide Prevention Gatekeeper Training Program among School Personnel." *Crisis* 38, no. 2 (Aug. 26, 2016): 1–11.

MacLeod, K. B., and E. B. Brownlie. "Mental Health and Transitions from Adolescence to Emerging Adulthood: Developmental and Diversity Considerations." *Canadian Journal of Community Mental Health* 33, no. 1 (2014): 77–86.

Maine Youth Suicide Prevention Program, www.maine.gov/suicide.

Miller, D. N, T. L. Eckert, and J. J. Mazza. "Suicide Prevention Programs in the Schools: A Review and Public Health Perspective." *School Psychology Review,* 2009.

Mullany, B., A. Barlow, N. Goklish, F. Larzelere-Hinton, M. Cwik, M. Craig, and J. T. Walkup. "Toward Understanding Suicide Among Youths: Results from the White Mountain Apache Tribally Mandated Suicide Surveillance System, 2001–2006." *American Journal of Public Health* 99, no. 10 (2009): 1840–48.

Randell, B. P., L. L. Eggert, and K. C. Pike. "Immediate Post-intervention Effects of Two Brief Youth Suicide Prevention Interventions." *Suicide and Life-Threatening Behavior* 31 (2001): 41–61.

Sales, M. J. *American Girls: Social Media and the Secret Life of Teenagers.* New York: Penguin Random House, 2017.

Shellenbarger, T., and C. Perez-Stearns. "From the Classroom to Clinical: A Family Educational Rights and Privacy Act Primer for the Nurse Educator." *Teaching and Learning in Nursing* 5, no. 4 (2010): 164–68.

Thompson, E. A., L. L. Eggert, B. P. Randell, and K. C. Pike. "Evaluation of Indicated Suicide Risk Prevention Approaches for Potential High School Dropouts." *American Journal of Public Health* 91 (2001): 742–52.

U.S. Department of Education. "Frequently Asked Questions about Section 504 and the Education of Children with Disabilities." Last modified October 16, 2015. www2.ed.gov /about/offices/list/ocr/504faq.html.

Walsh, E., C. Hooven, and B. Kronick. "School-Wide Staff and Faculty Training in Suicide Risk Awareness: Successes and Challenges." *Journal of Child and Adolescent Psychiatric Nursing* 26, no. 1 (2013): 53–61. https://doi.org/10.1111/jcap.12011.

Weber, A., and C. Haen, *Clinical Applications of Drama Therapy in Child and Adolescent.* New York: Brunner-Routledge, 2005.

Wood, C. *Yardsticks: Children in the Classroom Ages 4–14.* Turners Falls, MA: Center for Responsive Schools, 2015.

Wyman, P. A., C. H. Brown, J. Inman, W. Cross, K. Schmeelk-Cone, J. Guo, and J. B. Pena. "Randomized Trial of a Gatekeeper Program for Suicide Prevention: 1-Year Impact on Secondary School Staff." *Journal of Consulting and Clinical Psychology* 76, no. 1 (2008): 104–15. https://doi.org/10.1037/0022-006X.76.1.104.

Zenere, F. J., III, and P. J. Lazarus. "The Decline of Youth Suicidal Behavior in an Urban, Multicultural Public School System Following the Introduction of a Suicide Prevention and Intervention Program." *Suicide and Life-Threatening Behavior* 27 (1997): 387–403.

List of Digital Materials

MATERIALS ON THE FLASH DRIVE

Handouts are compiled in packets by curriculum section. Handouts and other resources that include the ⓈⓅ icon are Spanish translations that are available with the English versions in the digital files.

Hazelden *Lifelines Prevention* Handout Packet for Introduction to Hazelden Lifelines, Introduction to Youth Suicide, and Section 1: Administrative Perspective

Introduction to Hazelden Lifelines

- Hazelden Lifelines School Implementation Process
- Connecting Hazelden *Lifelines Prevention* to the *Olweus Bullying Prevention Program*

Introduction to Youth Suicide

- Warning Signs of Suicide (FACTS)

Section 1: Administrative Perspective

- Questions for Your Board of Education
- Readiness Survey
- School District Policy Template for Responding to Suicide: Intervention and Postvention Procedures

---

Hazelden *Lifelines Prevention* Handout Packet for Section 2: Faculty and Staff Training

- *Lifelines Prevention* Pre-test: Faculty and Staff
- "Educators as Partners in Suicide Prevention" Faculty and Staff Presentation Notes
- Warning Signs of Suicide (FACTS)
- Trusted Adult Card
- Frequently Asked Questions about Youth Suicide
- Resources for Suicide Prevention and Support
- *Lifelines Prevention* Post-test: Faculty and Staff

**Hazelden *Lifelines Prevention* Handout Packet for Section 3:
Parent Workshop**

- Sample Letter for Parents/Guardians Introducing *Lifelines Prevention* Implementation ⓈⓅ
- Sample Letter for Parents/Guardians Regarding *Lifelines Prevention* Lessons, Grades 5–6 ⓈⓅ
- *Lifelines Prevention* Pre-test: Parents and Guardians ⓈⓅ
- Resources for Suicide Prevention and Support ⓈⓅ
- "Raising Resilient Children in Challenging Times" Parent Workshop Presentation Notes ⓈⓅ
- Frequently Asked Questions for Parents ⓈⓅ
- Warning Signs of Suicide (FACTS) ⓈⓅ
- Starting the Conversation ⓈⓅ
- Addressing Behaviors That Concern You ⓈⓅ
- *Lifelines Prevention* Post-test: Parents and Guardians ⓈⓅ

**Hazelden *Lifelines Prevention* Handout Packet for Section 4:
Student Curriculum , Grades 5–6**

- *Lifelines Prevention* Pre-test: Students
- Session 1: What Do You Know?
- Session 1: The Thinking Tunnel
- Session 2: What Would You Do?
- Session 3: Courage Is
- Session 3: The Qualities of Helpful People
- Session 3: What Does It Mean to Find a Trusted Adult?
- Session 3: Trusted Adult Card
- Session 4: Help-Seeking Pledge
- Session 4: Lifelines Card
- *Lifelines Prevention* Post-test: Students

**Hazelden *Lifelines Prevention* Handout Packet for Section 4:
Student Curriculum , Grades 7–10**

- *Lifelines Prevention* Pre-test: Students
- Session 1: What Would You Do?
- Session 1: Questionnaire: True or False?
- Session 2: Warning Signs of Suicide (FACTS)
- Session 2: *A Teen's Guide to Suicide Prevention* Discussion Guidelines
- Session 2: Helpful Steps to Prevent Suicide
- Session 3: *One Life Saved* Discussion Questions
- Session 3: The Qualities of Helpful People
- Session 3: Trusted Adult Card
- Session 3: The Perfect Student: Role Play 1
- Session 3: College Crisis: Role Play 2
- Session 3: Poor Poetry: Role Play 3
- Session 4: Role-Play Discussion: Role Play 1: Owen and Alexa
- Session 4: Role-Play Discussion: Role Play 2: Olivia and Maria
- Session 4: Role-Play Discussion: Role Play 3: Seth and DeAndre
- Session 4: Help-Seeking Pledge
- Session 4: Lifelines Card
- *Lifelines Prevention* Post-test: Students

**Hazelden *Lifelines Prevention* Handout Packet for Section 4:
Student Curriculum, Grades 11–12**

- *Lifelines Prevention* Pre-test: Students
- Session 1: Middle School Assumptions
- Session 1: My Crystal Ball Predictions: Life After High School
- Session 2: When Things Don't Go According to Plan
- Session 2: When You Need to Take a Detour
- Session 2: When You Need a Friend
- Session 2: Resources for Suicide Prevention and Support
- Session 2: Lifelines Card
- *Lifelines Prevention* Post-test: Students

MATERIALS ON THE DVD

Section 2: Faculty and Staff Training

- *Suicide Risk and Warning Signs* video
- *Practicing the Warm Handoff* video

Section 4: Student Curriculum

Grades 5–6

- Grades 5–6 video scenes 1–9

Grades 7–10

- *A Teen's Guide to Suicide Prevention* video
- *One Life Saved: The Story of a Suicide Intervention* video

Grades 11–12

- *What I Know Now* video

About the Authors

....

Maureen Underwood, LCSW

Maureen Underwood is a licensed clinical social worker and certified group psychotherapist with more than thirty-five years of experience in mental health and crisis intervention. From 1985 to 2000, she was the coordinator of the New Jersey Adolescent Suicide Prevention Project. In this role, she initiated collaborative relationships between mental health and educational systems, provided in-service training, consulted on policy development, and assisted in the implementation of procedures for school-based crisis management. In addition to her other numerous publications, Maureen is the co-author of *Lifelines Intervention* and *Lifelines Postvention,* also published by Hazelden Publishing. In her role as the clinical director of the Society for the Prevention of Teen Suicide from 2008 to 2016, Maureen developed a series of online videos and resources for educators, parents, and students in youth suicide prevention. She currently maintains a group practice that specializes in suicide prevention.

John Kalafat, PhD

John Kalafat was a pioneer in community psychology. He was an internationally recognized expert in youth suicide prevention and crisis intervention who consulted with state, national, and overseas organizations. From co-founding a crisis counseling center to authoring books on youth suicide and divorce, John was at the forefront of his field. His publication of crisis-line evaluation has been central in guiding the National Suicide Prevention Lifeline. John was past president of the American Association of Suicidology, a fellow in the Society for Community Research and Action and the psychotherapy divisions of the American Psychological Association, and a professor in the Rutgers Graduate School of Applied and Professional Psychology. His career spanned forty years and embodied the "scientist-practitioner" model: his passion for research was driven by his love for getting directly involved with those who intervene with individuals in crisis. John, who passed away in late October 2007, has left a global legacy and a model for all of us to follow.

The Maine Youth Suicide Prevention Program

The Maine Youth Suicide Prevention Program (MYSPP) is a multiagency effort coordinated by the Injury Prevention Program in the Maine Center for Disease Control and Prevention (Maine CDC) in the state's Department of Health and Human Services. The long-term goal of the MYSPP is to reduce the incidence of fatal and nonfatal suicidal behavior among Maine youth ages ten to twenty-four. The MYSPP is guided by a plan containing twelve goals that mirror those in the National Strategy for Suicide Prevention. The program implements myriad activities, including a statewide Information Resource Center, statewide crisis hotline, websites for adults and youth, multiple training programs, data monitoring, fact sheets, and resource materials. Since 1998, the MYSPP has employed a public health approach to address youth suicide. The program is based upon the assumption that collaboration among state agency leaders and staff—along with significant input from service providers, youth, suicide survivors, and others—is necessary to plan and conduct youth suicide prevention activities. Much of the work of the MYSPP has been directed at providing training and consultation to school systems across the state to build competent school communities where all faculty and staff members believe they have a role to play in youth suicide prevention and are comfortable and knowledgeable about responding to youth in distress.

Other Titles That May Interest You

....

Hazelden *Lifelines Intervention,* Second Edition

Helping Students At Risk for Suicide

Maureen Underwood, LCSW, Judith Springer, PsyD, and Michelle Ann-Rish Scott, MSW, PhD, in partnership with The Society for the Prevention of Teen Suicide

Lifelines Intervention: Helping Students At Risk for Suicide is a whole-school program that educates the entire school community on how to address and respond to threats or signs of suicide and intervene before it's too late.

Order No. 3505

Hazelden *Lifelines Postvention,* Second Edition

Responding to Suicide and Other Traumatic Death

Maureen Underwood, LCSW, Fred T. Fell, EdS, NCSP, and Nicci Spinazzola, LMFT, LPC, BCETS, in partnership with The Society for the Prevention of Teen Suicide

Lifelines Postvention: Responding to Suicide and Other Traumatic Death is a one-of-a-kind program that educates everyone in the school community about how to successfully address and respond to any type of death or traumatic event that profoundly affects the school population.

Order No. 3510

Safe Dates, Second Edition

An Adolescent Dating Abuse Prevention Curriculum

Vangie Foshee, PhD, and Stacey Langwick, PhD

Safe Dates is the leading evidence-based program proven to reduce incidents of teen dating violence. This program helps teens recognize the difference between caring, supportive relationships and controlling, manipulative, or abusive relationships.

Order No. 9863

Voices

A Program of Self-Discovery and Empowerment for Girls

Stephanie S. Covington, PhD

Voices was created to address the unique needs of adolescent girls and young women. It encourages them to seek and celebrate their true selves by providing a safe space, encouragement, structure, and the support they need to embrace their journeys of self-discovery.

Order No. 4815

To order from Hazelden Publishing,
call **800-328-9000** or visit **hazelden.org/bookstore.**